GLOBAL
SOUTH
ASIA

Padma Kaimal
K. Sivaramakrishnan
Anand A. Yang
SERIES EDITORS

Making
New Nepal

From Student Activism to Mainstream Politics

AMANDA THÉRÈSE SNELLINGER

UNIVERSITY OF WASHINGTON PRESS

Seattle

Copyright © 2018 by the University of Washington Press
Printed and bound in the United States
Composed in Minion Pro, typeface designed by Robert Slimbach
22 21 20 19 18   5 4 3 2 1

COVER PHOTOGRAPH: Student activists protesting dismissal of the democratically elected
parliament, Bāg Bazār, Kathmandu, March 2005. Photograph by the author.
All interior photographs are by the author.

UNIVERSITY OF WASHINGTON PRESS
www.washington.edu/uwpress

LIBRARY OF CONGRESS CATALOGING-IN-PUBLICATION DATA ON FILE

ISBN 978-0-295-74307-3 (HARDCOVER), ISBN 978-0-295-74308-0 (PAPERBACK),
ISBN 978-0-295-74309-7 (EBOOK)

To Nepal's activists of generations past and present.
May future generations be inspired by your dedication
to your country and communities. Jaya Nepal!

Our view has been that none of our movements have been complete. The movement is yet to be completed. Today's students continue the movement.

—COMMUNIST PARTY OF NEPAL–UNIFIED MARXIST LENINIST minister on the difference between student movements of different generations, February 4, 2007

Contents

Preface

No Neutrals

In the spring of 2004 while conducting research on political consciousness in Nepal's universities, I was asked to give an interview to a political weekly, *Deshāntar* (Across the Country). Risha, a student activist I knew, said it would help publicize my research. I was hesitant. I did not want to draw undue attention during such a contentious period. *Deshāntar* seemed like the sort of mouthpiece (*mukh patra*) that Nepali political parties have. The newsstands are crowded with multiple daily, weekly, and monthly periodicals of every political stripe, and people know which mouthpiece represents which party. Risha admitted that *Deshāntar* journalists had direct access to Nepali Congress (NC) politicians and relied on them for analysis. But she assured me it was a respectable weekly that all people read, especially to understand the NC party line. I agreed to the interview but refused to answer any political questions. The interview was tame. The reporter asked me about my research, why I chose Nepal, and where I had traveled in the country. He even sent me proofs of the article.

The week of publication, I received an email from the director of the US Educational Foundation's (USEF) Nepal Fulbright Program asking if I was aware of the "exposé." When I explained that I had given an interview to *Deshāntar*, he asked me about an article in *Pratispardha* (Competition). The US embassy press attaché deemed the article bad publicity and forwarded it to the American Mission, the public relations office of the American Embassy in Nepal, which ordered him to refute the article's claims and demand a redaction. The article, attached to his email, was a brief biography of me in Nepali dismissing my claim to be a Fulbright researcher and asserting that I was an anti-Hindu CIA agent providing tactical support to the Maoists. It cited trips to the Maoist heartland—Rukum, Rolpa, and Dolpa—that I had taken during my college study abroad as proof.

Shocked to read my life details so grossly distorted, I immediately called Akash, another student leader, for advice. He informed me that *Pratispardha* was a small royalist mouthpiece, merely a tabloid. *Pratispardha* is published on Sunday instead of Friday like other weeklies, giving its writers time to peruse the competition and rewrite articles from a royalist bent. Their viewpoint, he said, "was based not on fact but on manufactured lies" and "hence the name, *Pratispardha*—it means 'competition.'" He congratulated me on being in good company. At various times, *Pratispardha* had depicted him as a Maoist, pro-Indian, and anti-nationalist to undermine his popularity. He explained that I had been targeted because of the *Deshāntar* article and asked why I had agreed to the interview. I told him that Risha had convinced me it would be good exposure. He laughed and said, "Well you received exposure for sure. Now everyone knows you are a threat to the monarchy. The activists [*āndolankāri haru*] will respect you."

This was my first public foray into Nepali politics. During a period of heightened political upheaval, I found myself researching activists who were defying state sanctions with anti-monarchical protests and came to learn that "in a revolutionary situation, no neutrals are allowed" (Nash 1976: 150). The Maoists had been waging a war against the government for almost seven years, which ultimately claimed seventeen thousand lives. Villagers were caught in the cross fire between the Maoist army and state security forces, and everyone was vulnerable to the random bombs that were detonated in public places. There were victims on all sides. Nepal's human rights record was disintegrating as the number of disappeared and murdered increased exponentially.[1] The US State Department had classified the Maoists as a terrorist organization until 2007 after an official cease-fire was brokered.

I did my best to resist advocacy because of the obvious complications it would bring to my informants and research, and my interlocutors were in any case capable in advocating for themselves. Instead, trying to avoid partisanship, I pitched my research as a non-biased exploration of Nepali student politics and their role in mainstream politics. A non-partisan approach turned out to be more challenging than I had expected, as my unwelcome publicity in *Pratispardha* demonstrates. I had little control over the way others perceived my research. My topic, Nepal's political struggle, almost implicitly said something about me, the researcher (Henslin 1972). Even as I observed from the sidelines, the students referred to me as the "observer activist" (*avalokan garne āndolankāri*) or the "sideline activist" (*sīdmā basne āndolankāri*). When I rebuffed them, they challenged me, asking, "You don't care what happens in Nepal?" Of course, I cared. I supported what the citizens wanted. In their view, this meant I supported them because they were fighting for the people's right to decide Nepal's future. To them I was an *āndolankāri*.[2]

Building rapport with the student activists meant I was "on their side" (Huizer 1973: 21), and outsiders placed me either where it suited them or where it made obvious sense. In Nepal's political field, people interpret others' actions as indicative of the spheres they operate within, discerning filial, social, and political interconnections. The notion of lack of bias is self-defeating. What I saw as an ethical research approach, my interlocutors saw as a limiting act that removed the prospect of political opportunity, of expanding one's influence through reciprocity and indebtedness.

Neutrality became more complicated for me after 2006, when the students were no longer unified. From 2003 to 2006 their strength had come through their numbers afforded by political unity. I was studying their political movement, and so I needed to work with all of them. Between 2003 and 2006, the opposition lines were drawn between those fighting for a multiparty republic and royalist supporters. Since their establishment in the 1960s, there had been deep mistrust among the student organizations in Nepal, which varied in severity across different campuses. After the king was dethroned by the Second People's Movement in the spring of 2006, I observed the students revert to interparty competition and political machinations, which showed how alliances and splits affected their shared political culture.

Student leaders became resistant to my work with other student organizations. After 2006, the focus of my study shifted from the student movement to student organizations and their interorganizational and intra-organizational practices. Soon my study became something else for them to compete over, and they complained that I was no longer a daily part of their lives—that I had "gone missing." This pressure pulled me in multiple directions as I attended separate meetings, going from campus to campus and juggling political programs throughout Kathmandu, missing key events when I had to choose between simultaneous political programs.

Nevertheless, I continued conducting a broad study of student politics. Satendra, the president of the All Nepal National Free Student Union (United) (ANNFSU [Akhil]), whom I had known for three years, had a penchant for attempting to undercut my claimed lack of bias. His machinations unwittingly connected me with Gyanu, the Maoist student president of the All Nepal National Independent Student Union (Revolutionary) (ANNISU [R]). During the 2006 peace talks, Satendra invited me to their rally to lobby their parties toward peace talk negotiations. When I arrived at their central committee's office, the secretary informed me that no rally was scheduled, but that nine student organizations were meeting to draft a joint statement demanding peace talks among the previous warring factions. It became apparent that Satendra strategically arranged for me to be sitting in his office when the other student leaders arrived. As others arrived, they greeted me with familiarity. The Nepal Student Union (Democratic) (NSU [D]) president suggested that we all catch up over tea, to the annoyance of Satendra, who refused. The meeting began without tea and without me. Satendra instructed me to wait so we could continue our visit after their press release was drafted.

Although I felt inconvenienced, I sensed an opportunity and waited. As the leaders were waiting to sign the press release, I introduced myself to Gyanu, who kept avoiding eye contact. I knew most everyone in the room, so I was confident when I remarked: "I've worked with all these gentlemen and their organizations for the past three years. You've been underground, so your organization is the missing link in my research. I hope I can work with you." He had been ignoring my phone calls and my research assistant's appointment requests. Our serendipitous meeting among the other student leaders assuaged his suspicion of me as a foreigner and convinced him that the other student leaders took me seriously. After that day, he answered my call, and within a week we scheduled our first meeting. Through that chance encounter, I was able to make inroads into the Maoist student union, and Gyanu became one of my long-term informants.

Through the unexpected challenges of forging relationships in Nepal's political terrain, I came to understand the field and actors within it. The limitations I experienced were the realities that structured my interlocutors' sociality. By working within the constraints of the field, I observed how Nepali politics works as a series of interparty and interpersonal alliances and competitions. More often than not we bonded over our shared experience of having no control as we tried to make sense of the ongoing political uncertainty together. The students let me in because I was trying to figure out politics, while they were figuring out their place in it. And through our fumbling we co-produced a particular reality, albeit for different ends. Our dialogical interaction was "embedded in both macro and micro social relations which defy a reduction to a simple equation of a powerful ethnographer operationalizing a research project focused on research subjects" (Holmberg 2011: 98). In that regard, the students and I were kindred spirits. Our connection came from leveraging each other in our own personal agendas: theirs political and mine research.

ETHNOGRAPHY AS POLITICAL PROCESS

An anthropological focus on democracy and social action must explore competing constructions of what is political: contested meanings, forms of power, and resistance (Paley 2002). It requires crafting ethnography as

open-ended analysis to elucidate the ongoing epistemic and social contestation of political process. This ethnography captures the dynamism and
stagnation of Nepali political life during the country's political transition in
the first decade of the twenty-first century. Political actors' conceptions and
categories, relational interactions, and political rituals and the forms their
political imaginary embodies are analyzed to apprehend what is political
to them.

The sustained long-term nature of this research has allowed me to understand politics as process, emerging from action and interaction. The student
activists of the twenty-first century's first decade provided me a firsthand
view into how they have shaped democracy through contestation and contradiction as they have negotiated what it meant for them both individually
and on the communal level. Through the ebbs and flows of their successes
and failures, I have come to understand the complexity of Nepali politics.
My interlocutors are not merely invested in ideology; they are personally
invested in the political networks and opportunities they see as their professional future.

This ethnography is based on research totaling thirty-four months from
2003 to 2015, in Kathmandu, with multiple field trips to over twenty-five
districts in Nepal, and on archival research in Delhi and Varanasi, India.
My research was a top-down project. I worked at the political center in
Kathmandu with the central committees of the student organizations and
political parties, from which I followed the students' political activities on
campuses and in districts throughout the country. I worked across party
and student organization lines with major political players.[3] The rapport I
established with the student activists in 2003 during their ongoing protests
provided me a firsthand view into their lives as activists, on the streets,
underground, and in the hospitals, courts, and jails. During this tumultu-
ous period, I was able to observe their internal organizational processes,
their interorganizational collaborations and competitions on campuses, and
their relationships with political party leaders. I was invited to students' and
politicians' homes and into their daily lives, where I observed how they
incorporate politics into the personal and the personal into their politics.

My day-to-day research differed quite significantly during the political
movements (2003–6) and afterward during the peace talks, the Constituent
Assembly (CA) elections, and state restructuring (2006–14). During the protest period, I followed students on the streets, observing their protest rallies,
and attended programs that the student unions and political parties held
on campuses and at other public gathering places, where I listened to

political speeches or just passed the time with students, who passively participated by being present but who also used these gatherings to socialize with their peers and rub elbows with party leaders. I visited student central committee and campus offices to observe the students' daily activities beyond the streets. In the evenings, I made the rounds to hospitals and jails with student leaders who were providing financial and moral support to their injured and detained cadres. I attended official and clandestine meetings between cadres and leaders whenever I was invited. I also followed student activists to their party leaders' houses or offices, in the morning before the day's activities began, where they paid homage, garnered political support or advice, registered complaints, elicited funds, and coordinated activities. During the Free Student Union (FSU) elections, I traveled to multiple campuses and observed the campaigning, voting, and ballot tallying, which gave me comparative data on competition in and among the student unions.

I also conducted formal and informal interviews with over one hundred student and party cadres, student leaders, ex–student leaders, politicians, ministers, campus chiefs and other faculty, policy makers, political analysts, and journalists, as well as international actors who supported the political process. I befriended a number of journalists and analysts with whom I regularly met to exchange reflections. Despite being rigorous, much of my research was spent having tea with interlocutors either waiting for something to happen or processing what had happened. During tea, I became familiar with the sociality of politics, which included moments of honesty but more often diplomacy, patience, and uncertainty while idling away the time between the big political moments.

After the 2006 political movement, I focused on the student unions' internal processes as they retreated back onto the campuses and out of the national spotlight. The post–peace talk period from 2006 through 2008 was heralded as a hopeful time. Yet for the students it was tinged with stagnation and uncertainty, as they waited for their parties to negotiate a new political frontier. I observed the student leaders' tense efforts to work cooperatively at the central committee level, while they also recognized that they were again competing with one another. I followed the conventions of the three largest student unions at the campus, district, and national levels, during 2006 and 2007, in preparation for the CA elections. And I shadowed student politicians through their CA election campaigns. Through my travels throughout the country, I observed students' role in national- and campus-level campaigns.

In 2009 and 2011, I returned to connect with student leaders and cadres whom I had maintained contact with throughout my research. I formally and informally interviewed them about contemporary political events at the national, party, and student organization levels. By this time many of them were transitioning into party positions, some successfully due to their popularity or established patronage connections, while others were stuck in a limbo between student leadership and minor party positions. During my research work through 2015, I consistently connected with the five student leaders whose narratives are featured in this book. I took all five of their life stories and questioned them on topics I had been asking them since 2003 to understand how their perspectives had changed over time and with experience.

Acknowledgments

I am blessed. I am blessed because there are scores of people who have supported, aided, and given themselves to this project over the past fifteen years. This good fortune, however, presents me with a dilemma. To those I neglect to mention here, please know that this book is a product of your influence and support.

To all those on the streets, in party and student union offices, at political rallies, in classrooms and campuses, jails and hospitals, ministries, and parliament, thank you for opening your world to me. It would be impossible to name you all, but you are a part of my research, just as you are a part of Nepali political history. Your knowledge, perspectives, and actions made this project rich and deep. To the five students whose narratives tie this book together, you will go unnamed here but not unrecognized by me or many who read this book. Thank you for sharing the past decade and a half of ups and downs. It has been an adventure.

My research project was generously funded by a USEF-Nepal Fulbright fellowship (2003–4), a Title VI Foreign Language and Area Studies grant (2005–6), a Fulbright-Hays research fellowship (2006–7), a Wenner-Gren research fellowship (2007–8), Cornell Sage fellowships (2005, 2008–9), and an Economic and Social Science Research Council (ESRC) grant (2012–16). I also received travel grants from the Einaudi Center for International Studies, the Society for Humanities at Cornell University, and the South Asia Center at the University of Washington. Michael Gill and Peter Moran supported me in their capacity as directors of the USEF-Nepal Fulbright Program, opening doors in the field and providing insight until the end. Constance Colding-Jones at the US embassy in Nepal supported my research even when the embassy was wary of it.

I am thankful to Cornell University's Anthropology Department for initially supporting my research and the University of Washington's South Asia Center, Tribhuvan University, and Oxford University's School of Geography and the Environment and Anthropology Department for providing me institutional homes and scholarly communities. I thank the University of Washington's Friday Harbor Laboratories and the Whiteley Center for generously hosting me as I worked on the manuscript. I am deeply grateful to Sunila Kale, Priti Ramamurthy, Cabeiri Robinson, Keith Snodgrass, and Anand A. Yang at the University of Washington's South Asia Center for continual opportunities that have allowed me to finish my book in Seattle.

I received formative academic guidance from David Holmberg, Kathryn March, Hiro Miyazaki, and Annelise Riles, which initially shaped this project. David Holmberg and Kathryn March trained me to be an engaged, empathetic ethnographer. Shambu and Banu Oja's and Krishna Pradhan's language tutelage enabled me to connect with my interlocutors and discern subtle elements of Nepali political culture. I have continued to be intellectually challenged on multiple continents. I thank David N. Gellner for his mentorship in Nepal and at Oxford and for his close reading of much of this manuscript. This book benefited from keen insight from my ESRC team, Jane Dyson, Craig Jeffrey, Dhana Hughes, and Jonathan Spencer. And interactions with Vibha Arora, Jo Boyden, Joanna Pfaff-Czarnecka, Anne De Sales, Deborah Durham, Nick Evans, Martin Gaenszle, Krishna Hachhethu, Michael Hutt, Lola Martinez, Filippo Osella, Tracey Skelton, Gérard Toffin, and John Whelpton have contoured this book's theoretical framework. I also received invaluable feedback from colleagues at the South Asia Research Cluster (SARC) and the Centre on Migration, Policy and Society (COMPAS) at the University of Oxford and in Kathmandu at the Social Science Baha, Martin Chautari, and Tribhuvan University's Anthropology Department.

A number of colleagues have provided consistent feedback and friendship in the United States, the United Kingdom, Europe, and South Asia: Iván Arenas, Anil Bhatterai, Bronwen Bledsoe, Sarah Byrne, Dambar Chemjong, David Citrin, Cheryl Colopy, Jason Cons, Sienna Craig, Dace Dzenovska, Rebecca Edwards, Rosalind Evans, Tatsuro and Yasuko Fujikura, Peter Gill, Peter Graif, Arjun Guneratne, Ashok Gurung, Susan Hangen, Ian Harper, Sondra Hausner, Pushpa Himal, Heather Hindman, Dan Hirslund, Amy Johnson, Brandon Kohrt, Satendra Kumar, Laura Kunreuther, Mahendra Lawoti, Chiara Letizia, Lauren Leve, Mark Liechty, Mara Malagodi, Andrea Nightingale, Pratyoush Onta, Anastasia Piliavsky, Janak Rai, Katherine Rankin, Jacob Rinck, Simon Robbins, Tom Roberston, Cabeiri Robinson, Jeevan Sharma, Sara Shneiderman, Bandita Sijapati, Anna Stirr, Bert Suykens, Mukta Tamang, Seira Tamang, Deepak Thapa, Mark Turin, Karen Valentin, Luke Wagner, and Ina Zharkevich. I am particularly appreciative for close readings from Bhaskar Gautam and Anna Stirr.

I owe a debt of gratitude to Devendra Neupane, my research assistant and translator. Devendra has worked tirelessly alongside me over the past fifteen years, never frustrated, unless on my behalf. This project would not be what it is if it not for Devendra's commitment and collaboration. I thank him for our many years of synchronous research and friendship. Sudip Gautam's guidance in Parsa district from 2013 to 2015 was an immeasurable contribution to my understanding Nepal beyond Kathmandu.

I would like to thank the following intellectuals and party members for their invaluable contributions to my research: Narahari Acharya, Rabindra Adhikari, Prakash Aryal, Yogesh Bhatterai, Ganeshyam Bhusal, Jitendra Dev, Pradip Giri, Anil Jha, Tanka Karki, Bijaya Kanta Karna, Suresh Ali Magar, Kedar Bhakta Mathima, Balmendra Nidhi, Shankar Pokhrel, Sahana Pradhan, Hari Roka, Yogendra Sahi, and Jhalak Subedi. I am also indebted to those who regularly kept my research from becoming myopic by providing me perspectives beyond mainstream party politics: Aditya Adhikari, John Bevan, Sam Cowen, Bhaskar Gautam, Prashant Jha, Sara Levit-Shore, Anagha Neelkantha, Suman Pradhan, Dinesh Prasain, Ashmina and Basant Ranjitkaar, Sophia and Shivanth Pande, Sushma Joshi, Astha Thapa, Manjushree Thapa, and Akhilesh Upadhaya. The India portion of my research benefited from the guidance and support of Anand Kumar at the Jawaharlal Nehru University (JNU), Jaya Regmi at the National Archives in Delhi, Alok Kumar of the Benares Hindu University (BHU), and Anju Sharan Upadhaya at the BHU Nepal Studies Centre. I thank Mona Adhikari, Deepak Bhatta, Rajan Bhatterai, and Dinesh and Pratikshya Prasain for their hospitality and for entrée into the Nepali community in Delhi and JNU student life.

I am grateful to Padma Kaimal, Kalyanakrishnan (Shivi) Sivaramakrishnan, and Anand A. Yang, the editors of the University of Washington Press's Global South Asia series, for supporting the publication of this book. Lorri Hagman has been a star in shepherding this project through to publication, and her editorial feedback has been invaluable. And I thank the two anonymous reviewers of the book manuscript for their productive critiques and suggestions as well as their encouragement on this book's contribution.

This project could not have spanned a decade and a half if I did not feel I had places to seek refuge. Thank you Laurie Vasily and Thomas Mathew, Vishwa and Kalpana Thakali, and Hirendra and Prathima Pradhan for making me a part of your families and always providing me a home and community in Kathmandu. To my family, I feel lucky that you are so big and keep growing. My parents, Mary and Jay Snellinger, and proxy parents, Mimi Dinova and Pam Cyr, have always been proud of me. My siblings— Lucy, Ani, Ann, Chris, Lisa, and Tommy—are mainly a lot of hard scientists and yet continued to support this endeavor even when they did not understand. Arianna, Brian, Cara, Christa, Devon, Grace, Jason, Jen, Kat, and Maija have anchored me while expanding my horizons. My husband, Jon Sequeira, has given me unending patience as I continue to drag him to landlocked places throughout the world. And, most importantly, he has believed in me always.

Abbreviations

ANNFSU (Akhil)	All Nepal National Free Student Union (United)
ANNFSU (Ekikrit)	All Nepal National Free Student Union (Unified)
ANNFSU-ML	All Nepal National Free Student Union–Marxist Leninist
ANNISU (R)	All Nepal National Independent Student Union (Revolutionary)
ANNISU (R) (Baidya)	All Nepal National Independent Student Union (Revolutionary) (Baidya Faction)
CA	Constituent Assembly
CPN (Maoist)	Communist Party of Nepal (Maoist)
CPN-ML	Communist Party of Nepal–Marxist Leninist
CPN-RM (Baidya)	Communist Party of Nepal–Revolutionary Maoist (Baidya Faction)
CPN-UML	Communist Party of Nepal–Unified Marxist Leninist
FSU	Free Student Union
NC (D)	Nepali Congress (Democratic)
NC (K)	Nepali Congress (Koirala)
NCP-ML	Nepal Communist Party–Marxist Leninist
NNSF	Nepal National Student Federation
NPU	Nepal Progressive Union
NSU (D)	Nepal Student Union (Democratic)
NSU (K)	Nepal Student Union (Koirala)
RPP	Rāstriya Prajātantra Parishad (National Democratic Party)
RPP-N	Rāstriya Prajātantra Parishad–Nepal (National Democratic Party–Nepal)
UCPN (Maoist)	Unified Communist Party of Nepal (Maoist)
UNMIN	United Nations Mission in Nepal

Note on Terminology and Transliteration

My transliteration is based on the standard diacritic practice for transliterating Devanagari script according to the International Organization for Standardization (ISO 15919), except when it comes to the letters च and छ. For these letters, I follow the standard Nepali transliteration practice *ch* for च (*c* in the ISO system), and *chh* for छ (*ch* in the ISO system). I use diacritics and transliterated terms throughout the text. I do not use diacritics for proper names and terms that are commonly used in English (e.g., Panchayat).

There is a debate in academic and ethnic activist circles regarding the designator "Nepali" versus "Nepalese."[1] This debate highlights the politics of recognition in postcolonial South Asia. During their colonial rule, the British used the term "Nepalese" to refer to people who were citizens of the nation-state of Nepal. In English, "Nepalese" was the accepted term until the past few decades, during which time the term "Nepali" gained currency. This shift marked a move away from colonial prescribed terminology to a term that more accurately reflects the ethnonym as it is spoken in the national language, Nepali (Nepali are the speakers of the Nepali language). Since the 1990s, however, there has been debate around these terms among ethnic activists, the contention being that "Nepalese" is more inclusive because the British colonial administration used it to designate all the citizens of Nepal, whereas "Nepali" implicitly excludes people whose mother language is not the national language, furthering the history of internal colonization and co-optation led by the Shah rulers. The Kathmandu Valley was the homeland of indigenous Newars; they called the land Nepal and their language was Nepal Bhasa (often called Newari in English). After conquering the Kathmandu Valley, the Shah monarchy relocated the central seat of its empire from Gorkha to Kathmandu and co-opted the Newar's place-name and communal designator, renaming their Khas language Nepali and the Shah monarchy's territory Nepal.

Nevertheless, I have chosen to use the term "Nepali" because it is the term that my interlocutors use. To make things clearer, I do not use "Nepali" as the noun referring to people but use it as a descriptor that details who or what I am specifically referencing. For example, I refer to the citizens of Nepal as "Nepali citizens," political actors as "Nepali political actors," and the state of Nepal as the "Nepali state." I only use "Nepali" in the noun form to reference the state language.

Making New Nepal

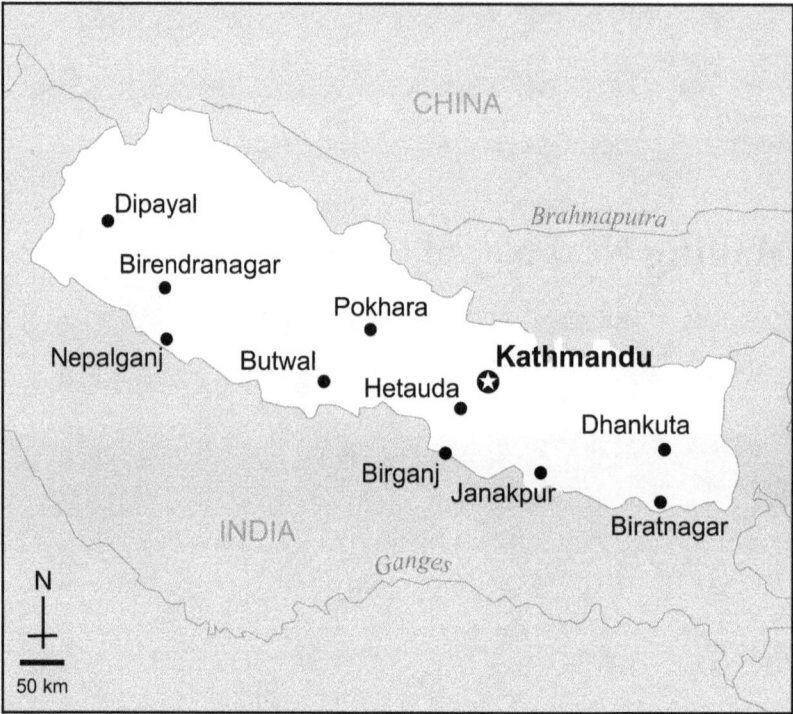

Map of Nepal. Data source: UN Department of Peacekeeping Operations, Cartographic Section.

Introduction

Political Opportunity through Activism

SAHANA PRADHAN LISTENED WITH INTEREST AS I TOLD HER OF my research on student politics. I was introduced to the leader of the Communist Party of Nepal–Unified Marxist Leninist (CPN-UML) at Basantapur Square in 2004, before she spoke to a crowd of over a thousand cadres who were participating in the Movement Against Regression (Pratigaman Birodhi Āndolan). For over a year, five political parties and their subsidiary organizations had been protesting the king's 2002 removal of Nepal's democratically elected government. The parties asserted that the monarchy had overstepped its constitutional bounds and were demanding that parliament be immediately reinstated. Before ascending to the podium, Sahana explained to me: "Student politics is the first learning place. It really matters to what extent one maintains what one learns at this stage. It is the first place you become educated. The firm understanding that is developed at this stage never gets erased. It is the basis for life."[1]

A week later, I observed a student cadre throw a rock at a police officer, striking his helmet. I recognized the student as the volunteer who had gingerly guided the esteemed political leader onto the stage as she had explained the importance of student politics to me. Our eyes met and he yelled to me as I stood on the sidelines: "This is the basis of our life."[2]

This vignette illustrates the centrality of student politics in Nepal's quest for democracy and the contradictory nature of seeking political opportunity within the framework of revolution (cf. Keniston 1968). Since the beginning of Nepal's democratic struggle in the 1950s, university politics has been the gateway into national mainstream politics, and student activists serve as the political parties' foot soldiers in their opposition politics against the state and other ruling political parties. This close-knit relationship between contentious politics and governance in Nepal's political history raises the following questions: What is the relationship between idealism and opportunism within political activism, since standing on principle now is seen as the path to powerful political office later? How has this relationship changed since Nepal's political situation shifted from a revolutionary context defined by a Maoist civil war and the downfall of a monarchy to an era of governing framed by restructuring the nation into a democratic, federal republic? During such politically contentious times, what is the role of political ideology, idioms, and practice in these young political actors' everyday lives, and how do they frame social categories like gender, caste, ethnicity, class, religion, and nation—categories that have tested the limits of democracy in South Asia?

The practices of Nepal's student organizations and people's transition from student activism to mainstream politics are useful analytic lenses through which to address these questions. Socialization into mainstream politics occurs through student politics. The student organizations are subsidiary organizations, or sister organizations, within which individuals receive both their social training and ideological indoctrination into Nepali party politics.[3] Thus, university politics serves as the training ground for student cadres and leaders. They move up the party echelons by organizing protests, strikes, and sit-ins and campaigning for their own positions on campuses and their parties' in general elections. Student activists have always been at the forefront, making radical demands based on the political ground gained by previous activist generations. This recent generation of Nepali student politicians came of age during a particularly contentious time. They were the foot soldiers of the political and revolutionary movements that deposed the Hindu monarchy and ushered in Nepal's democratic, secular republic, or, as they call it, "new Nepal."

This book explores Nepal's political transition in the twenty-first century by focusing on this generation of student activists. Based on multi-sited ethnographic research between 2003 and 2015, it is a snapshot of a generation's political coming-of-age during a decade of civil war (1996–2006) and ongoing democratic street protests (2003–6), which finally culminated in ousting the monarchy and establishing a democratic, secular republic. It tracks this generation's entrée into politics through street protest as they have negotiated the shift from revolutionary politics to working within the party system. Many activists exercised "judicious opportunism" as they ascended into national-level politics (Johnson-Hanks 2005). Some have progressed from student activism to the Constituent Assembly (CA), serving in both elected and party-appointed seats, while others are active in their parties at the national and local levels, and others have raised money from local and international donors to establish non-governmental organizations (NGOs) and think tanks. Examining their experiences beyond street protest and campus politicking brings their political narrative full circle. Analysis of five young leaders' stories of transition from student activism to mainstream politics elucidates how party leaders and international actors influence students' developing political identity and how, as full-fledged political entrepreneurs, these activists negotiate with established leaders to achieve their own agendas.

The concept of political regeneration is useful for demonstrating how Nepal's history of activism has shaped its political discourse and practice. Nepal's democratic struggle has always been a generative process in which each new generation attempts to establish itself politically by negotiating between previous acts of claim making and new political formulations. This case study thus illustrates how democracy works as a radical ongoing process rather than a formal sphere (Rancière 2004) and how the relationship between change and the status quo in Nepali national politics has created youth as a particular social category in politics. Youth works as a social mechanism for political reproduction and change, highlighting the dynamic nature of democratic politics.

THE EDUCATIONAL, POLITICAL, AND SOCIAL ROLE OF STUDENT POLITICS

Nepali university students have been integral to political organizing since the 1930s. Since the Rana regime, Nepal's college campuses have been one of the main places where the state has been challenged (Snellinger 2005). However, it was not until the 1960s that student organizations began to emerge in the form they now take as subsidiary organizations of political parties. The reason for this change was primarily the Panchayat ban on political party activities in the 1960s, which cemented the relationship between the mother organization (political party) and the sister organization (student organization). The student organizations fell outside the Panchayat government's ban on political organizations and thus became a convenient loophole to continue political activity clandestinely. During this period, political parties became dependent on student organizations to indoctrinate new converts and sustain their mission, if only on college campuses. As Akash, a Nepal Student Union (NSU) student leader, explained to me during our first formal interview:

> Yesterday, the student organizations' role was only to assist the parties.
> They were treated as nurseries, which used to supply plants for the parties.

In the nursery, the seeds used to be watered and fertilized. The role of
the student organizations was limited to this . . . to produce cadres. . . .
But now because of the students' movement and the faith that we have
obtained [from the public] our role is not that. . . . We have come to realize through the movement that we are the force with the most potential.
We are interfering to point a finger at the parties, saying that you cannot
compromise with the king in an inappropriate way. This means we are
also in the mainstream of politics.[4]

The relational dependence between mother and sister student organizations has been fraught since its genesis. All the student organizations, except
for the Maoist student organization, have clauses in their constitutions that
state they are independent entities from their affiliated political parties;
however, party interference is the status quo. The way the interference is
executed, and the degree of frustration it produces, varies depending on
party ideology and organizational style, which determines how in sync student organizations are with their parties' agenda. Inherent in this relational
dynamic is a more general tension between autonomy and organization as
well as agency and structure.

While all student organizations are affiliated with political parties, their
basis for existence is their presence on campuses. Each student organization
participates in the Free Student Union (FSU), which acts as the governing
student body on all university and college campuses affiliated with the
main university, Tribhuvan University, in Kirtipur, on the outskirts of Kathmandu. Each student union has a central committee based in Kathmandu
Valley that oversees the national operation of its organization, establishes
the organization's national agenda, and is the mediator between its political
party and the district and campus committees. The district committees
oversee the operations in each geographical district, and campus committees execute their union's operations locally on each campus, ideally by
winning seats in the FSU administration. Student unions must be registered
on the campus in order to compete for seats in that campus's FSU administration. FSU election day happens throughout the nation on every campus
simultaneously. The elections are supposed to occur every two years to
determine each campus's administration, but they are often postponed due
to the national political climate. This inconsistency is in part because elections need to be sanctioned by Tribhuvan University's chancellor, who until
2006 was the king and has since been the prime minister. In the off years,
each student organization is supposed to hold internal elections at the

Students entering campus through a police checkpoint to vote in the Free Student Union campus elections. Tri-Chandra College, Kathmandu, 2004.

campus, district, and national levels; however, the regularity of the student organizations' conventions is even less consistent than the FSU elections since their mother parties assume oversight of their national conventions.

Student unions have a potent incentive to secure an FSU majority on campuses because such victories provide access to financial resources and influence dictating campus policy and administration, which in turn allows them an upper hand in indoctrinating and recruiting general students and therefore maintaining their union's stronghold. The FSU administration's official duties involve overseeing the operation of the campus canteen, monitoring the student union budget, arranging campus construction contracts, and allotting coveted scholarship and hostel spots. Student unions also use political strong-arm tactics like holding campus strikes, enforcing lockdowns of the campus chief's and other administration offices, and sometimes escalating to vandalism and violence in order to sway faculty hiring and firing decisions, influence exam scheduling and grading outcomes, as well as protest student fee increases, rising national fuel prices, and other issues they claim affect students. Student unions have entrenched their position as mediators between the administration and students, serving as fixers who arrange students' identity cards, seats for exams, hostel

Newly elected campus leaders hoisted during an ANNFSU (Akhil) rally celebrating their FSU victory. Kathmandu, 2004.

lodgings, and scholarships. Indeed, campus politics is an inevitable reality for all students, who must rely on it to navigate the university bureaucratic process and other formal and informal networks.

During the time of my research, many non-partisan students and faculty considered student unions anachronistic because they no longer serve their original purpose of advocating for the student body. Instead, student unions are viewed cynically as holding the education and campus experience hostage. Unless general students have other connections in the campus administration, they cannot avoid dealing with the student unions. One student explained how it was necessary for every student to be on good terms with the student union members, otherwise nothing would get done because "the lower-level administration is in the student unions' pockets and the upper-level administration is scared of them."[5] I spoke to a number of campus chiefs, and none of them were overtly critical of the student unions; however, they all admitted that the student unions were forces with which they must contend and not always willingly or within the FSU administration's official mandate. One campus chief explained:

> The way I've been successful is to keep all the student union members happy. I give them all an audience. . . . Of course, I need to prioritize the FSU administration's decisions when it comes to their official mandate

since they were elected by the students. But on other decisions, I let them all know that I consider their views equally. . . . If one organization thinks I favor another one, they'll make my job miserable until I resign or get pushed out. Plus, I can't favor any one organization because I never know who will win the next FSU campus election or which political party will run the next government. Not playing favorites is how I survive.[6]

While campus chiefs must be diplomatic about the power the student unions wield, student unions' influence has degraded campus life over the past two decades. A vocal critic of the political interventions on Tribhuvan University campuses is Kedar Bhakta Mathema, the university's vice-chancellor during the late 1990s. He explained to me that since multiparty democracy was established in the 1990s, campus politics have become a zero-sum game that has gutted the university. The FSU used to be a proxy for multiparty democracy during the Panchayat government, but now both the teacher unions and the student unions are merely the proxies of the political parties' turf war for resources and influence, which has invaded all public and government institutions.

The student union members do not view their work as fixers or dissenters cynically because these activities are integral to the mix of idealism and opportunism that drew them to student politics, to protect the rights and welfare of students (*vidyārthī haru ko hak hit*). The student federations that spawned the contemporary FSU were established in late 1950s and early 1960s to advocate for "norm-oriented" goals like curriculum enlargement, improvement of campus facilities, and the quality of education (Altbach 1967). But the autocratic nature of the Panchayat government provoked dissent, and at that time any type of dissent became political. During the Panchayat era, student movements arose as "norm-oriented" but quickly developed into "value-oriented" movements in reaction to government suppression that obstructed student federations from making tangible demands on behalf of the student body.[7] It was at this time that student organizations became the activity of student politics, rather than a broader activity in which some politicians happened to participate (Baral [1977] 2006). Since that period, student organizations' mobilization, in all their key movements, has swung from norm-oriented to value-oriented demands due to government suppression (Snellinger 2007).

The most notable recent example of this phenomenon took place in 2003, sparking the student unions' joint movement supporting the parties' Movement Against Regression, which preempted the Second People's Movement

Students hang a poster to commemorate the first anniversary of Devi Lal Paudel's death, which sparked the students' unified participation in the Movement Against Regression. Rātō Ghar, Bāg Bazār, Kathmandu, 2004.

(Jana Āndolan II). The student organizations did not come out en masse against King Gyanendra's 2002 dismissal of the elected parliament until a student, Devi Lal Paudel, was shot during a traffic jam protesting oil price increases on April 8, 2003. A student leader explained to me: "It was at this time that we realized what was at risk. The issue was no longer the price of petrol but the principle of protesting the price of petrol. Our democratic rights were at stake and that changed the nature of the movement. It had to change. There was so much at risk, including the honor of a martyr."[8] Student cadres take to heart their original mission of norm-oriented student advocacy. When they shift into value-oriented activism, they elevate their mission to struggle for the "rights of the people" (*āmjanatā ko adhikār*). For student activists, advocating for material reform and fighting for fundamental rights are the idealistic motivators that justify the opportunistic elements of their political participation. Students navigate the tensions between politics as a dirty game and a form of public service by using their experiences of political struggle to bring the dichotomous positions of politics as an opportunity and politics as a sacrifice into unity.

The Nepali public views university politics ambivalently. On the one hand, the students' protests—which often escalate to vandalism, enforcement of nationwide strikes, campus closures, intimidation of university faculty, and other strong-arm tactics—are seen as a public menace. However, a few charismatic students always emerge as the future leaders of their party. During political movements, they come to embody hope for multiparty democracy.

In both the People's Movement (Jana Āndolan) of 1990 and the Second People's Movement (Jana Āndolan II) of 2006, the student activists' tenacity sustained the movements before the general public came out to the streets in support of the political parties. And students' protests provided the public an alternative vision of what could be possible. In 1990, they prefigured the end of the Panchayat political system by defying the ban on gathering and publicly dissenting, and their political demands included civil rights—the rights to consume, congregate in public, and organize politically and the right to a free press—which had mass public appeal. During the Movement Against Regression that led up to the Second People's Movement, youth leaders echoed public frustrations about the endemic problems of party politics and thus provided a face for their party's future at a time when the public was fed up with power politics. Student activists use their opportunity in the national spotlight during political movements to their advantage in order to cultivate public support to counter the limits their mother parties put on them and to build a constituency of support beyond the patronage-based dynamics in their political parties.

MAJOR PLAYERS IN NEPALI POLITICS

An exhaustive study of all the political parties and student organizations that exist in Nepal would be impossible, considering that there were 61 parties

TABLE 1. Political parties and affiliated student organizations included in this study

Parties	FSU Affiliate Sister Organizations
CPN-ML: Communist Party of Nepal–Marxist Leninist	ANNFSU-ML: All Nepal National Free Student Union–Marxist Leninist
CPN (Unity Centre–Masal) People's Front Nepal: Communist Party of Nepal (Unity Centre–Masal) People's Front Nepal	ANNFSU (Ekikrit): All Nepal National Free Student Union (Unified)
CPN-RM (Baidya): Communist Party of Nepal–Revolutionary Maoist (Baidya Faction)	ANNISU (R) (Baidya): All Nepal National Independent Student Union (Revolutionary) (Baidya Faction)
CPN-UML: Communist Party of Nepal–Unified Marxist Leninist	ANNFSU (Akhil): All Nepal National Free Student Union (United)
NC (D): Nepali Congress (Democratic)	NSU (D): Nepal Student Union (Democratic)
NC (K): Nepali Congress (Koirala)	NSU (K): Nepal Student Union (Koirala)
NCP-ML: Nepal Communist Party–Marxist Leninist	NPU: Nepal Progressive Union
Nepal Sadbhavana Party (Anandidevi)	Nepal Student Forum (Nepal Vidyārthī Manch)
Nepal Workers and Peasants Party (Nepal Majdūr Kisān Dal)	Nepal Revolutionary Student Union (Nepal Krāntikārī Vidyārthī Sangathan)
RPP: Rāstriya Prajātantra Parishad (National Democratic Party)	National Democratic Student Union–Nepal (Rāstriya Prajātantrik Vidyārthī Sangathan–Nepal)
RPP-N: Rāstriya Prajātantra Parishad–Nepal (National Democratic Party–Nepal)	National Democratic Student Union–Nepal (Rāstriya Prajatantrik Vidyārthī Sangathan–Nepal)
UCPN (Maoist): Unified Communist Party of Nepal (Maoist)	ANNISU (R): All Nepal National Independent Student Union (Revolutionary)

registered in the 2008 CA elections and 122 in 2013.[9] This book focuses on the main parties and student organizations that drove the political process from 2003 to 2008 (the appendix lists the parties featured in this study). Follow-up research with established informants addressed the political climate in 2008–15, which involved both party splits and mergers and the increased profile of regional and ethnic parties.

The five young leaders profiled in this book were central to the political movements between 2000 and 2006 and during the Maoist civil war.[10] They were chosen to represent the ideological spectrum and socio-cultural composition of the political landscape. I began serial interviews with all of them early in my research, addressing major conceptual and empirical topics. Their responses reflect their developing perspectives as they rose through the ranks of their parties and the political situation unfolded. Their stories demonstrate how techniques of political discipline from an individual, generational, and organizational level are mutually reinforcing.

These five individuals are university educated and have risen into the elite echelons of national politics. They were in the same cohort and worked together during the political movements between 2002 and 2006 and during the 2006–8 post–peace talks. Salini, Lagan, and Gyanu were presidents of their student unions, and the other two, Risha and Akash, vied for the NSU presidency with popular support but were stymied by the Nepali Congress (NC) party's intervention. Having been student leaders during a major political movement, all are positioned to serve as party leaders and government ministers in the future. Four are members of the three largest political parties—NC, CPN-UML, and Unified Communist Party of Nepal (Maoist) (UCPN [Maoist])—and one is from the Nepal Workers and Peasants Party (Nepal Majdūr Kisān Dal) in Bhaktapur, which, even with a small political following, has consistently won a few seats in all national elections and has a significant role in leftist politics because of its presence in the Kathmandu Valley. All five are middle-class; three identify themselves as working middle-class of agricultural backgrounds, and two are from professional families. They are from different caste and ethnic backgrounds: one male Brahmin, one male Chhetri, one female Chhetri, one female Magar, and one male Newar.

AKASH

Akash represents the prototypical high-caste male student leader in Nepali political history. He is a Chhetri whose family originally came from Solukumbhu district. He grew up in Kathmandu in an educated middle-class household and emerged as a promising leader after he was arrested for sedition in December 2003. He quickly became the voice of the young generation on the streets by simultaneously demanding the restoration of democracy and being a foil to the older party leaders whom the public blamed for the political quagmire that compelled King Gyanendra's takeover. He emerged into the national spotlight buttressed by the support of students, among whom he was beloved both within the NSU and on the Tri-Chandra College campus, where he began in student politics.

Akash has been adept at making political alliances within the NC while endearing himself to the public with his sharp critiques of his party and the political system. He used his notoriety during the street movement to keep the threatened NC leadership from marginalizing him into obscurity. At Tri-Chandra College, he entered into FSU politics with the support of Risha and some other well-connected NSU students who introduced him to NC leaders and rallied them to support Akash's bid for campus FSU president.

He handily won and from there was able to rise through the ranks of the NSU central committee through a combination of student support and party leadership blessing. His ambition became an internal threat when he angled to run for NSU president in the ninth convention, disrupting the rank-and-file promotions that the NC president, G. P. Koirala, supported. He agreed to take the position of general secretary with the understanding that he could run for the presidency in the next convention. He served as general secretary during the Movement Against Regression, establishing himself as a charismatic firebrand who eclipsed other NSU leaders.

Akash is a talented orator and sharp political thinker who has an uncanny ability for assessing the political situation and offering a game plan in effective sound bites. Having been educated in private primary and secondary schools, he has a good command of English, which made him a go-to source for the international press, foreign embassies, and international policy makers. During the Movement Against Regression, he provided the public with hope for what party politics could be in the future with leaders like him. The NC leadership obstructed his bid for the NSU presidency during the 2005 tenth convention. In what became known as the "Pokhara scandal," NSU convention members rioted in reaction to the rumor that the voter list had been tampered with to undermine him and vandalized the convention hall and vehicles in the vicinity, causing the NC to postpone the convention and insert an interim NSU central committee on the basis of "consensus." Akash continued to serve as the NSU general secretary. By the time the NSU had its convention in 2007, the NC was able to tempt Akash with a spot on its CA proportional list in lieu of running for president. He agreed and campaigned for a close compatriot, who, although not the choice of the top NC leadership, won by a large margin due to Akash's support. In the second CA election, Akash competed for the direct election in his Kathmandu constituency, number 4, which he won by a large margin. Akash has become less of a firebrand as he has emerged into national party politics, to the disappointment of many who were invested in the idea of him becoming a different type of leader. However, he still garners a lot of support locally, nationally, and internationally.

RISHA

Risha is extremely ambitious. She grew up in a family that has been active in NC politics for three generations. Her ancestral home is in Tanahun district, although her family was based on New Road, Kathmandu, dating back to when her great-great-grandfather was a colonel in the Rana army. After being educated in the Darbar High School, her grandfather took a divergent path and became a freedom fighter in the overthrow of the Rana regime. Rather than join the Panchayat administration, he fled to Chitwan and continued underground activities for the NC. After democracy was reestablished in 1990, her grandfather won local and district posts in Chitwan. Her extended family had property in the Maharajgunj neighborhood in Kathmandu that G. P. Koirala's family inhabited in the mid-1980s and eventually bought. During her childhood, Risha cultivated a close relationship with G. P. Koirala and his daughter, Sujata. They are the reason she entered into politics, and she believes deeply in the NC's democratic mission and is a staunch advocate for women's rights. She is one of five daughters, although she is the only one in politics, and three of her sisters have professional careers, with two of them working abroad.

Even with such close access to the NC's power center, Risha has had a challenging time securing positions of leadership. She was appointed vice president in the NSU, but her bid to compete for president failed twice. She now serves in the NC women's department and was on the 2013 CA elections' proportional list but was not appointed a parliamentary seat. Despite the obstacles she has faced, Risha has managed to work different angles to her advantage by promoting other students and political actors she finds promising, doling out favors, influence, and support whenever possible, and pressuring central and district leaders to endorse her causes.

Risha has also been adept at networking in international diplomatic and donor circles. During the Movement Against Regression she established herself as a female activist and was cultivated by a number of high-profile female foreign diplomats. With their support she networked beyond Nepal, in the United States, Europe, and Asia, attending international conferences on women's issues and political action, including the US International Visitors Leadership Program, and observing elections in multiple countries. She has used her contacts strategically, to learn how to organize, campaign, and finance programs, improve her English, and garner financial support.

In 2007, she established a nationwide network of women's organizations, drawing over 150 from all seventy-five districts to work together toward their common goals. She has continued to build this network and has secured funding from international organizations, including the Asia Foundation, NetCorps, the United Nations Development Programme (UNDP), and the United States Agency for International Development (USAID), to run training programs throughout the country, which utilize the women's organizations from her network to do community outreach

on issues ranging from political awareness of constitutional issues to repro-
ductive rights and health and hygiene. This work allows her to be financially
self-sufficient while garnering influence in the women's advocacy world
as well as in the political realms in places where she runs workshops. Her
political organizing and social work go hand in hand, both fueled by her
personal ambition.

SALINI

Salini was the female face of youth activism during the Movement Against
Regression, due in part to an iconic picture of her blood-stained face after
she was beaten by security forces during a protest. This picture came to
symbolize the youth force against the king in 2005 and 2006. Salini comes
from a rural village of Gulmi district. Her father was influential in resolving
disputes in the village, but, she claims, he was not involved in party politics.
Her family tilled about four hectares of mountainous, yet productive, land.
She told me that even though theirs was a modest life, her family was self-
sufficient for most of her time growing up. But as the cash economy crept
into their life, the more both her family and village struggled. It was her
teachers who helped her make sense of this situation, which laid the foundations of her political awareness. She became active in the CPN-UML student
organization in middle school and at that time resolved to finish her education so she could serve the country. She came to Kathmandu for her A-level
examinations, with a focus on nursing. Her activity in the All Nepal
National Free Student Union (ANNFSU) became her central focus, and she
shifted to a social science degree to balance her studies with politics. Early
on, she caught the attention of the Communist Party of Nepal–Marxist
Leninist (CPN-ML) leaders for having a quick mind and deft grasp of communist ideology. Her ethnic minority status also helped her standing, since,
as one leader told me, party leadership was keen to cultivate and promote
people from diverse backgrounds. That Salini is friendly, unassuming, and
approachable has allowed her to connect with cadres and leaders across the
political spectrum.

    After the notoriety Salini gained as a front-line activist in the Movement
Against Regression and the Second People's Movement, she worked her way
up the political hierarchy of the All Nepal National Free Student Union
(United) (ANNFSU [Akhil]), and in 2008 she made history again by becoming the first female president of any student organization after winning
the national election of the ANNFSU (Akhil). Since her presidential tenure
has ended, her political momentum has stagnated. She currently works in

the UML's ideology training and development department and mentors emerging student leaders. Many have noted that she has been sidelined since marrying and having a son. Nonetheless, she continues to be involved in party activities while maintaining her duties as the young daughter-in-law in an extended household. Like Risha, she was nominated for a proportional seat in the 2013 election and was skipped over for appointment. She criticized her party for this move, which garnered a lot of sympathy from the public.

LAGAN

I met Lagan when he was the chairman of the Nepal Revolutionary Student Union (Nepal Krāntikārī Vidyārthī Sangathan), which is the sister student organization to the Majdūr Kisān party. Lagan is from the Newar farming caste, Jyapu, and grew up in Bhaktapur. Although he believes in the party's mission to restructure Nepal to be a "purely socialist" republic, he was originally drawn to the party on a personal level. He explained that the party was integral to his community because his community was the party. His neighbors and family members were party cadres and leaders who opened schools, organized crop-harvesting labor shares, and saw to it that labor and resources were shared among the community. Lagan explained to me that the Majdūr Kisān party organically grew out of the farming system of the Jhapu caste in Bhaktapur. He grew up with the party, serving the peasant class and fighting for their rights. Inspired to craft his life by giving to his community through the party, he began by volunteering for party-organized community events, and then he became involved in the student organization and rose in leadership. By the time he was studying at Tribhuvan University, he was a chairman and charged with coordinating Bhaktapur students to participate in the Movement Against Regression.

After the Second People's Movement, Lagan decided not to chase parliamentary aspirations, but to refocus his political work on his community. He was frustrated that the government was ignoring the educational demands he and his fellow students made. He resolved that it was up to them to realize their own demands, and he became the principal of a locally funded secondary school. Lagan set a five-year plan for himself to institute the education system his student union was demanding, and then he returned to the party to ask what else they needed of him. It was mutually agreed that he could help connect the party and the community through his experience as a journalist, and he became a reporter and editor for the party's local newspaper. He refers to this undertaking as "mission journalism to establish a socialist system."[11] He has also continued his education, earning a master of philosophy in education, focusing on vocational training programs. He would like to pursue a doctor of philosophy in education while continuing in journalism because, as he sees it, his duty is to maximize his contribution to Bhaktapur's education, employment, and economic systems. The path Lagan has taken is a good example of how politics works locally in Nepal. The only difference is that due to Bhaktapur's proximity to Nepal's political center, Kathmandu, those like Lagan who focus on local politics are drawn into national politics when the mainstream parties need their party's support.

GYANU

If Akash represents the prototypical high-caste male political leader, then Gyanu is the other side of the coin. He is a politically radical Brahmin from a rural, agricultural family in Gorkha that struggled to make ends meet. The dominant ideology of his region was that of the CPN Masal faction led by Maoist chairman Pushpa Kamal Dahal, who is also known as Prachanda. Gyanu received his political indoctrination from his schoolteachers; the most influential was a Brahmin who died fighting in the People's War (Jana Yuddha). He started participating in ANNFSU student politics affiliated with Prachanda's faction in tenth grade, and when he shifted to Kathmandu for schooling he registered with the Communist Party (Ekata Kendra). By the time the People's War began, he was a central committee member of the party's affiliated student wing and a district chairman of Kathmandu. Between 1996 and 2000, he spent three and a half years in jail for being a Maoist rebel. During that time, he progressed up the party ranks, earning positions in absentia. He was released during the first major organized military operation and remained underground in Patan. He rose up the ranks while underground, moving around from Makwanpur to Rolpa and Dolpa, and then he walked down to Udyapur and Dhoti to run political programs but also participated in military operations. In 2004, he became president of the All Nepal National Independent Student Union (Revolutionary) (ANNISU [R]) and returned to Kathmandu.

When I met Gyanu in 2006, he was a cautious and measured individual who was dedicated to mainstreaming the ANNISU (R) on campuses across the country. He is a no-drama ideologue who believes that if people are made "aware," then they will support the Maoist cause. Student leaders from other organizations worked with him as much as they needed to; however, they kept him at arm's length, not trusting that he or his cadres would abide by FSU rules. Gyanu has had a difficult time transitioning into mainstream politics. He became frustrated with how quickly both cadres and leaders abandoned the Maoist cause to play the political game. When we met in 2009, he lamented how students were joining the ANNISU (R) out of self-interest and political opportunism.

Holding on to his principles, he gravitated to Mohan Baidya's fringe faction and was granted less and less opportunity by the Maoist ruling faction. Gyanu defected with Baidya in 2012 and participated in the election boycott of 2013 after the Unified Communist Party of Nepal (Maoist) (UCPN [Maoist]) and the first CA body abandoned the agenda of identity-based federalism. Since returning above ground in 2006, he has penned more than four books and fashioned himself as an intellectual keeper of the uncompromising Maoist flame. He has been a spokesperson for what direction radical politics in Nepal should take, writing op-eds and issues-based articles and participating in talk programs and debates. When I saw him in 2014 and asked him about his political path and how it differs from when we first met, he said: "My political life has not followed the course I expected because the country has not followed the proper path. I am still doing the same thing I was when we first met, speaking about injustice. But these days that makes me an intellectual, not a politician."[12]

The varying paths and evolving political perspectives of these five individuals provide analogue commentary of Nepal's state restructuring and their parties' role in it.

THEORETICAL FRAMEWORK

This case study of radical democracy focuses on the relational and performative dimensions controlling the agonistic nature of democratic politics. It speaks to the debate over democratic models' effectiveness articulated by voices beyond Nepal, including the Occupy movements and opposition parties that have boycotted elections in various Asian countries in the twenty-first century's first decade. Indeed, much is at stake in restructuring the Nepali state as various parties debate what democratic processes are suitable—multiparty democracy or a people's democratic republic, a proportional or first-past-the-post system, consensus or majority vote. Public pressure for inclusion, pluralism, and secularism has further challenged Nepali politics as a high-caste male enterprise. Shifting the optic to consider the stakes of political form beyond the democratic liberal purview, this book focuses on the rise of these young politicians into mainstream politics and shows that Nepal's democratic politics has always been a contentious act of claim making in which new voices struggle to reframe the terms of the debate (cf. Mouffe 2005; Rancière 1999, 2004) and over time become a part of the very system they fought to change.

The concept of political regeneration serves here as the central lynchpin to contextualize the history of activism and the socio-cultural processes that shape Nepal's national politics. Regeneration extends Karl Manheim's theory of fresh contact—in which each generation interacts with the world anew based on their accumulated socio-cultural history—by considering how generational relations mediate processes of social and political change (Cole and Durham 2007). Nepali youth activists highlight what has not been achieved by previous generations and in doing so ask the public to invest in them to improve the political system and, by default, to once again invest in multiparty democratic politics.

The category of youth is socially and politically contentious because Nepali student activists rely on it to bolster their claims of representing the young generation's "new" agendas, while their elders use it to dismiss youths' actions as immature or inexperienced (Durham 2004: 592). Analysis of youth as a political category—one defined by the complex dynamic between a traditional age-set structure, generational contestation, and the process of becoming political subjects as defined by global, rights-based discourse—reveals how power relations are mediated within Nepal's political hierarchy and demonstrates the circulation of political investment between generations in Nepal's unfolding political struggle.

As in other places, political action by youth in Nepal is affected by a shift in "patterns of temporality" (Cole and Durham 2007). The past, present, and future factor into the equations of Nepali students' being and becoming. Technological development since the modern industrial age has transformed how people experience both time and transition (13). These socio-cultural shifts have caused time to become integral to how people "shape livable presents and futures" (6). In my observations, Nepali student activists are struggling to shape a livable present, and therefore they postpone their aspirations and abstract them toward a future when they can be realized. Many scholars have theorized young people's techniques of waiting in order to cope with their socio-economic status.[13] The means by which these young Nepali activists cope with their socio-political status can be described as "not yet" (E. Bloch [1959] 1986), wherein their orientation to the future is open and they use the contingencies at their disposal to remain hopeful for what is to come (Miyazaki 2004). Their "let's see what will be" perspective cultivates hope since their critique of current politics challenges the public to reevaluate dominant norms and consider alternatives (Harvey 2000; Zournazi 2002). Thus, hope further underscores how youth works as a political category. Young Nepali activists capture political aspirations of the past and present and reframe them within a future "not-yet" orientation to direct the public toward tomorrow, when they will be national politicians (Snellinger 2016a).

Beyond youth activism, this book joins conversations in political theory and the anthropology of democracy. The young politicians who are the central focus of this book have come of age during a curious time in which international and regional forces have encouraged Nepal to liberalize the state, while the 2008 global financial crisis has made the limits of the neoliberal model apparent. These young politicians responded by negotiating a range of views, from Maoist revolutionary thought to monarchist loyalist traditions and to democratic pluralism, as they have moved from organizing mass-scale political movements to restructuring the state and society in a post–civil war peace process. Their perceptions of democracy and vision of how it fits into their society are affected by culturally specific factors such as patronage, networks of obligation, conceptions of self and group, dispute and resolution, and how power is linked to notions of reciprocity.[14]

These topical considerations have been central to postcolonial debates on what counts as political and how citizens' claims are articulated and interpreted within modern nation-states. Literature on this topic highlights a tension between the premodern and modern at the interface of global and local.[15] In anthropology, this dynamic has been framed as vernacularization (Merry 2006); the semantics of rights as discursive flow (Cowan, Dembour, and Wilson 2001); law as a normative site of regulation and production through which minority subjects are incorporated by the state (Povinelli 2002); and translation and translatability (Spencer 2007). Rights, however, are always based on earlier claims that are likely embedded more in local histories and idioms than in Western liberalism, particularly within the subaltern margins (Subramanian 2009).

But how does this dynamic work among a community that is only temporarily marginalized and whose political demands are partially motivated by desire for a place in elite, national politics? Activists from Nepal's first democratic movement onward have utilized external political principles to challenge the internal ruling system. In fact, the formation of the Nepali nation-state has developed in a field of "intercultural relations" since the 1816 Treaty of Sugauli, wherein an autonomous boundary was established between the Gorkhali empire's territory and British East India's occupied land to the south (Burghart 1984). The ways in which political values have circulated between local, regional, and transnational levels are central to understanding the role of political regeneration in Nepal's democratic struggle. Each activist generation has been shaped by its exposure to different political values on multiple scales.

The perspective of this case study thus differs from South Asian post-colonial literature of the subaltern. Although Nepal was never colonized, many have argued that it was quasi-colonized by the political elites who have governed since the Gorkhali empire consolidated the nation in 1768 (Jha 2014a; Malagodi 2013). A history of foreign dependence has also contoured Nepal as a nation-state, first during the British Raj, which has been extended since Indian independence, and over the past fifty years, as it has increasingly relied on foreign aid for state development, receiving the most official donor assistance relative to gross national income in South Asia (Upreti et al. 2012). Thus, Nepal's politics has always been a discursive conversation with external political principles from the South Asian region, the Cold War debates, and, within the past few decades, the global human rights and development regime. Due to the ongoing struggle to establish multi-party democracy, Nepali activists have leveraged external political norms to challenge the autocratic orders of the Rana regime (1846–1951), the Panchayat government (1960–90), and King Gyanendra's takeover (2002–6). In this regard, Nepali politics has always comprised a dialogical relationship between external and internal political values, making modern liberal rights discourse, communist ideology, nepotism, patronage, and non-transparency all constitutive dimensions of Nepali politics, each as universal and local as the other.

These different ideologies map onto the student activists' multi-scalar relationships. Out of necessity, these young politicians have followed the socio-historical trend of their forefathers by seeking influence through lateral and vertical scales to circumvent the limits they face from both state autocracy and political hierarchy. Their scaling techniques replicate the boomerang pattern that has propelled the spread of transnational networks (Keck and Sikkink 1998); they look outside their parties to garner support from national and international circles, which in turn forces their party elders to acknowledge their influence. Their scalar politics simultaneously underscore "inherited arrangements and emergent projects and relations" (MacKinnon 2010: 31), supporting the book's main tenet of political regeneration. These young political actors are not merely engaging in vernacularization by translating universal concepts into local idioms (Merry 2006). They are mediating Nepal's socio-political heritage while crafting a political horizon for Nepali citizens to invest in. By analyzing how these young activists have established themselves through relationships with influential actors on the local, national, regional, and transnational levels, this book demonstrates how political ideas, values, and practices actually circulate, through new and old relationships that vary in power, values, and histories.

This dynamic between different political principles and local idioms over time has not produced synthesis or established democracy as a set sphere. Rather, democracy in Nepal has been a continual process of dissensus. Dissensus is the contestation over political meaning—what was, what is, and what is yet to be—that forces democracy to be the ongoing formation of new political subjects (Rancière 1999, 2004, 2010). The formation of political subjects in Nepal occurs literally with each new generation that comes into politics and epistemologically as their political assertions generate new meaning. Dissensus in Nepali politics is fueled by youth, which serves as a social mechanism for reconfiguration within the process of political regeneration.

1 Manufacturing the State, Politics, and Politicians

WHILE I WAS COLLECTING ACCOUNTS WITH ACTIVISTS WHO HAD been underground and jailed during King Gyanendra's coup of February 1, 2005, a student activist friend with close ties to the police arranged for me to meet the police captain overseeing security at the ASCOL, Shankar Dev, Biswabhāsā, and law campuses. On the captain's day off, he invited me into the barracks so we could talk in a private setting. During our conversation, he said: "You know this is all a drama, right? Tomorrow we might be on the streets under the order of G. P. Koirala, or maybe even Prachanda, arresting royalist protesters. Our job is to stop the havoc and maintain security. We have no investment in suppressing any particular group. Our superiors decide that."[1] At the time, his justification seemed complicit. I did not push him to explicate. Instead, I immediately thought of all the disappearances the Royal Nepal Army and security forces were responsible for during the ongoing civil war. Only later, after the debates on army integration and the truth and reconciliation committee, did I understand his point. During our conversation, I was fixated on the "sides" of politics that were being enacted on the streets and hinterlands and entrenched through media representations and international assessments of the political situation. The captain was commenting on the ever-shifting terrain of collaboration, cooperation, and competition in Nepali politics.

Nonetheless, this "drama," as the captain called it, is shaped by traditional power structures. The effects manifest in two ways. The first is in how different political forces claim legitimacy in their contestations for and usurpation of state power. The second involves how these traditional power structures have determined the varying distribution of socio-political accommodation afforded to Nepali citizens, which in turn has shaped the demands different groups of citizens have made on the state. Political actors have merged these two effects instrumentally through their claim to be fighting on behalf of the people in their struggle for democracy, development, and nation building. Even King Gyanendra justified his two coups to "establish democracy on firmer foundations," claiming his grandfather King Tribhuvan, "the architect of democracy," as inspiration while following his father's Panchayat model (Gellner 2007: 50). What becomes apparent in how this political "drama" has unfolded is the degree to which the status quo is maintained with political change occurring incrementally.

THE POLITICS OF STATE AND SOCIETAL STRUCTURING

The state project is an act of ideology, one that is incomplete and is continually being negotiated. One of the leading tasks of the state project is to fog its incompleteness in order to appear legitimate, "which prevents our seeing political practice as it is" (Abrams 1988: 58). Rather, loose ends and slippages ensure that state construction is a dynamic process of dissidence, co-optation, and compromise (Sayer 1994). To grasp the contours of nationalism within state construction, "we have to understand the practical uses of the category 'nation,' the ways it can come to structure perception, to inform thought and experience, to organize discourse and political action" (Brubaker 1996: 7). In Nepal's case, this involves tracking the discursive and institutional processes that structured and maintained Nepal as a Hindu kingdom into the twenty-first century. Nepal's development as a nation-state was European in style; Nepal negotiated its territorial sovereignty in an "intracultural context" with the British. However, this formation "cannot be separated analytically from Nepal's intercultural field of relations" (Burghart 1996: 227). This process involved positioning the citizens vis-à-vis the nation-state through the principle of diversity into unity, first under the Shah monarchy and Hinduism and later through the Nepali language (Burghart 1984, 1996; Malagodi 2013; Onta 1996).

Nepal has been exclusionary since its birth and through its development into a nation-state. There is a rich scholarship documenting the exclusionary tenants of the Nepali state from the viewpoint of ethnic and regional dispossession, an issue that has mobilized the Maoists and the Janajāti (ethnic minorities) communities to question the basis of the Nepali state.[2] As a counterpoint, this volume focuses on elite contestations for state power.[3] The history of democratic party politics is in tandem with the state-making enterprise that has co-opted resistance sometimes through compromise but mainly through repression, a process that continually shapes activists' and politicians' assumptions and attitudes of the Nepali nation as a state.[4] The different political demands and claims of legitimacy political parties have made are in response to how the sovereign nation-state of Nepal was established.

Prithvi Narayan Shah, the Gorkha king, described the newly consolidated kingdom he attained from military conquests between 1743 and 1769 as a "true Hindustan," a "'garden' of four *varnas* and thirty-six *jāts*" (S. Sharma 2002: 25).[5] This maxim has come to glorify Nepal's diversity, but diversity that is contained within the "true Hindustan," which was strategically meant to contrast the Hindu kingdoms of North India that had been undermined by Muslim rule.[6] Shah established political legitimacy as the enforcer of the Hindu socio-cosmic order, and all later regimes used Hinduism to legitimate their rule. Shah's Gorkhali empire ritualistically maintained the Hindu realm (*deśa*) and later evolved into the sovereign nation-state of Nepal bounded by territory in accordance with the sociopolitical history unfolding in South Asia (Burghart 1996). The East India Company's defeat of the Gorkhali kingdom in the Anglo-Nepali war (1814–16) physically grounded the Hindu realm within the boundaries set by the Treaty of Sagauli. This treaty represents Nepal's first encounter with European political modernity, which imposed "a European-style linear and fixed border" distinguishing between Gorkhali territory and the East India Company's territory (Malagodi 2013: 71). The fixed inalienable border was the first step in creating a Gorkha polity whose sovereignty was recognized by Britain (72).[7]

When the Rana regime (1846–1951) seized power through the "Kot massacre" coup, it further entrenched Nepal as a Hindustan unified under the symbol of the Shah monarchy. To retain political legitimacy, Rana leaders established themselves as the administrative vessel through which the Shah monarchy ruled, diminishing the king to a ritualistic figurehead. During the Rana regime, state festivals and religious ceremonies left the confines of the royal temple and became public events.[8] Dasain is the largest ceremony and is still practiced today as an official state holiday, for which six days of leave are granted.[9] Essentially, Dasain was meant to ensure the Rana and subsequent governments' governing hierarchy by reinforcing hierarchal dependence. Superiors give *tikā* blessings on the forehead of all those who come and ask for it, and they also give gifts to junior relatives and servants. Inferiors who make an animal sacrifice for their family or household will also invoke their boss or patron when doing so. This ritual happens at the state level, with the king, army, and governing officials making sacrifices to the goddess Durga; in every stratum of society people honor their superiors and superiors' superiors in kind. This annual ritual is meant to reinforce the socio-political order of the entire country (Krauskopff and Lecomte-Tilouine 1996). During the 1990s, the Maoists and ethnic groups boycotted Dasain, the former to undermine state authority and the latter as a political act of re-embracing their Buddhist roots and defining themselves as "not Hindu" vis-à-vis the state (Hangen 2010).

In 1854, the Muluki Ain (law of the country) codified the Hindu social hierarchy into law (Höfer 1979). As the first attempt at legal uniformity, the Muluki Ain cemented an agenda of state-driven Sanskritization (Malagodi 2013: 79). The legal code subsumed all ethnic groups and tribes within the caste system, outlined behavioral sanctions on groups according to their assigned caste classification, and delineated the interactions between citizens according to caste tradition (e.g., from whom one can receive water or with whom one can eat, marry, or copulate). Throughout the Rana rule, local leaders from diverse ethnic backgrounds had to negotiate regime expectations to maintain varying degrees of local autonomy.[10]

In 1962, the constitution of King Mahendra's partyless Panchayat system banned caste discrimination, and legal statutes were adjusted to create caste equality in the eyes of the law (Höfer 1979). But the caste system was not abolished in the 1962 constitution or the democratic constitution of 1990 (Hoftun, Raeper, and Whelpton 1999; S. Sharma 2002). Many ethnographic studies have demonstrated that despite the central government's distance, its practices insidiously penetrated local tradition because the government administration incorporated leaders at every level, allowing them to profit through law enforcement and tenurial revenue collection.[11] Thus, the Muluki Ain was an act of not merely state building but social structuring that enshrined caste and ethnic-based discrimination, which exists to this day.

The ideological continuity between the Shah monarchy and Rana rule allowed King Tribhuvan to resume power after the overthrow of the Rana regime in 1950 (Whelpton 1991: 244). The 1959 constitution established multiparty democracy under constitutional monarchy and in "positivist legal terms" was the first to codify the monarchy as a Hindu kingship (Malagodi 2013: 86). This constitution was barely enacted because in 1960 King Mahendra staged a royal coup, banning political parties and establishing the Panchayat system. King Mahendra relied heavily on Hinduism to legitimize his Panchayat governing system; the 1962 constitution was the first to define Nepal legally as a Hindu kingdom, and it maintained the ban on conversion from the 1959 constitution (90–91). King Mahendra aimed to modernize Nepal while maintaining "the triumvirate of official Nepali national culture": Hinduism, the Shah monarchy, and the Nepali language (Onta 1996: 214, in Malagodi 2013: 91). In 1990, the political system shifted to multiparty democracy, but the three main pillars remained in order to preserve national unity (Malagodi 2013: 143). Those drafting the constitution justified their decision as having symbolic import meant to preserve social harmony; however, their constitutional nationalism perpetuated patterns of legal exclusion. By taking for granted the "essentially political idea of the inner unity of the Nepali State," the constitution makers never questioned whether the "ontological and ideational foundations of the Nepali state" (159) could be otherwise. Despite being a new institutional arrangement, ideologically it remained contingent on "'His Majesty' as a symbol of the nation" (20).

The process by which Nepal became a Hindu state was the result of institutional choices made by the ruling elite who wanted to establish their "ethnocultural version of the nation" (13) to maintain a particular social order. Entrenching Hinduism as the organizing state principle ensured their authority, whether in the guise of an absolute monarchy, Rana rule, a Panchayat monarchy, a representative democracy, or a democratic republic. Framing Nepal as a Hindu monarchy was the official agenda for 238 years. And every entity that has either supported or challenged the Nepali state has had to do so on these terms.

Elite ideology contends with this version of the nation through its political claims, demands, processes, rituals, and discourse. A stark example of this is that even politicians who have challenged the king's divine right to rule have gone to receive *tikā* from the king in an official capacity. The *tikā* blessing is also commonplace in political ritual across party lines. Even the Maoists adorned their soldiers' foreheads with the red rice paste and draped them with marigold garlands as they went off to the battlefields. And still today, after the abolition of the monarchy and the Hindu nation-state, politicians draw on Hindu religious metaphors in their speeches and political rituals. These metaphors envelop references to the nation and land to create a sense of solidarity and a sense of shared responsibility to act for the good of the nation. Such rhetorical devices are used seamlessly alongside democratic discourse, demonstrating their currency in traditional footholds of power.

VIKĀS (DEVELOPMENT)

Nepal may have relied on particular cultural and religious logics to organize itself internally, but its geographic position influenced how it projected itself externally. Nepal began engaging geopolitically in the era of modern nation-states, which shaped how it negotiated with foreign powers. The Panchayat government (1960–90) marked the end of isolationism, thirteen years after the Cold War's beginning and India's independence. Nepal's geographic position between India and China made it a nation of interest to both sides during the Cold War. Nepal opted for a policy of non-alignment, which allowed it to court India, China, the United States, and Russia for foreign investment to develop national infrastructure and governing structures.

India's development discourse certainly made an impact on Nepal. The Panchayat government was tasked with the challenge of the state acting as the "rational allocator and arbitrator for the nation" (Chatterjee [1986] 1993: 168). This presented a challenge to King Mahendra, who had recently usurped control from the squabbling political parties and subsequently banned them. He needed simultaneously to establish legitimacy within Nepal and externally to other countries as a sovereign nation-state with rational governance and administration.

The Panchayat government recognized the potential power and wealth that could be consolidated through the process of modernization (Panday 1999). King Mahendra linked development to the democratic project he was executing through local Panchayat councils that were "true to the soil" (Gellner 2015: 101). Development simultaneously pushed Nepal to become dependent on external powers as the Panchayat government tried to cultivate the state as the provider of basic necessities.[12] But since maintaining Panchayat power took precedence over the welfare of the citizenry, development ultimately produced little more than institutionalized corruption, serving the old and the new proprietary classes rather than the general public (Panday 1999: 254).

The benefits of development projects were threefold: first, they became an alternative revenue stream for government officials to amass wealth and political legitimacy through resource distribution; second, resource distribution through development schemes encouraged nationalistic loyalty from Nepal's diverse citizenry; and third, foreign investment legitimated and protected Nepal's borders from regional encroachment.[13] King Birendra's 1976 diplomatic initiative to establish Nepal as a "Zone of Peace" is most often described as a plan to attract investors, pitching Nepal as the Switzerland of South Asia (R. Shaha 1982).[14] It also juxtaposed Nepal's peace with India's communal violence. Manufacturing of such images encouraged international treatment of Nepal as a nation-state, which, to leery nationalists, also protected Nepal's sovereignty from Indian encroachment.

Although the post-1990 democratic government categorically abandoned the use of Panchayat government policies, it was not willing to forego the aid game and development dollars. With the deregulation of non-governmental agencies and many other services, Nepal went from being a socialized system to a liberalized one with minimal regulation. Every sector opened to foreign investment as both governmental and private endeavors negotiated the remaking of Nepal as a democratic, free market with an open civil society. At first, international NGO (INGO) discourse contributed to the image that things were changing in Nepal. But ultimately "NGO-ization" made Nepal vulnerable to all of the typical downfalls of poorly guided investment, reliance on transnational expertise, and the re-entrenchment of local power elites who emerged as middlemen (Pigg 1997: 265). Local elites quickly mastered the discourse of democratization, civil society, and empowerment in order to maintain their positions of power while funneling money as they saw fit (Harper and Tarnowski 2002). There is much research that documents how "distributional coalitions" (Pfaff-Czarnecka 2008) work together to become "civil society patrons" (S. Tamang 2002) whom beneficiaries are reliant upon and may even need to be obedient to (cited in Gellner 2015: 113–14).

INGOs and NGOs in Nepal positioned themselves as an alternative to the government by emphasizing their transnational networks and material resources (S. Shaha 2004). Development projects were no longer five-year plans implemented by the Panchayat government. Rather, donors came to the fore and people started to understand that USAID, the UK Department for International Development (DFID), the International Monetary Fund (IMF), and the World Bank, as well as private donors, were responsible (Hindman 2014a). Implementation was left to INGOs and NGOs, and the government was seen as largely peripheral. The fact that the democratically elected government was doing little for local municipalities further undermined the democratic parties' claims to represent and provide for its citizenry. Yet despite its pro-poor policies and democratic emphasis on empowerment, development perpetuated power imbalances between those who give and those who receive (Gellner 2015: 100). The Maoist People's War was fueled by the realization that both the democratic government and development aid contributed less to improving peoples' lives and more to corruption and maintenance of traditional power structures (Fujikura 2003; Hutt 2004; Thapa and Sijapati 2003). Their armed insurgency was a turning point for Nepal; foreign entities, in particular, used it to diagnose the country as going from a developing state to a soft state to, after ten years of armed conflict, a failed state (Fund for Peace 2013; Lawoti and Pahari 2010; Riaz and Basu 2007).[15] In this sense, Nepal had fallen victim to the new imperialism, development (Harvey 2003).

OPEN SOCIETY, PROTEST ERA,
AND DOWNFALL OF THE MONARCHY

The 1990 People's Movement was meant to transform the nation-state of Nepal. But it has since been criticized as a high-caste grab for power that had been generating for thirty years.[16] For many it was merely a regime change that had no central impact on their lives. Particularly in the country-side, people were vulnerable to the same hardships that plagued them for generations: poverty, feudal conditions, and marginalization. The rhetoric had nonetheless changed. Many received democracy by way of radio, magazines, and teachers emphasizing individual choice, progress, and success (Ahearn 2001; Fujikura 2003; Kunreuther 2014). Moreover, the landscape of the urban areas was altered in various ways. Deregulation allowed the private market to pick up where the government had slacked, namely, media, education, and telecommunications.[17] Furthermore, liberal free market principles rely on a stable state maintained by a strong civil society for an economy to thrive. The presence of donor agencies, NGOs, and INGOs fueled the desire to create a civil society in which everyone could participate and from which everyone would benefit (Gellner 2011, 2015). With the newfound protection of free speech enabling people to speak out and make demands, Nepal entered a protest era where most anything was open for contestation (Lakier 2007; Gellner 2011). Student groups and unions regularly protested government policy. Minority ethnic groups embraced their identity and history of marginality as a basis to demand equal access and representation through the Janajāti movement (Hangen 2007, 2010; Lawoti 2005; Shneiderman 2015).

The ultimate protest was a ten-year civil war (1996–2006) that polarized people between the ideologies of Maoism, multiparty democracy, and the monarchy. Different political actors asserted liberal democratic values, communist ideals, and minority rights to undermine the univocal vision of Nepal as a Hindu nation. The 2001 royal massacre—which shifted the line of succession from Birendra to his brother, Gyanendra, and his progeny, revealing the logical fallacies in the Shah monarchy's divine right to rule—soured many on the monarchy. When King Gyanendra's power grab in 2005 yielded little but erosion of civil liberties, economic hardship, and increasing insecurity, the possibility of becoming a democratic secular republic began to resonate. At first public sentiment was mixed over this king's 2002 and 2005 takeovers; many thought the parties' democratic project failed and peace and security were more important than the right to vote

This elder's T-shirt demonstrates how mainstream the idea of individual and communal rights and empowerment have become. Bagbana, Parsa, 2013.

for ineffective, corrupt politicians. In February 2005, a large sector of the population was cautiously optimistic; they thought the king's takeover was decisive and perhaps could bring stability to the country. But people became less tolerant after the king did not capitalize on the Maoists' four-month cease-fire to negotiate peace. Beginning in September 2005, the parties and the Maoists had been in a series of talks to establish a united agenda in which to regain power in the name of the people, which culminated in the Second People's Movement in April 2006. At that point, the demand for a republic became as audible as the call for "complete" democracy (*purna prajātantra*) was two years before.

After the fall of the king in 2006, peace talks were brokered between the political parties and Maoists, who then held peaceful Constituent Assembly (CA) elections in 2008. All parties accepted the outcome of the Maoist majority government. Nepal was officially declared a democratic secular

Party activists escorting a van announcing a political sit-in program. Jamal, Kathmandu, 2004.

republic during the first CA session in May 2008. Nepal entered the process of state restructuring to remedy the structural and symbolic violence caused by its construction as a Hindu nation. This era was coined "making new Nepal." The post-conflict period was an extension of local, regional, and transnational "intercultural relations" (Burghart 1984) coming together, again, this time to restructure the Nepali nation-state. Donor and diplomatic transnational agencies have been intimately involved in rebuilding Nepal. The United Nations Mission in Nepal (UNMIN) was a mediating force in the peace talks, the 2008 CA elections, and army reintegration, during which it followed the UN peace-building commission's standardized protocol for international intervention to establish liberal democratic state institutions in post-conflict countries.[18] By 2011, the UNMIN's mandate expired, and the CA refused to extend it, leaving many citizens asking what had become of "new Nepal." The post-conflict category employed by normative state-building agencies clearly did not map onto the everyday lives of citizens (Shneiderman and Snellinger 2014).

Instead, the political process diminished into "long-term provisionality" (Hindman 2014b). For five years, CA parliamentarians from different warring sides tried to maintain their multiparty consensus mandate to restructure the state and draft a new constitution as stipulated by the comprehensive peace agreement and the interim constitution. But consensus proved elusive, and the CA—which simultaneously served as the acting parliamentary body—shifted into the type of power struggles that threatened past democratic governments. After four postponements, the first CA expired on May 27, 2012, when the CA failed to reach consensus over a federal state structure, causing the prime minister to call for new elections after the Supreme Court refused a fifth CA extension. The second CA elections were held in November 2013. The centrist Nepali Congress (NC) secured the most seats, with the previous victors, the Unified Communist Party of Nepal (Maoist), coming in a distant third, and the royalist party, the National Democratic Party–Nepal (Rāstriya Prajātantra Parishad–Nepal [RPP-N]), coming in fourth with twenty-four proportionate seats. This reshuffle of power made the second CA less diverse than the original one. Between the peace talks in 2007 until the promulgation of the constitution in 2015, there were eight government reshuffles.

THE HISTORY OF STUDENT POLITICS

The 1950 revolution, which was coordinated between the NC and King Tribhuvan to overthrow the Rana regime, formalized the struggle for democracy in Nepal. However, Nepali university students played an integral role as early as the mid-1930s. The Rana regime's repression unwittingly created the situation in which students became politically aware and anti-Rana, in two ways. The first was political repression at the Tri-Chandra College campus. Tri-Chandra College, established in 1919 and first affiliated with Calcutta University, was Nepal's first tertiary institution. Originally, it was opened to allow Nepalese students to take Indian university exams domestically so they would not be exposed to radical politics on Indian campuses (Whelpton 2005: 83). In 1940, the Rana government cracked down on some isolated incidents of dissent over the poor quality of education, including jailing popular students, some of whom died while imprisoned. When Laxminandan Chalise was arrested for an essay critical of the Rana family, he is claimed to have said: "Friends! Life is nothing. I fulfilled my duty and you too shall not stray from your duties" (Ojha 2012: 42). Principal democratic activists who were mobilized by these events as Tri-Chandra students included Tanka Prasad Acharya, who started the Praja Parishad (People's Council), the organization that ultimately brought the demise of the Rana regime, and Ganesh Man Singh, founding member of the Nepali National Congress (43–44).

The second factor that spurred political awareness was the dearth of education institutions in Nepal, causing many to study in India. Those who were studying in exile in or had fled to India were exposed to the Indian Nationalist movement and participated in Mahatma Gandhi's satyagraha campaign, which greatly influenced these future politicians' struggle for democracy in Nepal (Hoftun, Raeper, and Whelpton 1999: 5).[19] They organized among themselves, establishing the Nepal Association (Nepali Sangha) and the Nepal Students' Association (Chhatra Sangha) at Banaras Hindu University in 1935 and the Association of Students of the Himalayas at Calcutta University in 1945. They actively coordinated with other Nepali exiles and migrants, including participating in the 1946 meeting that established the Nepali National Congress in Banaras, and then they returned to Nepal to organize their peers in Kathmandu to participate in the 1950 overthrow of the Rana regime.

The Jayatu Sanskritam (Victory to Sanskrit) movement of 1947 was the first organized student protest against the Rana regime.[20] This student movement originated at the Sanskrit Hostel (Tin Dhara Pathshala) of the Durbar High School. At the time, Sanskrit was the only subject offered to the Brahmin students studying for the Acharya degree. Both students and teachers saw the discrepancy in their education, opportunities, and salaries compared to the Rana elite who were studying English in the same building. These students were becoming politically aware in the 1940s while traveling to Banaras to take their exams amid India's independence movement (Ojha 2012: 52–76). There was mounting resentment over political repression at Tri-Chandra College and the second-class status of Sanskrit education in Nepal. Frustrated after their exams in Banaras were disrupted by Hindu-Muslim riots in 1946 and yet inspired by their participation in the first Nepali National Congress convention of January 26, 1947, in Calcutta and the subsequent jute mill strikes in Biratnagar, these Sanskrit students decided to demand concessions from the Rana government to expand their curriculum and allow them to take their exams in Nepal. Their request was ignored, and they went on strike from June 1 to June 15, 1947. The Rana regime submitted to expanding their curriculum; however, their other demands were ignored.

The students continued to rally for their unmet demands while insisting that humanities courses also be included in the curriculum. But the Rana government's tolerance had been exhausted; it ordered raids on the campuses, imprisoned students, and exiled forty-two others (Ojha 2012: 70). Many of these exiles returned to India and became active in the Nepal Praja

Parishad. The Jayatu Sanskritam agitators were instrumental in the Nepal Praja Parishad's 1950 revolution that ended the Rana regime and established multiparty democracy with a constitutional monarchy. During an inauguration of the semi-centenary of the Jayatu Sanskritam movement, Prime Minister Surya Bahadur Thapa declared that the Jayatu Sanskritam movement "sounded the bugle call" (73). These events marked the beginning of the entanglement of educational and political demands and the universities as central places for political organization in Nepal.

PANCHAYAT ERA

While university students participated in these formative struggles to establish democracy, student politics became an established institution during the Panchayat's rule (1960–90). When instituting the one-party system, King Mahendra banned all other political party activity, which drove the party leaders and activists underground. The political parties relied on the student unions to indoctrinate students to support the parties' democratic and communist struggles. During the Panchayat era, there were two forums to participate in politics, within the Panchayat party and its affiliate class organizations or in student politics on university campuses. Due to the political space afforded to students on the campuses, they became the hands and mouths of the underground parties. In time, student politics came to represent the struggle for multiparty democracy because the student organizations were allowed to engage in the open electoral competition within the Free Student Union (FSU) and thus became a proxy for multiparty democracy.

Similar to the Rana regime, the Panchayat government was leery of the students' potential to foment revolt against its one-party system. It tried to squelch dissent in a few ways. First, it infiltrated the Nepal Rāstriya Vidyārthī Mahasangh (Nepal National Student Federation [NNSF]). The NNSF was created in 1949 by communist supporters and was central in overthrowing the Rana regime. During the years of tentative democratic rule in the 1950s, the NNSF went from being a cross-platform federation to a pro-communist, anti-Congress organization. After King Mahendra's dismissal of the multiparty government, the NNSF became directionless as pro-palace students inserted themselves into the organization. The leftist students abandoned the organization, and the NNSF became defunct until 1969.

The government also attempted to curb dissent by targeting student organizations under the National Directives Law of 1961. It asserted that student unions fell under the rubric of class organization in the Panchayat system.

This move galvanized the students against the government. They demanded the right to organize student unions freely nationwide. Since they were unable to gather publicly to make their demand, students began organizing zonal and district committees to maintain a student front despite government crackdowns. Nepali students outside of Nepal, in Banaras and Calcutta, also provided support by instituting the Democratic Social Youth League and the Democratic Youth Group.

In response to the mounting student organizing, the Panchayat government instituted the Nepal Student Organization (NSO) as a pro-government class organization in 1962. The other student unions were in fact formed in reaction to the Panchayat government's attempt to indoctrinate students through the NSO. The anti-Panchayat students came to revile the NSO, and during protests in 1966 they targeted the NSO's offices in retaliation for police crackdowns against their demands for a free student union, standardized fees, and other educational requests. In response, the government repealed the National Directives Law against student organizations and disbanded the NSO, allowing students to organize the FSU.

Unwittingly, the Panchayat government turned the FSU into a multipartisan endeavor. With the right to organize freely on campuses under the guise of FSU activity, different political factions began instituting their own organizations. The progressive and leftist students established the All Nepal National Free Student Union (ANNFSU) nationally in 1967, which destroyed the anti-Panchayat opposition unity the students had maintained until that point. Nevertheless, the Panchayat government was unwilling to sit on the sidelines of the FSU activity on campus. In 1968, pro-Panchayat students created the Rāstriya Swatantra Vidyārthī Mandal (Nationalist Independent Student Council [NISC]). Students who participated in the NISC were groomed for future positions in the Panchayat government. They were known by the derogatory term "mandale," deriving from the term "mandal" (council), for policing so-called anti-national activities on campuses.

In 1970, the NC officially established its own student union by the reinstituted name Nepal Student Union (NSU), in order to fill the political vacuum after multiple leftist factions defected from the ANNFSU. During the inaugural convention, there was a police crackdown and over one hundred students were arrested for participating in political activities. After three months in jail, they were released on July 9, 1970, under a Supreme Court habeas corpus ruling, which also declared that student organizations within the FSU were not political organizations and thus had the right to organize. The NSU finally held its inaugural conference in 1971 (Ojha 2012: 191).

The Panchayat government again tried to curb partisan student activity through its institution of the 1971 National Education System Plan (NESP). The new educational policy was a step toward American education; it introduced a semester system with regular exams and attendance, which left little time for politics.[21] Many who were student and party activists at the time continue to regard the education policy suspiciously as a Panchayat machination to eliminate dissent rather than improve education under the pressure of foreign aid. NISC students violently enforced these new education policies on campuses from 1975 to 1979, a period known as the "mandale terror" (Ojha 2012: 150). One of the key demands the students made during their political movement of 1978–79 was to roll back the NESP mandates affecting higher education and disband the NISC student organization.

Another plan the Panchayat government introduced in the hopes of tamping dissent was the Back to the Village campaign through the National Development Service (1972–79). Implemented as part of the 1971 NESP policy, this program required master's students at Tribhuvan University to perform a year of service that involved practical training in first aid, agriculture, teaching, and local development; a ten-month village stay working with local Panchayat officials; and the submission of a village report to the central government. Over 90 percent of the districts participated (Messerschmidt, Gautam, and Silwal 2007). As frustration mounted over the confusing implementation of the service program, students put forth a twenty-eight-point demand to the government, which led to region-wide strikes in 1975. Ultimately, negotiations with the government failed because the students did not maintain a united front. The program was the Panchayat's answer to sustainable development that would also provide surveillance of local administrators (Gellner 2015). But in reality, the students took advantage of this process in order to politicize village leaders and broaden their underground political networks. The program served to unify the country, but in ways unforeseen by the Panchayat government.

The next major student agitation was in 1979. It began as a small protest of conscience, but the result altered Nepali political history by setting the stage for the nationwide referendum that allowed banned political parties to campaign nationwide in 1981 (Rana 1995: 422–25). On April 7, 1979, two hundred students marched to the Pakistani embassy to protest the execution of Z. A. Bhutto. "Protests against a dictatorship abroad were transparently protests against authoritarianism at home" (Gellner 2015: 107). In this instance, the police manifested such authoritarianism by refusing to let the marching students enter a main thoroughfare and block traffic at a time the king was scheduled to be in the area. Clashes broke out between the students and policemen. The students' gathering was no longer about Bhutto's execution but was instead about their own suppression. In the days that followed there were protests throughout the country, with police brutality causing several deaths. Such an escalation had not been expected on a nationwide scale, and King Birendra ordered a royal commission to investigate the students' demands.[22] The student action committee, which consisted of three students, Bal Bahadur K.C. (NSU), Sharan Vikram Malla (ANNFSU), and Kailas Karki (NNFS), reached an agreement with the commission, which ended the new education policy, abolished university entrance exams (making entrance accessible to all who passed the National School Leaving Examination); allowed for independent unions on a national level; and dissolved the National Independent Student Forum, the pro-Panchayat student organization.[23]

Despite significant reform achieved at the university level, the students were frustrated with the lack of state-level reform. The three representatives of the student action committee bore the brunt of their fellow students' frustrations the next day, May 22, 1979, while reporting their bargain with the government. An outcry arose over the lack of broader political change. The students painted Bal K.C.'s and Sharan Malla's faces black, hung garlands of shoes around their necks, and paraded them through the streets for their alleged deceit.[24] The demonstration grew to about twenty-five thousand protesters and culminated in the burning of a government newspaper office and the destruction of public vehicles in front of the Royal Nepal Airlines Corporation office.

On May 24, 1979, King Birendra announced that he would hold a nationwide referendum allowing people to choose between a multiparty system and the Panchayat-style government. He even permitted the underground parties to campaign for the referendum throughout the country. Many leaders were suspicious of such a move, though eventually the parties worked together to campaign for the national referendum. Ultimately, the government won the referendum.[25] The Panchayat system's victory was suspect; many believed election irregularities occurred. Ganesh Man Singh, the NC's general secretary at that time, claimed, "Only foolish men can believe that a free and fair referendum will be possible under Panchayat Rule" (Hoftun, Raeper, and Whelpton 1999: 91). Nevertheless, the role the 1979 student movement played in opening things up politically cemented students' place in politics. By 1980, claims such as the following were being made: "It is clear that students and politics are synonymous words. One cannot be separated from the other. In the absence of any one of them, the nation loses its spine. Students are one of the means to make politics strong and powerful" (Amatya, Agrawal, and Pradhan 1980: 3).

For the next decade, the parties were officially banned but operated marginally in public. They were visible; they had offices and political programs, but they were not technically allowed to do so and thus were constantly vulnerable to surveillance, arrest, and the risk of being shut down. The student organizations, in contrast, were legally sanctioned entities that openly organized on campuses. At this time, the dynamic between the student organizations and the political parties began to shift. Previously, the political parties were more dependent on the student organizations, but after the national referendum the parties became a viable political option. The parties relied on the student organizations to host political programs and arrange logistics and publicity as well as conduct political indoctrination on the campuses, but less so as a means to maintain party survival.

REINSTATEMENT OF DEMOCRACY

The student unions, along with other professional associations, were key in mobilizing the mass protests of the 1990 People's Movement that led to the reinstatement of multiparty democracy under a constitutional monarchy. The student organizations had already been coordinating among themselves in the six months leading up to the People's Movement. In August 1989, they held a nineteen-day convention and drafted a nine-point program to create cooperation and coordination with other anti-Panchayat organizations. In December 1989, seven student organizations issued a joint statement declaring they would "prepare the atmosphere" by publicizing and rallying the public to participate in the People's Movement (Ojha 2012: 252).

The lines of communication and influence established between the parties and their sister organizations in the previous few decades allowed the students to carry out the activism that party leaders were still unable to undertake, primarily getting people to the streets.[26] Though directives were given from the top, the students oversaw much of the protest strategy from hour to hour over the chaotic two-month course of the movement. Unlike in the past, this movement was not merely opposition from the elite political leaders backed by party cadres or a student movement. The agitation ballooned to include the urban public nationwide. Over the course of the movement, protests, sit-ins, strikes, torch rallies, blackouts, and signature campaigns were mounted by every type of professional, political, and communal organization. After a protest of eighty thousand people in Patan, activists were able to seize control of the city and cut it off from Kathmandu by digging trenches at all points of access (Ogura 2001). They declared Patan to be a zone free of the Panchayat government. At the movement's peak, an estimated half million people congregated in the center of Kathmandu, which was thought to be the largest gathering recorded in Nepali history (Hoftun, Raeper, and Whelpton 1999: 131). For the third time in Nepal's political history, student activists were instrumental in securing the possibility for their parties in government.

The only political campaign of note during the early years of reestablished democracy was ANNFSU's Kalapani campaign (June 5–20, 1998), in which students marched to the border to protest Indian encroachment, although many viewed it as a stunt manufactured by the Communist Party of Nepal–Unified Marxist Leninist (CPN-UML) to whip up nationalist fervor.[27] Only Maoist-affiliated students pursued contentious politics focusing on socio-economic justice in the 1990s. They actively enforced a boycott on the 1994 midterm election, including booth capturing in Rolpa (Ojha 2012: 273). They heavily recruited and indoctrinated campus students, and after their mother party declared revolution in 1996, they continued recruitment surreptitiously. Maoist student activists also oversaw the indoctrination of primary and secondary students and teachers in their stronghold areas, enforced nationwide school closures, collected taxes from private schools, and pressured the Private and Boarding School's Organization Nepal (PABSON); they also served active duty as soldiers.

Since multiparty democracy was reestablished in 1990, student organizations have taken on a very different role. They are still mobilized by the parties, but the dynamic in which the parties were dependent on them, as they were during the Panchayat era, has changed. Student organizations quickly fell into the role they serve today as subsidiary organizations, providing a gateway into national party politics. In the 1990s, norm-oriented student movements became the institutionalized way to put pressure on the campus administrations, opposition parties, and government-sponsored industries to prioritize educational and economic issues. Because these agitations were disruptive to public life and their benefits beyond partisan opposition were disputable, the Nepali public dismissed the students' activism as partisan antics carried out by party appendages. Their new ability to pursue careers in party politics also undermined their role of being at the forefront of democratic and social activism. Since the 1990s, student activists have had to negotiate this tension to establish legitimacy with the public, while also navigating the prescribed hierarchy of their party.

CONTENTIOUS POLITICS IN THE TWENTY-FIRST CENTURY

The student activists on whom this book focuses entered into politics during a contentious period that demanded they embrace their role as the parties' foot soldiers by taking up value-oriented political action. The national political situation from 2001 to 2007 can be understood as a tripartite struggle for power between the Maoists, the king, and the political parties. Exercising article 127 of the 1991 constitution to restore national security, the king twice—in 2002 and 2005—seized the reins of the government by dismissing parliament and instating royalist bureaucrats, namely, to oversee the Royal Nepal Army's protracted armed conflict with the Maoists. The student organizations spent four years on the streets protesting the king's dismissal of the democratically elected government in what came to be known as the Movement Against Regression.

Their protests and demands were more radical than their mother parties. They demanded a republic in a joint statement released by the seven student organizations on December 18, 2003, after three of their leaders were arrested on charges of sedition.[28] At the time, the Maoists were the only other political faction publicly demanding a republic. The students used their radical stance to pitch themselves as an alternative to the other political options available, many of which had disappointed in the past. Even the king's government recognized the students' public influence; security officials prioritized arresting student leaders over many party leaders during the king's 2005 coup. The state of emergency in February 2005 became the tipping point that pushed the parties and the Maoists together to negotiate a twelve-point agreement in Delhi (ICG 2005). Their unity allowed them to organize nationwide mass protests in April 2006 (the Second People's Movement), which ultimately deposed the king. The student organizations were central in mobilizing and sustaining the April uprising.

I returned to Kathmandu in the fall of 2009 to find that the students' perspective was notably different from when I departed right after the 2008 CA elections. They wistfully made references to a third people's movement (*jana āndolan bhag III*) and told me that they were ready because the movement had not been completed. They were grappling with the fact that reconstruction could not fulfill all of their aspirations to remake "new Nepal," especially not at a pace as rapid as their protests. Their longing to be on the

A joint student-union program addressing the relevancy of the monarchy after the release of student leaders who were arrested for sedition. Tri-Chandra College, Kathmandu, 2004.

streets also highlighted their political position; they had derived a sense of meaning from street protest because it allowed them to contribute to nation-wide politics in a palpable way. After the *āndolan* was over, they were relegated to peripheral tasks such as campus politics, leaving them on the sideline of national politics. Along with the general public, they were watching their leaders bumble their way through the reconstruction process. Rather than euphoria, the students felt inertia as they waited to rally their troops once again.

By 2013, the FSU was marred by widespread anarchy and lethargy. Reports of hooliganism, financial embezzlement, criminal activity, and campus clashes led the student unions' reputations to decline rapidly after the 2008 CA elections (Bhusal 2013). This dynamic, however, was nothing new in the ups and downs of Nepali politics. The students' tactics are consistent but serve different ends at different times. Their actions may be dismissed as cynical politicking in one context while applauded as noble activism in another. Is there a difference between compensating students injured in clashes with the police during the state of emergency and those injured in campus clashes with other student unions? Is there a difference between

Student volunteers on crowd-control duty at a Movement Against Regression rally. Ratna Park, Kathmandu, 2004.

burning tires and effigies and destroying government vehicles on the streets to demand the reinstatement of democracy and destroying campus property and detaining campus administration when FSU orders are defied? There is of course a difference in the intent, but not starkly so. It underscores the complexity that student unions and their members embody: a mix of idealism and opportunism. Some of this can be credited to the increasing professionalization of politics in the post-1990 democratic era; however, the dynamic emerges from their historical relationship with the political parties. The scenario of growing anarchy in the student unions in 2013 demonstrates that the opportunistic elements of their political calculation were overshadowing their idealism. Nevertheless, from my conversations with student cadres across the political spectrum, it is apparent that political idealism is central to their personal narrative, which they frame within the larger historical narrative of ongoing democratic struggle.

EDUCATION: AN ELITE ENTERPRISE

The historical correlation between education and political power has structurally determined who can rise in party leadership. Education has always been an exclusionary enterprise in Nepal;[29] at first, access was determined by one's relation to the ruling elite, and then as education became a more mass-based, democratic enterprise, access to quality education became market-driven. Both factors have perpetuated the dominance of high-caste presence in politics. Even after fifty years of policies expanding educational facilities, the literacy rate of the population is 61 percent, the net enrollment rate of the university-age population (seventeen to twenty-two years old) is 8.1 percent, and the mean number of years of schooling for adults is 8.1.[30] Educational outcomes continue to fall along caste lines in ways eerily similar to the demographic makeup of political and state leadership.[31]

Both the Shah monarchy and the Rana regime governed according to the Vedic dharmashastra system (Burghart 1984; Joshi and Rose [1966] 2004). The Kshatriya caste rulers relied on Brahmin priests to maintain their ritual relationships with the gods from whom they divined their ruling power. Members of royal and elite families were educated and trained to fulfill their appointed duties, which were often paternally inherited, namely, caste-based occupations (Caddell 2002). Historically, educational institutions were scarce and men went to Banaras to study. The Rana regime established a few educational institutions with the specific purpose of educating elites to serve the government administration, including the Durbar High School in 1883 and Chandra Intermediate College (later renamed Tri-Chandra College) in 1919. The ruling government maintained strict control over enrollment, both doling out seats and banning people based on political whims. The 1947 Jayatu Sanskritam student movement was a manifestation of growing resentment over the inequalities the Rana government created through its limited education policy. Jayatu Sanskritam cemented the tradition of political demands coming out of educational demands. The perpetuation of high-caste elites governing Nepal stems from this history, in which one's access to education required connections to study domestically or the financial means to study abroad.

The Rana regime had no interest in mass education, viewing it as a threat to its political authority. Attempts to establish a broader network of schools were squashed, and punishments for accepting or giving tuition were enforced (Whelpton 2005). Hugh Wood (1965: 120), the USAID education adviser to the Nepali democratic government, described the state of education at the end of the Rana rule as abysmal, with 8.5 million people illiterate. The illiteracy rate was 98 percent at the time (Whelpton 2005). In the final decades of Rana rule, however, restrictions on private tutoring were eased somewhat, some rural educational institutions were established by returning Gurkha soldiers, and a plan was initiated to open fifty public schools based on Gandhi's Basic Education program (NEPC 1956; Wood 1965; Shields and Rappleye 2008). This program was expanded during Nepal's first decade of tentative democracy. The education policy of the 1951–59 multiparty democratic government viewed the expansion of education as a way to facilitate modernization and strengthen a unified national identity (Caddell 2002; Shields and Rappleye 2008). Education had become an instrument to further the nationalist project of Sanskritization (Joshi and Rose [1966] 2004). There was a focus on teaching the Nepali language in the hope that other languages would disappear (NEPC 1956: 8). By 1959, the medium of instruction in basic primary education was Nepali, at the expense of other languages, which lowered retention rates among ethnically diverse communities (Shields and Rappleye 2008: 268).

After King Mahendra instituted the Panchayat government in 1960, mass education took national priority. The king's express purpose for instituting the Panchayat system was to develop Nepal and its citizenry to eventually govern themselves instead of being at the mercy of elite power politics. Cloaked in egalitarian language aimed at expanding the educated base, the education policies of the Panchayat government promoted a nationalist ideology that supported the king, Hinduism, and the Nepali language (Onta 1996; Ragsdale 1989; Skinner and Holland 1996). King Mahendra's intents dovetailed with the post–World War II Great Society era that replaced colonial relationships with aid and development support. Literacy rates increased from 8.9 percent in 1961 to 12.16 percent by 1971, although female literacy was only 3.4 percent, while male literacy increased to 21.9 percent (LeVine 2006: 23).

The 1971 NESP was the main piece of education policy of the Panchayat government. Its preface addressed education's elitist roots in Nepal: "The plan is primarily aimed at counteracting the elitist bias of the inherited system by linking it more effectively to productive enterprises and egalitarian principles" (quoted in Hayes 1976: 760). Funded by USAID, it unified the system of public education under a central government body that administered schools through the district education offices. This shifted the locus of power to the education ministry in Kathmandu, transferred teachers into the state employment structure, and stripped local interest groups of any previous power they had to shape educational provisions and access (Carney and Bista 2009). Between 1970 and 1980, the number of schools increased by almost 40 percent (LeVine 2006) and student enrollment expanded rapidly (Stash and Hannum 2001). Those who lacked education were deemed backward and further stigmatized since education provided the basis for assimilating into an ideal Panchayat citizenry (Ragsdale 1989).

In the 1990s, education became more closely intertwined with development and social mobility (Caddell 2005; Liechty 2003; Pigg 1992). The national education policy aligned more closely with the UN's Education for All campaign that donors pushed, which aimed to achieve universal basic education globally.[32] As a result, the Ministry of Education shifted from its traditional policy-making function to administering and managing aid (P. Bhatta 2011). At the same time, the government was under pressure to liberalize many public sectors, including education, which caused a decentralization of the management process and a complete transfer of school management to local communities by 2003, unfortunately without the appropriate resources or support (Carney and Bista 2009; Edwards 2011). A burgeoning, largely unregulated, private school sector filled in where the government had retreated (Caddell 2006; Shields and Rappleye 2008).[33] Despite education outcomes improving, all these factors have led to an increase in educational inequality, wherein the distinction is no longer between educated and uneducated (Skinner and Holland 1996), but now there are more subtle variations to what educated means (Caddell 2006: 469). Financially, private schools spend an average of eleven times more on each student than public schools spend, which has resulted in better educational outcomes (Mathema 2007).[34] The disparity between private and public schools not only exacerbates class disparity, but it also falls along caste and ethnic lines.[35] Some have argued that these factors gave momentum to the Maoist insurgency (Pherali 2011; Shields and Rappleye 2008).

Top government leadership has figured prominently in higher-education policy and administration. The king was appointed chancellor of Tribhuvan University when it opened in 1959, and he maintained veto power as the national university system expanded with campuses nationwide. After multiparty democracy was reinstated in 1991, the constitution stipulated that the king remain the chancellor of Tribhuvan University and Mahendra Sanskrit University, but as a figurehead who merely rubber-stamped official activity, including appointments and curriculum. Although the position of chancellor was meant to be symbolic, so was the position of constitutional monarch, yet the monarchy used article 127 twice since 2001 to expand its powers. During the royal takeover of 2005, King Gyanendra's government floated a proposal to make the king the active chancellor of all universities under the Tribhuvan University system, including the nation's only private university, Kathmandu University. This move drew suspicion among party activists, who were leery of the king reasserting control over the universities as means to maintain his illegitimate rule. The 2005 New National Education Act released by the king's governing council further confirmed this suspicion by reinserting a photograph of the royal family into textbooks. A number of student leaders and cadres were arrested for burning these new textbooks and were then immediately rearrested upon their release for burning more textbooks in the jail courtyard. One of the arrested student leaders explained to me: "We need to let the public know that the king wants to take over everything, even the minds of their children."[36]

Non-state actors' access to education has been politicized since the 1950s (Caddell 2006). Each regime has revised its education system to institute the relationship between the state and the people according to the regime's ideological view (Onta 1996). The Maoists' imprint on education has been a more recent example of this process (Pherali, Smith, and Vaux 2011). Since the 2007 shift to a democratic federal republic, there has been no reform of the university administrative structure. Rather, the prime minister has merely replaced the king as chancellor of the Tribhuvan University system and administration appointments are still politically motivated. In 2008, the National Planning Commission's three-year interim plan instituted higher-education reform suggestions from the Tenth National Development Plan (2002–7). The reforms that most affect student life are a semester-based grading system that evaluates attendance and exams and daily biometric monitoring of teaching staff to decrease faculty absenteeism. These reforms have had a direct impact on student politics since attendance requirements limit the time students can dedicate to their activism. Donors involved in the peace process encouraged the interim government to institute these university reforms to stem campus unrest. The political parties also had a vested interest in their student activists returning to student life without disrupting the governing and state-restructuring process. These maneuvers highlight how education institutions are the domain of the ruling power's national project; education is indeed "politics-driven policy" (Singh 2013). Education institutions continue to be a battleground for nationalist, democratic, monarchist, Maoist, and international forces. Student activists have historically been at the center of these vying agendas, and the general student population falls victim to an ongoing turf war that has diminished higher education (Mathema 2007; Snellinger 2005).

CONCLUSION

The generation of student activists featured in this book entered into politics at a time when it seemed the tenets of Hindu monarchy were to be rooted out. The way they contend with political values such as human rights, democracy, liberalism, secularism, and inclusion is grounded in the values and assumptions that have shaped Nepal's socio-political institutions, which have been informed by two intertwining narratives: Nepal's national history and the history of political struggle. Just as the Panchayat nationalist history was contoured to legitimate the Gorkhali empire and obscure other histories (Onta 1996), Nepal's modern political history is framed to inspire each new generation to participate in the democratic struggle. The political movements (*āndolan*) provide episodic momentum and the activists (*āndolankāri haru*) are the characters of this narrative. A CPN-UML minister underscored the struggle's dynamic when he said, "Our view has been that none of our movements have been complete. This means it has yet to be completed."[37] Thus, each new generation is invited to play a role.

One student leader defined the activists' role in this way: "We follow the principle that no change comes without struggle. It is for this principle that the student organizations were formed. When the need comes, we must fight."[38] Student activists have indeed pressured the state to react, reform, and rebuild itself (Tarrow 1996). Unfortunately, their political leaders are rarely able to enact their vision fully. The lingering status quo with incremental political change perpetuates a sense of the unfinished and reenergizes students every time democracy is under threat. To some this process may seem like a self-serving cycle, but political actors have cultivated a historical narrative that emphasizes this process as a struggle for higher political ideals. This was substantiated for me during a discussion with Gyanu. Near us a group of rowdy young men were taking up more than their share of public space. At one point in our conversation Gyanu said, "If I did not understand the historical struggle of the Nepali people, then I would be like them, with nothing to do, no opportunity, no direction, merely adding to the problems."[39]

2 Discipline and Sacrifice in the Dirty Game of Politics

THE PRESIDENT OF THE NEPAL REVOLUTIONARY STUDENT UNION, the sister organization to the Majdūr Kisān (Workers and Peasants) party, remarked in 2006: "Politics has four aspects. The first is power. This means to extend one's influence over others in the most far-reaching way possible. The second is conspiracy. This means that everything is fogged. There is a belief that one would lose the extent of one's influence if one were to be transparent in one's action or engage in discussion. When one is not, it breeds distrust. The third is thought, which really means ideology. And the fourth is credit, which in Nepal comes out of our patronage system."[1] This view of politics is common. The stated purpose of student politics is to protect the rights and welfare of students (*vidyārthī haru ko hak hit*). Politics, however, is equally considered to be a dirty game in which power struggles hold the government, the streets, and the campuses hostage. Why, then, do students invest in politics? How do they justify this investment as a contribution to society?

When I asked student activists and politicians why they chose to pursue politics, nearly all began by discussing politics as a social service (*sāmājik sevā*). The consistency of their immediate response was uncanny. What followed varied. Sometimes respondents provided a more refined articulation of their public service commitments; at other times, they segued into the secondary reasons why they had chosen a political path. The ways they couched their political commitments highlighted their ambivalence regarding the unsavory aspects of competitive politics. Even general citizens were discomfited by the agonistic elements of democracy, as the wife of an ethnic party leader articulated: "The Panchayat era was better because there were no conflicts between neighbors and other villagers. Now we have lots of parties and lots of conflicts along with them" (Hangen 2010: 108). Public sentiment has become even more jaded since this observation was made, particularly after the Maoists transitioned into party politics and proved themselves indistinguishable from the other parties in their practices of power politics and rent seeking (cf. Hirslund 2012). The Nepali public often dismisses as duplicitous the claim that politics is service. I, however, could not dismiss the idea so easily because I heard it too consistently from my interlocutors. To understand this dynamic more fully, I asked my informants if politics could be taken up as a profession. What became evident was that their entry into politics through activism allowed them to navigate the inherent contradictions politics engenders and to unify the "politics as social service" and "politics as opportunity" dichotomy. Their responses resonate within South Asia's socio-historical context that links public figures with social work.[2]

POLITICS: SOCIAL SERVICE OR PROFESSION?

The tension between service (*sevā*) and politics (*rājnīti*) is rooted in how the nation, citizenship, and nationalism have been defined. The nation-state of Nepal was constructed in moral terms, in which the cosmological and the physical overlapped (Gellner 2003a). From 1742 to 1815, the Gorkhali empire established sovereign rule by linking the territory that now defines the modern nation-state of Nepal to Hindu cosmology (Burghart 1984). With the Treaty of Sagauli in 1816, the realm became territorially bounded to establish Nepal's sovereignty vis-à-vis British occupied India. The legal code of 1854 went further by turning inhabitants of the realm into subjects of the realm through a caste-based classification system (Höfer 1979). In 1960, King Mahendra followed this tradition by ontologically collapsing the divine and the terrestrial in order to justify the Panchayat system as the Shah monarchy's governing system. His public addresses emphasized that "both king and citizen are devotees of the nation-state and there is an identity between Nepal *deśa* and the Nepalese people" (Burghart 1984: 120). In order to promote his two key policies of unity and development, he drew parallels between religious duty and national service (*deśa sevā*) to pursue national policies like "nation building" (*deśa banāune*),"national construction" (*deśa nirmān*), and "national development" (*deśa vikās*).

King Mahendra strategically emphasized devotion as the foundation of national identity to create a unified polity. Service was reinforced in school curricula as investment in education became increasingly central to the Panchayat government's nationalizing agenda. Educational curricula since the 1960s have encouraged students "to 'serve the nation,' 'be great,' and to do so with 'humility'" (Madsen and Carney 2011: 119). While the governmental discourse of *sevā* stems from the Panchayat period, the undertaking of public service by interest or political groups was strictly prohibited due to the controls on public organizing. Service was to be done on an individual basis or through Panchayat-mandated clubs confined by the nationalistic sentiment of *deshprem* (love of country) (K. Adhikari 1996, in Heaton Shrestha 2010).

Sevā is not only a government agenda to engender nationalistic sentiment; it has also been the basis for establishing authority and garnering influence locally throughout South Asia. People are often selected to their village council based on the "social work they did" (Ollieuz 2011: 35). Local leaders are expected to coordinate groups of people, raise salaries, mobilize local development, and solve local disputes; therefore, they need to demonstrate their ability to be dependable and diplomatic and to build alliances. The way a person publicly establishes himself or herself as capable of these tasks is through social work. Once he or she is either elected as the *pradhan panch* (community leader) or recognized as a *pancha bhaladami* (mediator / social worker), then his or her service and community leadership become mutually reinforcing.

That service is done on behalf of the community is key to this dynamic. In South India, becoming a big person is an active process of cultivating a public self, which necessitates managing the self within and through the community (Mines 1994). Similarly, in village decision making in Nepal's hill region, a leader earns prestige and continual communal support by heeding the collective advice of the group and serving as decision announcer rather than decision maker (Miller 1990: 167). The importance of neutrality during dispute resolution works similarly in Nepal. Arbitration is not possible unless everyone recognizes the authority of the mediator (Ramirez 2000). The mediator demonstrates impartiality based on a track record of working on behalf of others, thus making dispute settlement and authority mutually constitutive (Suykens and Stein 2014).

If we extend these ethnographic observations to service, we can better understand why political actors frame politics as service to address the underlying political ambivalence. After the reinstitution of democracy opened up the political field in 1990, political party actors sought to usurp influence and co-opt authority at all levels of government and other public spheres of influence from which they had been excluded for thirty years. One of the key ways they did that was by replacing the traditional elites—the tax collector, the *pancha bhaladami*, and the *pradhan panch*—in resolving local disputes and problems (Hachhethu 2008: 61). Thus, "adjudicating disputes continues to be an important factor in shaping the public image and authority of Nepal's newly dominant authority figures: political parties" (Suykens and Stein 2014: 14). This history informs my interlocutors' understanding of their politics as *sevā*. Service is the socio-culturally sanctioned way to establish oneself in one's community, become recognized, and demonstrate authority.

NGO work has elicited a similar ambivalence, which has co-opted the discourse of service as nation building through "people-centered development" but has been derisively coined "'dollar kheti' (dollar farming)" (Heaton Shrestha 2010, in Gellner 2009: 9). A human rights lawyer referring to NGO-ism as a chronic disease spreading throughout the country asserted: "It is diverting the strength of the youth away from socio-political and anti-imperialist movements. The people who could be leaders in these movements are running away with excuses of political corruption, poverty, and unemployment. They have been smart enough to define NGOs as parallel to social work and that NGOs offer them name, fame, wealth, and even political gain" (Siwakoti 2000: 136, in Heaton Shrestha 2010: 182). Gopal "Chintan" Siwakoti's concern that the uptick in NGOs in the 1990s is eroding socio-political reform points to another element that underpins the way my interlocutors frame their politics as service, which is activism—the act of intervening with a specific intent to affect the status quo.

A particular discourse has developed out of Nepal's democratic struggle over the past sixty-five years that collapses activism and politics together (cf. Gellner 2009, 2010; Snellinger 2007). Scholars focusing on the Maoist war have examined how people's participation "was not simply a mechanical response to an economic problem or an expression of frustration in the face of individual deprivation," but "it entailed rather, a commitment to, and participation in, a particular—revolutionary—way of envisioning the world" (Fujikura 2003: 24; see also Lecomte-Tilouine 2006). The commitment to a way of envisioning the world is, however, not solely the domain of the Maoist movement. In India as well, the "culture of representative democracy is a way of imagining the world" (Kaviraj 1998: 148). My interlocutors' articulations of political commitment can be understood as a collective expression of how they envision the world and how they want to assert that vision to ensure it becomes reality.

In political theory, politics has two sides: the assertion of a better life for all and the distinct opportunity to enforce how and who benefits from that better life (cf. Mouffe 2005; Rancière 1999). Politics in practice is also linked with power and access to resources. A leftist student leader from a small student organization framed this paradox in Nepali politics, explaining:

Naturally, the people who have come to politics cannot work in both
the private and public sectors. . . .Our society perceives political participation as twofold. On the one hand, there is the negative perception that one
who becomes a political leader becomes spoiled. On the other hand, it is
perceived as a social responsibility. For that reason, a person who desires
to be involved in politics should have a clean image. He should not have
greed and vested interest. He has to think about the future of the society
and the country. He could not be a politician if he thinks only about himself, his family, or his region. The politician has to be able to represent the
society as a whole. I suppose in this sense, the ones who do pure politics
are useless in the eyes of the contemporary society since they could not
give the proper attention to their household. . . . Those who put politics
second, after managing their family life, are the opportunists.[3]

Politics is meant to serve something higher than you or your family because
politicians are expected to speak for all (cf. Miller 1990). Nevertheless,
political actors draw on the shared kinship paradigm to construct the necessary intimacy and sense of social duty to index the "mutuality of being"
(Sahlins 2011: 10) in which people eschew "the individual self in favour of
relations" (Piliavsky 2014: 23). The ubiquity with which filial metaphors
are mapped onto political relationships elucidates this sentiment. A family
is idealized as working toward a common goal, the maintenance and betterment of the shared lineage; similarly, a party works to enact a shared ideology into practice.

The presumed selflessness that underpins filial obligations also obscures
the hierarchical dimensions of client-patron relations in politics. The
emphasis on kin relations simultaneously denies and embraces the patronage tradition pervasive in Nepali politics. But patronage and service are not
necessarily at odds, because in South Asia "the local logic of patronage is
not about profiteering." "On the contrary, it is a radical denial of individual
self-advancement. Patronal munificence and the client's service (sevā)—
both of which ought to be markedly selfless acts—affirm social relations,
connectedness and society as ultimate values. . . . Giving and serving as
such are necessarily exertions for another's sake. Shows of patronal munificence display the will to give away, something the picture of self-serving
appropriation turns upside down, making it impossible to grasp the inner
rationale of patron-client proceedings" (Piliavsky 2014: 22). My interlocutors' political articulations of service to country (desh) and people (janatā)
echo the Panchayat nationalist discourse that strategically linked the

inhabitants of the territory to the Hindu realm; rhetorically, munificence was first bestowed through the king and later through democratically elected statesmen. The discourse of politics being service signals selfless dedication in a social order in which politicians are both patrons and clients, a dynamic that has become more entrenched since multiparty democracy instituted open elections wherein political mandates come from voters but authority is interlayered and contingent.

My interlocutors' claim that their political commitment is like religious devotion further elucidates this dynamic. Such an articulation is not an outlier but echoes other scholars' observations regarding Maoist conceptions of martyrdom as linked to Hindu notions of sacrifice and renunciation, "the Brahmanic and ascetic self-sacrifice to the fire" (Lecomte-Tilouine 2006: 68); sacrifice underpins how Youth Communist League cadres make meaning of their political action (Hirslund 2012); and sacrifice and martyrdom are common affective themes in revolutionary music (Stirr 2013). Many of my informants asserted that the ideal-type politician is an ascetic. Yet they also noted the contradictions of being a statesman in contemporary times. A second-tier leader of the CPN-UML described the political transition from ascetic to corrupt in the following anecdote:

In the feudal era, there used to be the landed gentry and the peasants. Some used to grow crops, whereas others could afford to put their time toward politics in the name of social service. . . . It was an upper-class pursuit. Society gradually underwent change. Yesterday's feudal mode of production no longer exists. The capitalist mode of production was introduced, and the people tended to migrate to the towns from the villages. . . . The class that has come into modern politics is not from the landed gentry, nor is it *sanyāsī* [renunciate]. The leadership has come from the middle class. Middle-class people rarely rise to the upper class, except one or two. One who goes to the upper class is one who has linkage with power, one who has been successful at balancing resources and opportunities.

What has happened here is an interesting picture of the statesman. His image is that of the *sadhu* [holy man] and *santa* [hermit]. He is the one who claims to be devoted wholeheartedly to serve the people and the nation. He is the *yogi* [ascetic] who is determined to perform what Mahatma Gandhi was not able to accomplish successfully. But he has the monthly expenditure of more than sixty thousand rupees. This is the amount he spends on his lodging and food. He travels in a Pajero that cost more than 5 million rupees.[4] Ten years ago, he was not a leader. But now he lives in a grand building, which he owes to his links to power and resources. My political peers have grand buildings, even boys my junior. They are not landed gentry, producers, service holders, peasants, or farmers. In addition to that, they are not laborers, managers, nor do they have any firms. They are only politicians. But where does their money come from?[5]

His explanation touches on many of the factors that underpin the tension between politics as service and opportunity.

The first tension addresses the class elements in the traditional pursuit of social service. The landed gentry historically "served" the community. It is thus suspect when people without means pursue politics, because they are unable to do so selflessly. A student explained this to me by referencing the writing of B. P. Koirala, who is known as the father of Nepal's democracy movement. Koirala had written that if one cannot afford to feed oneself or one's family, one should not enter into politics but find other ways to contribute. This student reasoned that a politician, like everyone else, needs to survive. But corruption must never be a temptation. Therefore, to be selflessly dedicated to politics, one must have some property to support oneself.[6] Another campus leader made that clear when he lamented that politics is only for the educated wealthy: "If your family cannot invest in you, you will not be able to invest in the country, at . . . the level of full-time politics. If you cannot do it full-time, people do not consider you selfless. Rather, you are looked upon as an opportunistic dabbler. You can see how that keeps those who must earn their food through labor away from politics."[7] Only those with resources could pursue politics in a "selfless way" (*niswārtha dānga*), making the landed gentry the vanguard of political progress.

There is a moral logic of selflessness in South Asian politics (Piliavsky 2014: 23). Nepali activists are keenly aware of that, as David N. Gellner and Mrigendra Bahadur Karki (2010) concluded from a survey of two hundred activists: "The popular image of activists in Nepal allows that they should have, or paradigmatically do have, non-economic interests and that they are pursuing other-directed goals" (145). Accordingly, this campus leader admitted that one of the most anxiety-producing accusations is that he only looks after his own self-interest (*āphno swārtha herne*). I often heard this dismissal bandied about as a way of expressing disappointment in an individual politician or student leader. Many student activists expressed concern to me that the public was not supporting the Movement Against

Regression because politics had come to be seen as a self-interested enter-prise. In fact, the general dismissal of politics as social service speaks to the breakdown of the social contract that underpins patron-client dynamic in politics. The shift from selfless to self-interested marks the shift from politi-cal patron to political fixer.

Another point that emerges from the CPN-UML leader's anecdote quoted earlier is that the allure of politics mirrors the paradox of politics. Statesmen must translate their political ideals into material form within the institu-tional and state structures. The fall from grace he describes is grounded in the political history of centralized state power, which since the 1960s has been routinized through the dissemination of policy and resources from the central state to the local level. The Panchayat government relied on vil-lage elites to enforce its mandate, which reinforced the positions of state bureaucrats and more marginally tribal leaders. After 1990, those who fought for democratic freedom took the reins of state power. They not only became the decision makers in all matters pertaining to the state, but they also gained access to state resources and the accompanying influence. After these underground and exiled democratic activists became state caretakers, politics shifted markedly from an ascetic endeavor of the landed gentry to a corrupt endeavor of opportunity seekers. As a new type of distributional politics was instituted in the 1990s, democracy became a guise for resource usurpation, with public allocation a mere afterthought (Pfaff-Czarnecka 2004). The Maoists, who took arms against this trend, were subject to asper-sions of self-interest as they transitioned from revolution into parliamentary politics (Hachhethu 2009). Even power-sharing measures like the All-Party Mechanisms (2008–12) appointed to govern locally through consensus have led to rampant corruption and lack of accountability locally.[8] All of this demonstrates that the politicians and political actors who convinced the public to rise up against the status quo in the People's Movement, the Peo-ple's War, the Second People's Movement, and the sub-national Madheshi movement fighting for regional autonomy in the south (2006–8) eventually neglected their duty as community leaders and patrons working selflessly on behalf of others.

The Nepali case makes clear the difficulty that political actors face in weaving together the ideals of selflessness and service and the mundane aspects of resource distribution and agonistic politics in order to establish the authority necessary to maintain the public's faith. As a Nepal Student Union (Koirala) (NSU [K]) cadre explained:

> Politicians have to make the people be more inclined toward them than
> toward God. God never tells you to take your life for him, but a leader
> may even tell you to die for the political cause. A leader has to be able
> to make his cadre follow an ideology or an ideal. For all this to happen
> one has to be qualified and well-rounded, one has to be able to manage
> everything, even supporting his cadres in order to enable the success
> of the political cause. That is why money is essential to politics. It's so
> worldwide. Leaders must have command of money and resources. This
> is a must.[9]

His frank explanation outlines what is required to fulfill the obligatory
dynamics of patronage-based politics. A student leader associated with the
NC Deuba faction, NSU (D), emphasized this point, saying that "politics is
glamour." He clarified: "It is difficult to become a leader. But once you arrive
at power there is prestige [*ijjat*].[10] People will follow he who has power and
resources. And that is the reason people are attracted to politics."[11] Both
points by these student leaders echo the understanding of why, as Anastasia Piliavsky (2014) indicates, "people cast their chiefs, patron-deities,
ancestors, elders and MPs in the role of 'patrons,' not only entitling them
to special honours and privileges but making them responsible—obliging
them to provide, protect and stand accountable for their actions" (34). Those
with authority are indeed elevated in Nepal; however, patronage has a
fraught history due to the systematic exclusion it continually produces.[12]
While some studies document how certain social groups cultivate relationships with state power (Clarke 1997; Shneiderman 2010), the ability to create
reciprocal relationships with politicians and state patrons has been uneven,
and there is general dismissal of the political enterprise as corrupt, cynical,
and sycophantic (cf. Bista 1991). This history of marginalization informs
the discourse of politics as service, making it necessary to obscure the role
that power, leadership and influence, and wealth play in politics. Politics as
social service tempers the image of politics being a dirty game.

LOCATING ONESELF IN POLITICAL HISTORY

The shared ambivalence around politics as opportunity and politics as service affects what gets emphasized in political discourse. Deconstructing this
discourse elucidates how people make meaning of their political participation on a personal and social level. A key way that occurs is through the
rhetorical cultivation of political history. Students and politicians call

Joint-party sit-in at Democracy Wall during the Movement Against Regression. Ratna Park, Kathmandu, 2004.

attention to specific political movements to highlight the ongoing impact their parties have made. "Contests over ownership of key symbolic events of past historical struggle are shot through with claims to be the true activists and the true heirs to the activists of the past" (Gellner 2010: 4). And while political actors assert proprietary claims over this history, these events of historical struggle are referenced to such a degree that they have become abstracted to mean something larger than the specifics of each event. A political imaginary has been created—a shared ideal of what politics has been and should be and what is possible. The oratory tradition of political speeches further entrenches this political imaginary. Politicians publicly link their version of *āndolan* history with metaphors of land, country, and shared cultural values to emphasize their party's provenance.

This rhetorical cultivation of political history also reinforces different actors' position within the political structure. To be in politics one must be an activist. This dynamic is mutually reinforcing; one enters the annals of political history by participating in an *āndolan*, and in order to have a political career, one needs a spot in this history. All students, regardless of their political affiliations, refer to themselves as *āndolankārī* (activist) with pride, and many even embrace the term *krāntikārī* (revolutionary).[13] The Maoists

and leftists more regularly claim the title of *krāntikārī*, but student organizations across the political spectrum use these terms to designate themselves
as agents for change. I was surprised to hear students greet each other with
the term *krāntikārī* at the NSU (D) 2007 national convention. The NSU (D) did
not participate in the joint seven-student-union movement in 2004, and
Sher Bahadur Deuba, its party president, had served as a king-appointed
prime minister during the Movement Against Regression.[14] Still, the students
considered themselves revolutionaries because they were part of the NC faction that stood up to G. P. Koirala's dynasty and revolted against strong-arm
tactics they thought were stymieing the NC's internal democracy. Like other
student organizations, they highlighted their defiance in order to link themselves to a larger political struggle. By doing so, they were asserting themselves as contentious political actors.

Being recognized as activists by the state further reinforces political
actors' place in the political history and bolsters their sense of purpose,
even leading to individual notoriety. In March 2004, during the Movement
Against Regression, I observed how the king's government banned public
gathering in particular areas of the city. People caught protesting in these
areas were arrested. The designated "no-protest zones" were the heart of
where the seven political parties and their student organizations had been
demonstrating for over six months. Political cadres from every echelon
gathered to defy the royal decree. For the first few days the police made mass
arrests, rapidly loading up police vans and shipping trucks. Protesters were
not deterred. As soon as they were released, they immediately returned to
the streets. In response, the security forces began to blockade the no-protest
zones, so the protesters gathered in smaller groups in arterial junctions
around Bāg Bazār and marched toward the center through the gullies. I followed one group of protesters through Jamal toward Ratna Park. A group of
about a dozen security forces were waiting to head us off at the footbridge
on the Jamal side of Rani Pokhari (Queen's Pond). The police captured
protesters from the front line and tried to throw them into the police vans.
The protesters struggled from the police officers' grasp while trying to negotiate with them. They begged the police to let them reach Ratna Park. At
Ratna Park, they would not resist.

Puzzled, I asked a student why they were resisting now but would acqui-
esce once in Ratna Park, and he responded: "Ratna Park was the heart of
the 1990 People's Movement. It was where thousands from the general public [*āmjanatā*] joined hands with activists and marched toward the palace
to make the king surrender. We are activists [*āndolankāri haru*], we expect

Art exhibit on Democracy Wall commemorating party activists' contributions to the Movement Against Regression. Ratna Park, Kathmandu, 2004.

arrest, but it means more to get arrested at Democracy Wall. For many it's like a rite of passage. Others respect you if you've been arrested in Ratna Park."[15] Getting arrested was not enough to mark participation in the movement. The urban landscape was affectively imbued with a political history that inspired these activists to emulate the democratic history in a particular way. They were acting out what had come before in order to feel connected to the larger history of democratic struggle.

Being arrested is beneficial for student activists beyond cementing their place in the annals of *āndolan* history. It gives them exposure both publicly and within their own parties. That became apparent in 2005 when I was invited to join some NC central committee members to visit their student leaders who had been detained at the central jail in Hanuman Dhoka during the state of emergency. I had tried to meet these students alone, but the security forces denied my request. When they saw me with the political leaders, they apologized, saying they were "not aware of who I was." We were led to the police chief's office. It was a large office and the couches surrounding the perimeter comfortably accommodated our entourage of over a dozen. The police chief sat at his desk and chatted with the leaders seated to his left, while we sipped tea and waited for them to bring in the arrested students.

As the students entered, the atmosphere was relaxed and everyone was jovial. The main NC leader asked the students if they were all right, if they were being treated fairly and getting what they needed. They nodded silently as the police chief looked on. The leader then said: "I remember all the times I stayed here. What years? It was definitely in 1960 and then a couple of times during the Panchayat era. It was less crowded then, and you couldn't bribe the officers for cigarettes." He then turned to the police chief and said: "You weren't here then, were you? You were too young. I think you must have been a schoolboy *mandale* when I was here."[16] Everyone chuckled. The police chief shook his head and said that he was not here at the time; he began his post in 1978. Then, pointing to a second-tier leader, he asked: "You were jailed here then, weren't you?" The other NC leader nodded and eagerly began recalling his experiences. The leaders and police proceeded to reminisce for over twenty minutes about their times in jail together. All the while, the students sat silently and listened.[17]

Later Akash, who was one of the arrested students, told me that he will know he has achieved the status of party leader when he is "sitting in their seats" telling of his experience to other arrested students in the police chief's office.[18] His aspiration demonstrates how the experience of jail makes one a part of the political lineage. By jointly claiming the title of *āndolankāri*, political actors connect across the generations, mapping the glory of the ongoing political movement onto the past and using it to make claims on the future.

The whole process is mutually reaffirming. The shared experience allows activists and police to establish relationships, which shift depending on political dynamics and who dictates state power. It also allows politicians to embrace their roles as activists who have effectuated political change and eschew their role in maintaining the status quo when governing. By doing so, they are indicating they have been in the students' shoes, contributing to the democratic struggle before them. The students' reputation as activists enables them to make their mark as well as provides them a sense of their contribution. They may be a part of the Free Student Union (FSU), but everything they do is ultimately for their party. It is on the streets during their public protest that they are able to critique the political system in which their parties participate. The political leaders allow them this space because they know that if the public supports the students, then the public will support their parties. Once they have resecured their parties' power, however, the students are expected to retreat back onto the campuses and allow their parties to govern.

Student activists relish the freedom the streets provide and use the *āndolan* to establish authority within the confines of party politics, in which their ability to influence is limited. They must rely on relations of patronage in order to rise in the ranks of the parties (Hachhethu 2002; Pfaff-Czarnecka 2004; Upadhya 2002), while simultaneously convincing the public that they will be effective as politicians and provide alternatives to their mother organizations' policies. These idealistic articulations of autonomy both contest and conceal the underbelly of the political constraint they face. It gives purpose to the students' struggles, allowing them the conviction they need to sustain the dedication and passion for their activism, which is often a protracted and uncertain endeavor. Their vulnerable position further underscores their dedication to politics as service because it highlights selfless dedication to their political cause.

This dynamic emerged starkly during the so-called post-conflict period (2008–15), which was initially heralded as a hopeful time but soon was marked with a sense of stagnation and uncertainty. Many student activists have waited on the sidelines while their parties negotiated their positions in the new political frontier of the secular federal republic. Some student leaders, like Akash, have gained the opportunity to participate in the CA and parliament. But most of the student leaders and activists had to find new roles for themselves beyond street protest. It has been difficult for many of this generation to come to terms with the way the political structure has limited them. The five activists highlighted in this book demonstrate different paths taken to overcome these limits. Despite their varying experiences, the *āndolan* serves as a fixture that reinforces what they have accomplished, what influence they have garnered, and how they would like to move forward. Ultimately, political instability has been the opportunity in which student activists of this generation have found meaning and a sense of purpose. And the historical narrative of the *āndolan* provides them with a sense of perpetual struggle that reinforces the larger political community and their place in it.

IDENTITY OF STRUGGLE AND SACRIFICE

Narratives of suffering and sacrifice further underpin activists' belief that politics is service. Sacrifice and suffering substantiate political identity across ideological lines because these experiences unite individuals in their political organizations and the larger institution of politics. In the early years of multiparty democracy, the public recognized the party activists' sacrifices from their having done their time during Panchayat rule.[19] This recognition has given currency to political sacrifice in general. As a result, tropes of struggle and sacrifice have become instrumentalized to mobilize student activists within the party's agenda. Narratives indexing struggle and sacrifice unite political actors by shifting attention away from internal hierarchies by creating unity out of shared experience.

During the Panchayat-mandated ban on party politics (1960–90) many party activists spent time underground, jailed, or in exile. These experiences became a de facto rite of passage into Nepali politics and as a result bolstered people's sense of their participation as sacrifice and struggle. The most recent example of this is the Maoist students' experience during the People's War. The ANNISU (R) is a recent offshoot of other communist organizations and thus they pay homage to the same communist lineage.[20] They foreground their own underground experience, which began during the Maoist People's War (1996), while connecting it to leftist history since the 1950s. Their shared experience of hardship buttresses the strength of their individual and organizational discipline (cf. Hirslund 2012; Zharkevich 2009). ANNISU (R) students form their personal identities, their organizational identity, and their internal culture based on their experiences of shared sacrifice and struggle during the People's War. Their master referent for their mobilization is the people (*janatā*) (see Hirslund 2012: 94–95). ANNISU (R) students repeatedly emphasized to me that the opportunity to observe the common people's struggles (*janatā ko sangarsha*) informs and continually reinforces their political ideals. They take pride in recognizing the urgency of social inequality while also being young enough not to be invested in the status quo traditions of feudal society. They believe their generational awareness of class struggle during a revolution allows them a new repertoire in which to frame socio-political progress and the means for achieving it. Many ANNISU (R) students described the experience of being underground during the war as formative; some even claimed it as their coming-of-age (Snellinger 2010; Zharkevich 2009).

My ANNISU (R) interlocutors nostalgically recalled their life underground. Even those who lost partners, relatives, or friends and those who spent time in jail and endured torture still embrace the experience. It allowed them to witness the everyday realities of suffering induced by poverty. As one student phrased it: "We came to see what our political ideology and struggle are based on." They attribute their deep connection to the people to their experience underground. Another student explained: "I think that had I not gotten involved in this political movement for change,

I would have been born and died like any insect in the world. I've been able to win many people's hearts and read many people's minds. I would never have gotten the chance to know about the people in their real-life situations. We obtained knowledge about the diversity of suffering as well as joy within the Nepalese society."[21] In addition to observing the reality that inspired their party's ideology, they derive political authority from having lived through it.

The experience of being underground enabled them to transcend their traditional identities and social backgrounds. They believe that their relations with all sectors of Nepalese society allowed them to break from those past identities and study Nepal from a purely class perspective. They also learned about their own capacity to endure suffering only after being underground. They articulated a resolve in their capacity to sacrifice for their political ideals because they have and they saw progress from it. For example, an ANNISU (R) leader, after describing how they had dug a hole and buried dozens of their cadres in Myagdi, looked me directly in the eye and said: "We now know what we need to do to make our ideal real."[22] They have built their identities around this conviction. They pride themselves on knowing better than other student activists what is at risk, and they believe it is worth it to achieve their ends. Other student organizations dismiss the Maoists' use of violence and claim to have a longer history of sacrifice to reference, dating back to the repressive times of the Rana regime, through the underground years of the Panchayat era, and including every student political movement since the first in 1947.

As much as people's personal experiences strengthen their political resolve, tropes of sacrifice and struggle are also instrumentalized by leaders who repurpose political history for their own agenda to establish authority or to mobilize others for a particular cause. A striking example of this was during the national convention of the NSU (D) in July 2007. It was highly disorganized, causing cadres to wait for days for the convention to launch. Each day was full of the unknown. Many student delegates were anxious they would be cut from the voter lists because of rumors that the lists were being manipulated. While the delegates were uncertain of their own status, they also did not know who the official candidates were, since many aspiring candidates were at the mercy of their political leaders' decisions. Each morning, the delegates lingered on the streets outside the hall for the day's program to proceed. They waited for hours only to receive their directives immediately before the program began. The general cadres never knew what to expect regarding the convention schedule: when they could review activity

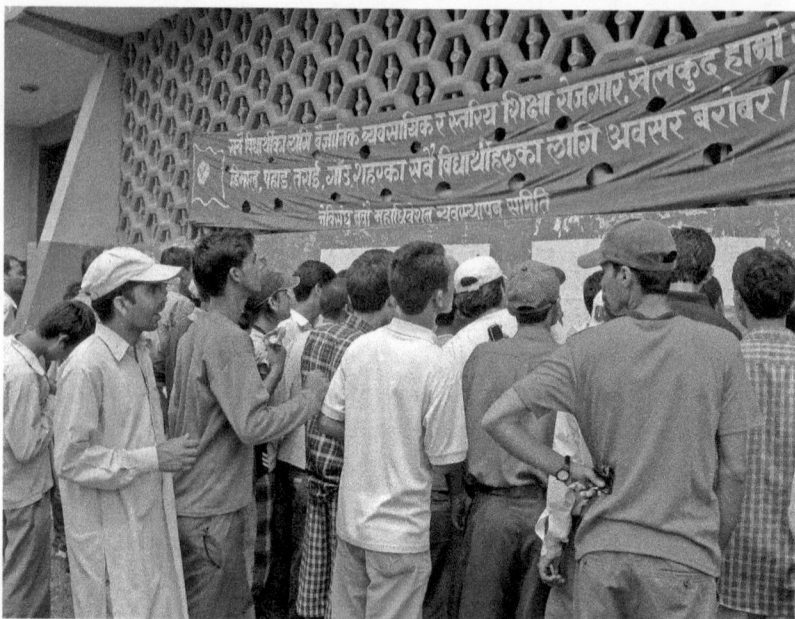

NSU (D) cadres reviewing the voter list while waiting for their national convention to begin. Nepalganj, Banke, 2007.

reports, when they could vote for amendment proposals, when the voter list would be released, or when elections would take place. Since the processes lacked transparency, the atmosphere became ripe with rumor and speculation on the smallest minutiae (when the convention gate would be unlocked) and broad conspiracy theories (whether the student and party leaders were stalling in order to rig the election for their gain). Many delegates became sick with heatstroke and dysentery; others fretted about the upcoming exams they were unable to prepare for.

Finally, at the closed session the delegates were awaiting the presentations of the political, educational, fiscal, and social reports to prepare them for approving new constitutional amendments, when the student leaders reluctantly admitted to the inconvenience they had caused their cadres. The then-current president sympathized with the students, acknowledging the difficulties of enduring the heat and mediocre food and accommodations in Nepalganj. Reframing the uncertainty of their political process in order to mobilize the students, he then said: "I want to remind you that we too, your leaders, are suffering. We are not sleeping until we complete this convention in a healthy and successful manner. We are willing to suffer because we are dedicated to the norms of democracy and providing you with your rights, just as we know you are dedicated to the struggle to not only fight for, but maintain, democracy in Nepal. Your experience at this convention will strengthen your dedication to struggle for your country."[23] Rather than admit the adverse impacts their disorganization had on their student union's stability, they avoided the impending fallout by couching it in the narrative of democratic struggle. The students responded dismissively, saying that their leaders had become full of themselves (*Thulo manchhe bhaisakyo*, or "He has become a big person") and no longer considered the impact their actions had on those who voted them into leadership. Yet these students tolerated it because they had an ideological and social investment in politics. They justified the hardship they endured through the very same rhetoric of democratic struggle.

Student and political leaders use democratic struggle as a crutch to galvanize the public as well. Referencing political history and the *āndolan* as an ongoing struggle is to eschew the political stagnation that often results from interparty power politics. This emerged quite clearly when I escorted Risha to a workshop she was conducting in Gorkha district in 2011. The workshop's purpose was to facilitate dialogue between women, youth, political leaders, and parliamentarians about how inclusion should be implemented in the constitution, sponsored by the Asia Foundation, NetCorps, the UNDP, and USAID.

An NC parliamentarian had traveled with us to participate in the workshop as a representative of the CA's inclusion and equal rights drafting committee. He did not attend the first day, nor did any of the local politicians. Rather, Risha and her co-facilitators taught the audience about inclusion, the new affirmative action policies, and federalism and what impact these issues had on their lives. The next day participants broke into small groups and brainstormed suggestions on how to properly implement these provisions. In the early afternoon, the groups presented their suggestions. This program was meant to be interactive, with the parliamentarian listening to the groups' suggestions and dialoguing with the participants.

Toward the end of the presentations, the parliamentarian showed up, along with the local politicians. He arrived just in time to give his speech. He apologized halfheartedly to the audience about missing their presentations and promised to take the posters they made back with him to the CA "to make sure they were heard."[24] He was late, he explained, because he was visiting the families of the martyrs from the People's War. Nothing was lost on the audience. Gorkha is the home district of Baburam Bhattarai, second in command of the Maoist party. The district experienced a heavy Maoist

Homage to political forefathers and martyrs adorns the stage at a NSU (K) district convention. Bhadrapur, Jhapa, 2007.

and army presence during the People's War. Local NSU students and NC cadres lost their lives at the hands of Maoists. The parliamentarian referenced these local martyrs to emphasize the sacrifice the NC had made. He continued to name Gorkha martyrs from earlier political movements. Then he returned to the current situation and explained that the CA process was a continuation of this political struggle and that the public needed to keep faith in the NC in order to do justice to their local martyrs. He did not address inclusion or the federal setup but instead concluded by saying that the *āndolan* was ongoing and they must be patient, that things come slowly.

The two sentiments, that the *āndolan* continues and that political change comes slowly, are commonly articulated in Nepali politics. "The movement continues" (*Āndolan jārī chha*) was a signature slogan during the Movement Against Regression. And during that time, a number of leaders countered public impatience with the lack of political progress, saying that change was coming slowly. This infuriated many student activists who thought it was an excuse given by apathetic leaders. However, as these activists have matured, they too have developed a better perspective on the gradual emergence of political progress. Salini admitted this to me in 2011 when I asked her if her political perspective had changed at all since the days of the Movement

Against Regression. She recounted how she used to be idealistic and thought that her efforts would change society. But as she explained: "I've come to understand that society and individual life are very different things. The evolutionary process of society is very slow and it takes a long time to see results. It may take centuries, and people don't live for centuries." She reassured me that she is not frustrated or hopeless, only that her view has matured. She said: "I know I'm contributing because the role of student politics is to fight for the students. This is why we're motivated to get involved in politics. We believe it creates social change, but I now realize this happens over generations, not just in one."[25] Her realization allowed her to frame her cohort's sacrifices in a generational history of political struggle. This process is not unidirectional acculturation. Rather, it is the process of political regeneration in which the unfinished is passed to the next generation, and they understand what is left to be done from their unique socio-historical position.

"PESSIMISM OF THE INTELLECT AND OPTIMISM OF THE WILL"

While student activists frame their activism as serving the betterment of students and citizens to distance themselves from the unsavory aspects of politics, their dedication to political causes also works on a sociological level by reinforcing personal belonging and enforcing a sense of what politics ought to be. The students substantiate their political dedication by enacting it in everyday life. They also judge others' behavior and commitment according to this ideal mode of political being. This technique of social discipline is akin to Michel Foucault's ([1984] 1992) "techniques of the self," which everyone both enforces and has enforced upon them.

This dynamic became apparent as I gathered interviews. During my initial research, I began interviews by asking people to shed light on their personal background in politics. As I did more interviews, I noticed that the more leftist individuals were, the more they avoided detailing their personal life.[26] Gyanu's response to my inquiry sums up this trend: "Our history lies within the history of the organization where we work and in our political movements. We are different in the sense that bourgeoisie first think about 'I' and 'my' and only then go to [think about] 'ours' [hamro]. In our case the foremost thing is 'our organization,' 'our history,' and 'our movement'—'I' is a secondary factor. You have to understand us and our organization in this light. In spite of all this, I would like to tell you [what you want to know] since 'we' are public figures."[27] He then detailed his own background.

After I noticed this trend, I removed the word "personal" from my inquiry and merely asked people to shed light on their political backgrounds. Even then, I received responses such as "My political background is the history of the party."[28] In response to my perplexity over this statement, a UML leader explained that leftist students are taught historical materialism to identify how the past has shaped their social position. By embracing the history of the party as their personal political history, they are disconnecting from the traditional roles they were born into and adopting their shared communist agenda.

Another way I observed how leftists orient their everyday lives in line with their ideology was in the shared value of optimism (āshābādī). Maoist students kept emphasizing that one "must be optimistic, and must cast aside cynicism [nirāshābādī]."[29] After hearing this sentiment articulated in different contexts, it became apparent that they were referring to something more than merely being hopeful. After the tenth time hearing this, I interrupted the student cadre and asked: "I have often heard this point from Maoist students to differentiate themselves from other student activists. What does the word āshābādī mean for you?" He explained:

> We locate our life within our political struggle. We believe that we have
> to be optimistic to achieve our aim. We have to be optimistic in our work
> and struggle. We need to be determined and undeviating, not just in our
> lives but also in our lifestyle. In our smallest action we must live up to our
> ideals. If we do not live up to our aim through our daily lives, then how
> do we expect it to manifest in society? This is the difference between us
> and others. This is the difference between an optimist and a cynic. It's
> not about our personal gain but that of the society.[30]

The context in which I pressed this student may have invited his tone. We spoke at a Maoist student co-op at the edge of Kathmandu Valley. I was there visiting to get a sense of how they lived and how the organization inserted itself into their everyday lives. His explanation, nevertheless, captured what other students insinuated through their use of the words "optimism" and "cynicism." Politics as direct action fuels the shared sensibility of politics as service. Action (or activism as they conceive it) involves a self-conscious transformation of oneself through attempts to transform society, akin to being reborn (Hirslund 2012: 163). The idea of rebirth noted by Dan Hirslund is a maturation process particular to the Maoist movement, in which one becomes "conscious" (cf. Zharkevich 2009, De Sales 2003, Pettigrew and Shneiderman 2004). The young co-op director emphasized this by clarifying that optimism was regularly impressed upon Maoist cadres in their trainings and discussions. They came to this shared ideal through indoctrination.

The Maoist students' emphasis on optimism captures Antonio Gramsci's maxim "Pessimism of the intellect, optimism of the will." It was the masthead for *L'Ordine Nuovo: Rassegna Settimanale di Cultura Socialista*, the weekly journal he edited. This tenet was grounded in the critical theory logic that a pessimistic intellect is necessary to observe the inherent opposition of dialectical epistemology (cf. Gramsci 1924). But in order to avoid despair, a pessimistic intellect must be coupled with the conviction to effectuate positive change, an act of will regardless of the challenges one faces. A pessimistic intellect without optimism merely creates a stagnant cynic.

It should be noted that the Maoists were well positioned to meld their theory (or political ideals) with their practice more effectively than other student organizations at the time of my research because they had not yet made the transition into party politics. When I began working with them soon after the civil war ended, they were still maintaining the discipline that war had required of them. Such conviction was necessary since their mission was a complete restructuring of society—politics, culture, family, and individual lives—whereas other student organizations' missions were more narrowly defined, a struggle to institute multiparty democracy.

The ANNISU vice president explained the organization's holistic approach in this way: "If we are only seeing the branches of a mango tree and expect that it will bear mangoes, our thinking will not be holistic since a mango tree has its roots—if they are rotten then the branches cannot bear fruit. In the same way, if we say that we are concerned with the educational sector and don't care about other sectors like politics or labor, then we will never be able to obtain our objective."[31] That is why other parties have not been successful, he explained, because they do not imbue every facet of their lives with revolutionary struggle. Their family and private lives are disconnected from their political lives, which they leave behind on the streets.

Of course, the Maoists do not have sole claim to this holistic approach to politics. Many student cadres emphasized living their ideology. An All Nepal National Free Student Union (Unified) (ANNFSU [Ekikrit]) central committee member explained that the organization determines members' leadership capabilities according to how fully they incorporate sacrifice and devotion to class struggle into their everyday lives.[32] Self-sacrifice for party ideology is a political value trumpeted across party lines. An ex-student leader from the NSU (K) articulated that through his explanation of what makes an effective organization. The most important matter for a political organization is not its ideology but its activists' commitment to that ideology. This commitment, he explained, must be directed toward a mission over and above the students' private affairs.[33]

The ANNISU (R) leaders themselves hit up against the challenges of inspiring their cadres to imbue their everyday life with the party's mission after their party won a plurality in the 2008 CA elections. When I met Gyanu in 2011, he was pretty despondent over the number of students who joined the ANNISU (R) not out of dedication to the Maoist cause but due to the "lure of opportunity." He noted the challenges in trying to instill ideological commitment: "After we were victorious, so many students joined that we could not keep up with their ideological training. Plus, many weren't really interested since they joined out of self-interest. We did not anticipate this. We thought the more cadres the better. But they've eroded our party."[34] The Maoists' transition into the political mainstream had been predicted by political scholars (cf. Hachhethu 2009). This unfortunate outcome is part and parcel of the general way that party politics in Nepal has developed, emerging out of *āndolan* to seize control of the governing apparatus (Snellinger, forthcoming).

CONCLUSION

There is a deep ambivalence as politics has shifted from a social service of the landed gentry to a professional opportunity for statesmen. Party cadres regulate themselves and others with discursive categories such as commitment, struggle, sacrifice, optimism and cynicism, and selflessness and self-interest in order to grapple with the unsavory elements of mainstream politics. It allows them to frame their politics ethically and to guide their mode of political being.

Students also make politics personal through their embrace of these tropes. This was starkly revealed to me after interviewing a female student from the ANNFSU (Akhil). We took a bus together to her union office. On the bus, she told me that she had hepatitis A and this was her first outing in a month. As we waited for our separate appointments in the student union's central office, she began to yawn. She must be tired, I quipped. She shrugged as she continued yawning and pointed to a poster behind the president's desk. It was a picture of Krishna Bhattarai, a formidable leader of the UML who was active underground for much of Panchayat rule. Below his portrait was the quotation "In politics there is no such thing as exhaustion." The student had just told me her life story. I knew that she had not experienced a fraction of the hardship Bhattarai had, but she still identified with him and his commitment because she was carrying on the mission he began.[35] Like many of her activist peers, she created her identity based on his ideals, demonstrating how politics is personal for them. By drawing on the previous generations' political struggle and focusing on what is left to be done, they elevate their individual participation to the level of service to a larger cause and embrace the opportunities that may come from their activism despite public scrutiny.

3 The Political Category of Youth

CHANDRA, A FORTY-FIVE-YEAR-OLD NC MEMBER, EXPLAINED TO me why he kept being introduced as a youth leader at CA campaign rallies in 2007: "I am still a youth because my aspirations remain unfulfilled. What I have fought for has yet to be attained. What I fought for as a student is what students are still fighting for. We fight together. Maybe after the Constituent Assembly elections it will be attained. Maybe then I will become a central committee member of the Nepali Congress and be introduced as a party leader. Maybe."[1]

Chandra has a long history in student and party politics. He was active in the 1979 student movement that led to the 1981 nationwide referendum, the 1990 People's Movement, the Movement Against Regression from 2003 to 2006, and the Second People's Movement in 2006. I asked a number of students attending these rallies why he was introduced as a youth leader. One student reasoned that Chandra was younger than the master of ceremonies, and so he referred to Chandra as a youth, while others suggested that Chandra was labeled a youth leader to welcome young people and inspire in them dedication to the party.[2]

This mislabeling of Chandra and the explanations I received are emblematic of what youth engenders in Nepali politics. In Chandra's words, youth is a state of deferment for things to come. It does not map onto notions of youth in the Nepali cultural context or in Western policy norms. The reason lies in Nepali political history, specifically the role of student politics in the process of becoming a politician and the need for young political actors to cast themselves as the "hope of tomorrow" in order to get out from under the thumbs of their political leaders.

Anthropology's disciplinary focus on youth developed in tandem with predominant social science paradigms.[3] From the 1920s through the 1960s, both cultural and social anthropology assumed that adolescence was a universal experience, preparation for adulthood in the linear life-stage process. Margaret Mead (1928) documented coming-of-age, E. E. Evans-Pritchard

(1940) classified age-set systems, and Victor Turner (1969) coined the term "liminality" to describe the ritual space people embody during coming-of-age rituals. What differed from culture to culture was not the social production process itself, but the details in which it occurred. More recently, anthropology's focus on young people has shifted from adolescence to youth in order to highlight the tension between individual agency and social structure. This shift to youth as the sociological marker focuses on individuals' particular socio-cultural situations (Bucholtz 2002). The category of youth does not assume that childhood or adolescence is a bracketed classification that serves as a rehearsal to becoming an adult. Rather, it "imparts to youths as to adults a degree of consciousness that goes beyond any one situation" (Amit-Talai 1995: 231). What underpins this contemporary logic is the postmodern view that individuals make strategic choices navigating the opposing tensions of social structure and individual agency. For this reason, the category of youth is a valuable mode of analysis for anthropology that allows us to track change in processes of social reproduction (Cole and Durham 2007). As the focus on youth increases in both scholarly and policy realms, we find it becoming a more flexible category of the social that is continually being contested and renegotiated by a number of individuals both within and between societies.

Although this is true in Nepali politics, youth takes a particular cultural form that is a mixture of modernity—grounded in the cultural tenets of the Hindu life cycle, traditional age-set structure, and generational interaction—as well as postmodernity, a contested category of being and becoming defined by global, rights-based discourse (Snellinger 2009b). The Hindu life cycle is a high-caste male cultural paradigm in which the opportunity for education and training is integral.[4] The very experience of university education, out of which Nepali politics comes, cordons off youth as a discreet period of individual cultivation.[5] At the same time, student activists are potently aware that they have little influence in mainstream politics because they are young and must defer to their party seniors. Thus, they assert their youth position, highlighting their new agenda as the coming generation of political leaders. "The accepted 'awareness that each moment is part of a range of cultural possibilities' (Amit-Talai 1995: 231) is the very reason why youth has the political currency it has; this socially acknowledged category allows flexibility. In politics flexibility means malleability to the advantage of oneself and one's group" (Snellinger 2009b: 44). Their claim making is political action meant to establish influence through youth empowerment.

"Let Me Write My Constitution Myself," placard of the youth campaign for new Nepal. Birganj, Parsa, 2013.

Youth is instrumentally employed to mediate power relations in Nepali politics. Students assert themselves as the youth generation to counter their leaders' dismissal of them as immature and their reluctance to grant the students autonomy. The student's explanation that the master of ceremonies introduced Chandra as a youth leader because Chandra was younger than he was captures this dynamic. Leaders often dismiss the generations younger than they are as youth because the leaders see all those they socialized into politics as youth (*yubā*). A CPN-UML leader's explanation captures this dynamic:

One day, after I put my son and daughter on the bus, the conductor said to me, "Please, grandfather, quickly get off or stay on." My daughter, after returning home, expressed surprise that the conductor called me grandpa. But in politics, I am still a youth. [*Laughs.*] . . . You are questioning this, no? [*Laughs.*] . . . Life expectancy is about fifty-five years, no? In this sense, how many people can really be in the youth stage? It may be natural to say "youth" to a person who is up to thirty, perhaps thirty-five. In [the context of] Nepali politics, Girija Prasad Koirala views Ram Chandra Paudel as a youth.[6] I think the word was invented by those in power in

order to minimize challenges from those who are their juniors. . . .
["Youth"] is a derogative term [used] to sideline the juniors from the
power in the pretext that they are not mature and experienced enough.
Thus, this is a word invented to exclude some people from power.[7]

Youth is not a fixed sociological category in the Nepali political context, but
is relationally determined within each interaction; it is indexical as it shifts
from one situation to another, making it discursively contentious (Durham
2004). Youth conceptually maps onto the more general cultural construction of small person and big person (*sānō mānchhe / thulō mānchhe*), which
is another indexical construction that determines position in Nepal's political hierarchy.

Ultimately, the ways in which the youth category is manipulated reveal
that politics has become a holding pattern—extending youth beyond the
globally accepted age range of eighteen to thirty years—since opportunities
for leadership positions have diminished, while still serving as a social
designator in the political hierarchy. Therefore, the category of youth has
been extended to incorporate people of additional generations into "micro-
categories of emergence and waiting" (Snellinger 2009b: 62). This intergenerational dynamic is rooted in the socio-historical relationship of reliance
between the parties and their student unions. Thus, youth in Nepali politics
encapsulates political regeneration.

INTERNATIONAL AND NATIONAL CONVERGENCE ON YOUTH POLICY

Nepal's policy approach to youth issues emerged in coordination with
global development schemes. This process, however, was not as starkly
donor-driven as Nepal's education policy has been since the 1990s (Carney
and Bista 2009). Rather, there has been a complex convergence of priorities
fueled by different motives, both paternalistic and supporting claims for
autonomy and empowerment. Over the past five decades the transnational
position on young people has shifted from a position of legal protection to
include promotion and empowerment (cf. Baker and Hinton 2001). Con-
verging international consensus around the need to invest in the youth
demographic as a discrete political group through rights-based programs
was spearheaded by the United Nations. In 1965, the UN General Assembly
adopted resolution 2037, titled "Declaration on the Promotion among Youth
of the Ideals of Peace, Mutual Respect and Understanding between Peoples."

Between 1965 and 1975, the General Assembly's Economic and Social Council emphasized participation, development, and peace as key priorities for national and international youth-related policy. In 1979, the General Assembly designated 1985 as the International Youth Year: Participation, Development, Peace (resolution 34/151). It launched an awareness campaign to bring international attention to the needs of youth (aged fifteen to twenty-four years old) and promoted their active participation in economic and social development. The UN declared August 12 as International Youth Day, creating an annual tradition of calling together government ministers who oversee youth's well-being, to discuss policy and implementation strategy (UN 2010: 11).

In 1995, on the tenth anniversary of International Youth Year, the World Programme of Action for Youth was adopted by the UN General Assembly as a policy framework to provide guidelines for national action and international support. It identified ten fields of action, and then in 2007 adopted five more, and they included education, employment, hunger and poverty, environment, substance abuse, juvenile justice, armed conflict, HIV/AIDS, intergenerational conflict, and gender discrimination (i–ii). The Programme of Action was divided into three phases that focused on (1) analysis, drafting of the program, and adoption by the General Assembly in 1995; (2) implementation (1995–2000); and (3) further implementation, assessing progress, and identifying how to improve outcomes and long-term implementation (2000–2010) (12).

In Nepal, a history of youth-focused policy dates back to the Panchayat-era attempts to strengthen nationalism. The Panchayat government established the national student council (*rāstriya vidyārthī mandal*) to cultivate college students into the Panchayat administration. The national student council, like the other student organizations, competed for political influence on campus, and indoctrinated its members and other students through its FSU activities. Additionally, in the 1970s and 1980s, Queen Aishwarya inaugurated youth programs, including the national youth house (*rāstriya yubālaya bhaban*). These overtures were meant to demonstrate the government's youth-friendly position and to tamp down dissent.

Another youth-focused program was the National Development Service (1972–79), which was implemented as part of the new education policy of 1971. Its purpose was to integrate students' education with service, enabling them to be key contributors in the nation's development (Vaidya 1992: 129). Master's students were required to spend ten months in a village on community development through teaching, agricultural training, medical service, or administrating development and then draft a report on the village's progress. This program was the Panchayat government's answer to sustainable national development by connecting the newly educated youth with the nation's rural villages and towns, but it was also an attempt to cultivate national pride and connect these newly educated professionals to rural Nepal (cf. Messerschmidt, Gautam, and Silwal 2007).

The first youth policy initiative after Nepal's institution of multiparty democracy was the creation of the Ministry of Youth, Culture, and Sports in 1995 by Sher Bahadur Deuba's government. It was housed in the Ministry of Education office complex in Kaiser Mahal. This ministry's directive was unclear, and thus, in 1996, Minister Purna Bahadur Khadka (an NC-affiliated political appointee) named Kedar Bhakta Mathema to oversee a high-level commission to assess the situation of youth and provide recommendations. The commission recommended that His Majesty's Government (HMG) draft and approve a youth policy to outline the government's and the non-governmental sector's minimum responsibility. It also suggested that a national youth council be devised to coordinate policy and oversee a youth volunteer service program. The commission highlighted youth employment as a serious issue of concern and urged a comprehensive youth employment policy with a five-year plan and the establishment of national youth development centers that would work throughout the country to promote training and guidance on employment opportunities, particularly emphasizing self-employment. It also called for the promotion of education in rural and urban areas and mechanisms to promote youth development at the village development committee level (HMG 1996).

The Ministry of Youth, Culture, and Sports survived until 1999, but little of its annual budget of NR 2.01 billion (1.06 percent) went to youth issues, nor did it institute any of the high-level commission report's main recommendations.[8] Nevertheless, the Deuba government did break the mold in the Ninth Plan and separated youth from adolescents by dedicating subsection 14.2.1 to "youth mobilization." It identified education, culture, employment, health, sports, crime involvement, and substance abuse as major priority areas, which echoed the World Programme of Action for Youth that the UN General Assembly adopted in 1995 (National Planning Commission 1998). The policy suggestions in this plan mirror the suggestions of the 1996 high-level commission report; however, none of these suggestions had been instituted by the creation of the Tenth Plan. In the Tenth Plan, devised by the last HMG of Nepal, youth issues were given even less priority, with no direct mention of how to accommodate youth. However, in 2002, during Sher

Bahadur Deuba's tenure as King Gyanendra's appointed prime minister, a draft of the National Youth Policy (NYP) was written, but it was never presented to parliament. Bureaucrats in the Ministry of Youth, Culture, and Sports drafted the policy by consulting the 1996 high-level report and other countries' national youth policies.

Like most reports and plans, little of the youth-related policy proposals translated into legislative action before 2007. Rapid government turnover during the fractious decade and a half of multiparty democracy was the main reason. Between 1990 and the CA elections in 2008, the prime minister changed fifteen times, and that does not include King Gyanendra's direct-rule stints in 2002 and 2005. New administrations make their mark often by breaking with the agenda of the previous administration. Thus, each administration's grand plans, policies, and reports fade on the back shelves of ministry archives as the bureaucrats busy themselves working with new political appointees to craft alternative plans and policy proposals, which are unlikely to be instituted.

The drafting of the NYP did not become a serious endeavor until after the peace talks between the Maoists and political parties. Chapter 24 of the 2007 Interim Three-Year Plan (UN 2007) was dedicated entirely to youth issues. It outlined a special policy to mobilize youth in the development of the nation decreed by the 2007 interim constitution. The policies and objectives focused mainly on employment but also included devising an NYP, creating a national youth commission, and adopting affirmative action and inclusion policies for marginalized youth communities in response to the emerging demands of the People's War and the 2006–8 Madheshi movement. Other proposed policies and programs echoed the suggestions of the 1996 high-level commission report and demanded coordination between the government, donor agencies, and NGOs. In 2008, Maoist prime minister Pushpa Kamal Dahal provided the needed political will by issuing the directive to create the NYP (which was finally published in 2010), the Ministry of Youth and Sports, and broad-scale education and employment schemes. These directives had the support of all sides—far-left parties, democratic parties, royalists, the general public, and donor agencies—mainly because the majority of democratic activists and Maoist combatants were youths. All parties recognized that to keep them loyal they must address their young cadres' concerns.

Transnational actors' post-conflict intervention played a central role in fueling this momentum. Donor agencies correlated investing in youth opportunity with maintaining peace and stability. During the peace talks and the writing of the interim constitution in 2007, the UN Country Team's Peace and Reconciliation Plan advocated the World Programme of Action for Youth. The ten-member UN Youth Advisory Panel for Nepal was formed in October 2008 as part of the UN Country Team's agenda. The UN Country Team heavily prioritized youth issues that were considered integral to attaining the Millennium Development Goals outlined by the UN Development Assistance Framework for 2008–10. The government of Nepal and the UNDP signed an agreement to ensure young people's rights in accordance with the Convention on the Rights of the Child (UN 2010). The National Planning Commission also tried to address young people's employment challenges by crafting the National Plan of Action for Youth Employment (2008–15) with technical cooperation from the International Labour Organization (ILO). It emphasized employability, equal opportunity, entrepreneurship, and employment creation (National Planning Commission 2008). The estimated total budget was NR 14 billion, little of which was allocated or spent on developing programs.

Nepal's increased focus on youth policy materialized from a combination of international pressure for youth-supported policy and the increasing political influence of generations of student activists who have risen through the political ranks to governing positions. The central impetus for the 2008 NYP, however, was a consensual post-conflict agenda that equated pro-youth policy with sustainable peace. Student activists have used the international priority on youth empowerment to bolster their own political position by claiming the youth demographic as the public sector they represent.

GENERATION OF THE TWENTY-FIRST CENTURY

Student politicians' consistent position on the front lines of each political movement since the Rana regime and the interdependence between the political parties and student unions that developed during the Panchayat era bolstered the students' ability to assert the global language of youth empowerment to their advantage. During the first decade of the twenty-first century, the students heralded themselves as future leaders with new agendas as a strategy to make their mark during political upheaval and ensure their future in democratic politics, while also perpetuating the discourse of youth empowerment.

The politicians and political leaders who protested against the state from 1996 to 2006 (during the People's War, the Movement Against Regression, and the Second People's Movement) were the stewards of multiparty democracy on university campuses during the Panchayat government ban (1960–90). When King Gyanendra curbed their political reach from 2002 to 2006, they immediately mobilized their affiliated student unions to extend their influence onto the streets in the form of opposition politics. There was, however, a key difference in the orientation of the student activists' generation during King Gyanendra's rule and the generations of the Panchayat era. The student leaders protesting the king's 2002 autocratic takeover had professional aspirations in politics. During the Panchayat era, there was no guarantee that student activism would ensure any political advancement; the only way to make politics a professional endeavor was to join the Panchayat government. From the 1960s through the 1980s, students fought for their right to assemble and for democratic exercise on campuses, whereas the student activists of the twenty-first century recognized that their charge to lead the street protest was an opportunity to appeal to the public for support directly. As youth who could bring change tomorrow, they appealed to the public to reinvest in multiparty democracy in order to guarantee their own political futures. They used their position strategically to ensure their political advancement and bypass the limits they encountered by both King Gyanendra's repressive rule and the factionalism and patronage within their parties.

The students framed themselves as the politicians of the twenty-first century. They argued that the king and the monarchy were twentieth-century relics that were unable to address the needs of the country as it went forward into the new millennium. This narrative was not new; democratic activists had equated liberal democratic politics with political modernity since they overthrew the Rana regime (cf. Joshi and Rose [1966] 2004). Even the Panchayat government's main motive was to guide the country into modernity so that at some point in the future it would have an educated and aware citizenry that could participate in democratic politics in an informed way (Gellner 2015). The link between a multiparty system and political modernity was this notion of development (*vikās*).[9] The drafters of the 1990 constitution viewed the Westminster model as "synonymous with 'political modernity'" (Malagodi 2013: 117).

The student activists in the Movement Against Regression and the Second People's Movement, however, fought to reinstitute regime change in a more radical way than their predecessors, by questioning the validity of the monarchy itself. The student union alliance leading the Movement Against Regression was the first cross-party alliance to demand republicanism (*ganatantra*) on the streets, with only a few political outliers such as Narahari Acharya from the NC and the Maoists, who had made republican demands since the mid-1990s. Their republican stance simultaneously distinguished the students from their leaders' democratic political establishment and positioned them as an alternative to the Maoists' republican agenda. The Maoists fused their agenda with support for multiparty democracy in 2003 by passing a resolution called "Democracy in the 21st Century" (Hachhethu 2009: 58).[10]

In response to King Gyanendra's 2002 takeover, the parties used vague political rhetoric to hedge their bets. Some politicians called for *purna prajātantra* (pure/full democracy). Others found the demand for any form of *prajātantra* problematic, because *prajā* (people) retains a sense of subjecthood and thus cannot exist without a ruling entity, in Nepal's case, the *rājā* (king) (Malagodi 2013: 136). One student explained to me that *prajātantra* was the democratic setup of the 1990 constitution that gave the king article 127, the power to override the democratically elected body for the security of the nation, which Gyanendra took advantage of in 2002 and 2005.[11] Those who were leery of monarchical power but not radical enough to take a republican stance demanded *lōktantra* (democracy; literally "folk/community rule"), a term that comes from the Sanskrit root *lok*, which means "folk" or "community" and thus has no linguistic or historical connection to the king. Rhetorically, these different demands for democracy's reinstitution represented the range of political attitudes from traditionalist to radical.

A handful of student leaders called for a republic in their speeches at a protest program celebrating Democracy Day on December 16, 2003, and were subsequently arrested and charged with sedition. Such a charge had been rare in the post-1990 political era, indicating a step backward to Panchayat autocracy during which free speech was curtailed. Student activists reacted violently, setting fire to government vehicles and hurling bricks at police, and demanded their leaders' immediate release. The government responded to the mayhem by quickly withdrawing the sedition charges and releasing the student leaders, a turn of events that further emboldened the students. Since the king's government was unable to enforce sedition charges, the student unions used the opportunity to form their own joint movement, comprising seven of the FSU organizations. Their mission was to radicalize the discourse of the Movement Against Regression by making demands that their more conservative parties were not willing to ask for. The students embraced protesting the king's autocratic actions as an opportunity to distinguish themselves from their party leaders.

Within the confines of the streets and campuses, students asserted their own political agenda. I observed them continually experiment with their

Student union cadres igniting an effigy of the king, during the Movement Against Regression. Bāg Bazār, Kathmandu, 2004.

protest tactics to cast themselves as bolder than their party leaders. In doing so, the students were reformulating knowledge, assumptions, and expectations. By presenting the public with alternatives to what was, their tactics implicitly posed the question, can't it be otherwise? This rhetorical strategy was necessary for them to make a future beyond serving as the parties' foot soldiers. That they made it a project of their own came through in distinct ways. They declared Padma Kanya Campus, an all girls' college that served as a base of operation for much of the 2004 street protests, as a republican zone (*ganatantra kshetra*). Establishing this zone demarcated the public campus as something outside the state's reach, a place beyond the no-protest zones that were instituted from March 2004 through 2006.

Another protest tactic that distinguished the students was a series of mini-referendums they held on campuses nationwide. General students across the country were asked to choose between an active monarchy, a constitutional monarchy, or a republic. The student unions rolled out these referendums over a six-month period beginning in the spring of 2004. Each campus referendum was staged with absurdity to gain media coverage, and results were released to coincide with media outlets' release of their own countrywide political poll data. These referendums were not statistically

Banner over the Padma Kanya Campus's entrance: "Republic Bazaar gives a hearty welcome to everyone who has come to participate in the people's movement. —FSU, Padma Kanya Campus, Republic Bazaar, Kathmandu." Bāg Bazār, Kathmandu, 2004.

sound. News articles at the time raised doubts about whether the results of the referendums were indicative of public sentiment because they were not executed in a systematic fashion.[12] Nevertheless, they still made a clear statement: the monarchy was not long for this world, perhaps not even for one generation, because students overwhelmingly supported a democratic republic.

These young activists, however, recognized that without their leaders' blessing they would not have had the leeway to pursue such contentious protest tactics. Years later, Akash explained to me that he was given permission by the formidable NC president G. P. Koirala to make republican demands: "The political leaders allowed us to be radical because they wanted to pressure the king. They didn't realize that we believed in republicanism and were not merely demanding it to ensure their success. They didn't recognize that we were inspiring the public. This did not make them happy."[13] The students' contentious politics resulted from a symbiosis of forced dependence between mother and sister organizations, wherein the parties mobilized the students to circumvent the limits put on them by the monarchy and the students relied on the political leaders for patronage to ensure their political future.

Even King Gyanendra's government recognized the students' potential to counter the established political authority. Before the king's state of emergency was declared in February 2005, the Rāj Parishad (King's Council) released lists of political activists whom security forces were to detain under the Terrorist and Disruptive Activities Prevention and Control Ordinance. These lists were ranked in order of priority from A to C, with those posing the biggest threat on list A. More student activists than political leaders were on list A.[14] Many student leaders were arrested or fled underground and were subsequently arrested. When recalling their experience of arrests, habeas corpus trials, and rearrests, a number of student leaders admitted that it was unsettling but beneficial because it also gave them public exposure. Salini explained: "It was terrifying. I did not know where they were taking me. They put a hood over my head and drove me around the valley. Everything was so uncertain. . . . But due to my arrest, my profile was increased. It showed that the king's people took me seriously."[15]

Akash's experience was even more dramatic. He was not captured immediately because he had fled underground. He even avoided attending a regional conference that I organized with the American Mission for youth leaders in South Asia, because it took place a week after the king declared the state of emergency.[16] I visited Akash in hiding while I was in Kathmandu to attend the conference. The day I departed, he shifted his location in case someone had noticed a foreigner regularly visiting the area and reported it. For the next month, he regularly moved around to outrun the police. He was finally apprehended a month later, but not in obscurity. The BBC reported that one of the "country's most wanted men" had been arrested (Haviland 2005). Ten days later, when he was released on a court-ordered habeas corpus ruling, many people came to felicitate him, only to see him rearrested on the steps of the jail compound for inciting an illegal gathering. Reaction came from not only students but also onlookers from the general public, who up until this point had not defied the state of emergency. At his second habeas corpus hearing, people from all public sectors attended. This chain of events threw Akash into the limelight, and the support he received foregrounded his political potential. Although the crackdown on Akash and his counterparts as threats was unintentional, it actually bolstered their political position. Akash pushed this further and in all his speeches after he was released directly asked the public to question the utility of the monarchy.

As these events demonstrate, the student activists used their youth position to real political effect. By casting the status quo as something that was cutting off their future, they created an unofficial discourse of power that simultaneously asserted their potential while depicting dominant narratives of power as anachronistic, of a bygone century. The students embodied the possibilities that youth encompasses as a political category: something new, something different from what is. By doing so, they were implicitly asking the public to consider what type of politics and politicians they wanted. As one student leader explained: "It's up to us, the youth, to show the world what Nepal's democratic potential is. We will begin among our own sector, and eventually it will become institutionalized by our society."[17] By finding space within the political limits they encountered, the students presented themselves to the public as an alternative and allowed the public to put hope in their future.

POLITICS OF EMERGENCE AND WAITING

The students recognized that youth claims resonate both locally and globally, and they strategically used their youth position as an alternative voice and new vision to ensure their political longevity. When asking what "new Nepal" should be, many students advocated for a central role for youth. One student leader proposed a youth parliament, with the simple argument that "new Nepal" equals new rules and policies that must come from new leadership, which only the new generation can provide. However, this orientation of "us as the new and all previous generations as old" is not unique to this generation, as one UML leader explained: "I used to say that my father was orthodox, an old and conservative person. It was so because my father was not able to perceive the change of the times. In the same way, my son labels me as orthodox because he uses the Internet, whereas I belong to the age of plough and spade."[18] Indeed, the student activists I worked with were not the first to dismiss previous generations for having a limited conception of what is possible. This is in fact how political regeneration operates; each generation creates new demands and political formations that fuel political change over time. The student activists of the first decade of the twenty-first century distinguished themselves from their predecessors by harnessing the global language of youth empowerment and liberal democracy because they understood its currency among foreign donors and transnational agencies. They were resonating with what mattered to contemporary power brokers, and in turn these organizations lobbied the king and their political leaders on their behalf. This, in kind, demonstrated to the public that these young activists themselves were influential and worth investing in.

The connection between political regeneration and youth as a political category can be conceptualized in how generational interaction socially mediates the process of political reproduction and change. Just as the political category of youth draws on the Hindu life cycle, interaction in the political hierarchy is similar to the high-caste Hindu joint-family dynamic. The family is idealized as an egalitarian unit in which members work together for a common good. Yet in the high-caste joint family there is tension (Bennett 1983). An apprehensive inter-reliance exists between the relations of old (patriarchs) and young (sons), or, in the case of the political parties, between those currently in power and future leaders. The longevity of the shared lineage or ideology requires codependence. A political party benefits when members remain together rather than split into smaller groups, but this "interdependency is fraught with tensions between competition and solidarity" (Snellinger 2006: 357). Filial metaphors commonly used in Nepali politics are leveraged in particular ways. Politicians use filial references rhetorically to connect with a crowd or to draw fellow political actors into fictive kin relations to establish networks of obligation. Risha pointed out to me that these filial metaphors are so normative that nobody thinks about them as deliberately constructed: "Even the party structure mimics the family—we are the sister organization and our party is the mother organization."[19]

Just as an extended family is sustained by intergenerational cohesion, the political parties are sustained by intergenerational interaction. Generations (pustā) forge the past, present, and future of parties. Generations are generally defined in reference to political movements because each political movement marks the new set of students stepping into activism. A bond is created among each new cohort as they forge their path into politics through the political movement. The political movement is the first opportunity for activists to distinguish themselves from the activists who came before, and future political movements will inevitably distinguish this cohort as well. A Maoist leader explained this to me as the law of dialectical development, or, as he phrased it, "negation of the negation as continual revolution"[20] The new (or young) will challenge the old order, the very people who brought them to the position in which they could be a challenge, because the old order challenged those before them. In this cycle of tense reliance, the parties and sister organizations fight for common causes; however, each movement brings different experiences of struggle, demands, and achievements, which are the very things that differentiate each generation. Just as memory is conceptualized within the different movements, the movements differentiate the generations. This is the cycle of political regeneration.

But as Chandra's situation demonstrates, mapping generations onto political movements is not straightforward. During the Panchayat era, people identified their peers and drew camaraderie according to the first political movement in which they participated; however, multiple generations were not collapsed into inaccurate age categories as they are today. An NC leader explained that this change occurred after multiparty democracy was instituted in 1991. Before then, the political landscape consisted of the old generation, the leaders, and the new generation, those who did not hold power within the party but, being junior, were still learning and in need of cultivation. After multiparty democracy, holding positions of power within the party has meant determining the makeup of government by negotiating with other parties and doling out seats to party members. These positions come with many perks and little risk. The octogenarian leaders, who are in the life stage of renunciate (*sanyāsī*) and should be withdrawing from society, have refused to retire, creating a surplus of adults in the political wings and causing the traditional life stages to become askew. The simple distinction between old and young has become anachronistic. Now there are over four generations in party politics, all at different ranks that roughly correlate to different political movements.

Thus, youth has come to incorporate these additional junior generations, causing a misalignment between the political category of youth and culturally specific and globally prescribed definitions of youth. Youth, however, is not merely a category in which similarly aged people are grouped together. Within it, there is also a hierarchy by which one wields one's influence and higher position over those who are either younger or less influential. Influence over others further entrenches one's superior position. But one's position is always relational; in some scenarios one is in the position of leader and in others that of a youth activist. Evans-Pritchard (1940: 263) argued that an actor's position is determined in the relational context of social interaction. However, he was referring to interaction between the age-set systems, the discreet grouping of men according to their initiation-rites cohort. The key word in Evans-Pritchard's analysis is "set." Which set or cohort one was a part of determined one's position in each interaction. However, in Nepali politics, multiple cohorts are still considered youth, making it a malleable designator. Which are youth is based on the dynamics of each social interaction in which status or age can be the determining factor.

The emic concept of "small person and big person" (sānō mānchhe / thulō mānchhe) in Nepali culture can further elucidate this dynamic. Most people are both big and small people in different aspects of their lives. People simultaneously embody these multiple modes of being. To achieve big-person status in all interaction is the ultimate goal of a leader. In politics, only leaders are no longer youth because they are big persons in every social interaction. Until then, like Chandra, one can be dismissed as youth whether or not one fits within the prescribed youth age-group, because youth as a political category comprises all those who are waiting for more to come. Thus, the youth stage engenders varying degrees of emergence, "micro-categories of emergence and waiting" (Snellinger 2009b: 62). As an NC leader explained, "People make meaning of this waiting through their attempts to impact politics in any way they can."[21]

Many student activists are in a similar position to Chandra. They are stuck in limbo between student politics and party politics. They had positions of leadership in their student organizations and now they find themselves in a liminal space, again rejoining the ranks of burgeoning leaders, this time vying for positions in their parties, mainly in ancillary youth, women, or ethnic wings.

Risha, Salini, and Gyanu acutely experienced this situation after 2009. They have struggled to gain their footing in party politics for different reasons. Gyanu's trajectory fell victim to the ideological splits in his party. He was not in Prachanda's camp that maintained governing power, and thus there was no place for him to gain an official foothold. Rather, as he explained to me, he continues to write his manifestos and be a voice for the Maoist radical fringe: "I've taken up the role of intellectual [buddhijībī]. I must stay true to the party, so I influence with my thoughts and writing rather than from a seat of power."[22] For Risha and Salini, their gender has adversely affected their ability to get ahead. Salini fared a bit better than Risha in student politics itself since she was elected president of her student union, the first woman in Nepali political history. Nonetheless, they have both been shunted off to peripheral departments, the women's wing and the training and ideology department. They also experienced the disappointment of having been listed on their parties' proportional list in the 2013 CA elections and then not appointed to seats. Both campaigned vigorously for their party during the CA elections.

All three continue to give speeches at student functions, consult regularly with the current leaders of their student unions, and cultivate new students. Risha has also stepped beyond politics to garner the influence she has not found within it. She developed a national network of women's organizations in which she had cultivated and trained many women to advocate for themselves. On the way to Gorkha for a workshop on gender and inclusion, a middle-aged facilitator from Dhanusha admitted: "Risha is our *bahinī* [younger sister], but really she is our guru. Even though she's young, she leads the cause for women."[23]

There is no guarantee that these activities will advance the political careers of Risha, Salini, or Gyanu, but they are important for maintaining their relevancy. By mentoring others and serving their parties as "former student leaders," they are further expanding their sphere of influence. The interlocking processes of mentoring and being mentored are integral to the dynamics of intergenerational interaction within political parties. It is the sociality that undergirds political regeneration. People invest in each other in order to maintain a presence and, they hope, garner some political capital through alliance and reliance among generations.

ESTABLISHING POLITICAL AUTHORITY
BEYOND STREET PROTEST

Through the drafting of the NYP in 2008, youth leaders were invested in propagating a particular meaning of youth—one out of sync with general cultural norms—to stake their claim and establish political authority in post-conflict Nepal.

Approved by the ministerial council in 2010, the NYP mandated the establishment of the Ministry of Youth and Sports and the National Youth Council to execute pro-youth governing policy.[24] Drafting the NYP had multi-partisan support since it fulfilled a central post-conflict priority to address the needs of young people to prevent them from becoming disillusioned and compromising the postwar reconstruction. The NYP drafting committee participants all pointed to young people's central role in ensuring state reconstruction as the motivating factor for establishing the NYP: "The youths have rendered an outstanding contribution to every political change, founding of democracy and other social movements in Nepal. The peaceful popular movement, decade-long armed conflict, Madhesh movement, Tharuhat movement as well as movements for identity and recognition, which took place in the past, have raised a demand to specially address the existing situation of the youths. The need of a policy for youth has, therefore, increased" (Ministry of Youth and Sports 2010: 1–2). One drafting committee member pointed out that "youth are the pillars of development" in all societies and that a "new Nepal" needed to demonstrate this to itself and to the world by creating a national youth policy.[25] For youth leaders, however, the NYP and resulting National Youth Council were quid pro quo compensation they felt entitled to for their service as political movement leaders.

The drafting committee boasted inclusion of various youth demographics.[26] It was made up of people who advocated for youth across sectors. But most striking was the lack of inclusion by age. Only three of the committee members were younger than thirty years old, and none were under twenty-five; the majority of the members were older than thirty-five. Political parties' youth and student wings also dominated the committee, which caused rifts between participants from the political and social sectors (INGOs and NGOs) on a number of issues.

The most contentious issue was the debate over age range. The majority of the politically affiliated members advocated for the age range to accommodate political party reality, sixteen- to forty-five-year-olds. Non-politically affiliated drafting committee members saw this as ridiculous, bordering on cynical. As one individual critical of the political wings' logic explained:

> The youth, who represented the political parties, they don't fall in the sixteen to twenty-nine age range. They belong to the thirty-five through sixty age demographic. It seems to me that they were drafting the policy for themselves . . . for their own sake rather than for the youth throughout the nation. For this reason, they took a very strong stance. . . . We opined that it's just like feeding the food meant for an infant to a twenty-two-year-old person. We disagreed with it. That was the debate. I wrote a note of dissent on it. They even said that I must be punished for this.[27]

The non-political participants advocated for an upper limit of twenty-nine years of age. They reasoned that, like the 2002 policy draft, it needed to surpass the UN-sanctioned upper age limit of twenty-four years because of the scarcity of economic and educational opportunities in Nepal.[28] The original draft drawn up the committee's coordinator, Udaya Raj Pandey of the CPN-UML, set the upper age limit at thirty-five. However, the youth-wing participants affiliated with the five main parties argued for forty-five based on their own constitutions.[29]

There were three main concerns regarding the sixteen to forty-five age designation. The first was that it incorporates multiple generations, wherein both parents and children are within the same demographic category, possibly incorporating up to three generations (Asia-Pacific Interagency Group on Youth 2011). The second was that resources allotted for youth programming will be spread thinner among a larger population and will inevitably dilute the impact of any youth-related policy. The third concern was that, for official budgetary and policy purposes, it throws Nepal's statistics off from both national and transnational donor norms. According to the introduction in the NYP document, Nepal's youth (sixteen to forty) comprise 38.8 percent of the population (Ministry of Youth and Sports 2010: 1). However, Nepal's youth population according to the UN standard (fifteen to twenty-four) is 19.97 percent of the population, and it is 27.82 percent according to the National Planning Commission and the ILO's youth target group (fifteen to twenty-nine) (Central Bureau of Statistics 2012: 65). Thus, the NYP throws off the uniformity of prescribed universal norms, highlighting the relative underpinnings of youth as a social and political construction.

Many hours of debate ensued among the drafting committee members over this issue. The committee eventually agreed to compromise and cap the age at thirty-five. Yet, despite a lack of support from the majority of the drafting committee and all of the consulting experts warning against it, the age cap was increased to forty years old in the final draft that was presented for endorsement. The CA government's ministerial council approved it.[30] Advocates for the older age cap argued that it was consistent with youth-wing policies from the Panchayat rule and that it was important in making the policy inclusive.[31] Those who supported a cap of twenty-nine years of age were thoroughly disappointed, and seven of them did not endorse the final policy. Four of the dissenting participants boycotted the remainder of the drafting meetings once they realized that they could not change things; the other three attended but stopped participating.

The age designation of youth as sixteen to forty in the NYP is illustrative of the contemporary social reality outlined in the previous section; youth has become a holding pattern that incorporates additional generations waiting to emerge into adulthood. One drafting participant aptly noted, "We have a disease in politics—one is seen as a youth until one holds a position."[32] The political youth-wing participants used the drafting of the NYP as an opportunity to create positions for themselves in both politics and government. As a Youth Communist League participant candidly explained: "We reasoned that we can target this [sixteen to forty] age range to develop political leadership. As for the UN provisions, its underlying logic for determining the age range is meant for providing services, whereas we have political reasons behind our choice. We felt that youth should be defined politically, too. We made it this age range in order to ensure the involvement of youth from the parties' sister organizations."[33] All of the youth-wing participants who supported the sixteen to forty age range were apprehensive that older people would step in and take over the leadership duties of the National Youth Council if the NYP set the age limit too young. Their anxiety was rooted in their own political experience.

This situation, however, is not merely about older people usurping opportunity; it also demonstrates the endemic mistrust in young people's abilities. That elders refuse to give responsibility to young people perpetuates the stereotype that they are inexperienced. The outcome of the NYP further demonstrates that social bias against youth in politics has been internalized even by youth leaders. As one youth-wing participant stated: "The fifteen to twenty-four age range incorporates those who've just passed their teenage years. We doubt that this age-group may be able to perform well. Therefore, we included more mature persons."[34] The Ministry of Youth and Sports representative who sat on the drafting committee echoed this prejudice, explaining that individuals thirty and older are more experienced and can therefore think and plan more constructively than those in the fifteen to twenty-four age range. He did admit, however, that elder youth also have a tendency to dominate the younger youth.[35]

The political youth-wing members wanted to reserve the leadership level of the National Youth Council for people aged thirty-five to forty-five. Their reasoning was that people of this age would command the respect necessary to avoid interference from elders because they have had the longest experience working as youth and for youth.[36] People aged twenty-five to thirty-five would assist in instituting the National Youth Council policies, allowing them to gain the experience to lead the council in the future. And the NYP policies would benefit those aged sixteen to twenty-five.[37] Of course, the unspoken factor fueling their ambition to oversee the National Youth Council is access and control over state resources and the authority earned when distributing those resources.

It is clear that the youth-wing participants envisioned the NYP's institution to mirror their political organizations, a tiered age hierarchy in which leadership is reserved for elders. Only within the political category of "youth" do they have the standing to take leadership, and they want to ensure that party leaders do not usurp their newfound sphere of influence. By taking advantage of the external pressure that transnational organizations and donor agencies were putting on Nepal's post-conflict government to prioritize youth-related policy, these youth leaders were establishing political

NC (D) party elders occupying the stage of the national convention of the NSU (D). Nepalganj, Banke, 2007.

authority beyond campus politicking and street protest. The obvious down-side to their logic is that it perpetuates the tension between the generations. The political agenda of designating youth as sixteen to forty years of age in national policy further frustrates young people by structurally entrenching the political precedent of older people speaking for the young.

CONCLUSION

What does it mean for Chandra to be in a state of deferment? The socio-political dynamic of Nepali politics has forced him to postpone his personal and political aspirations. However, Chandra and his cohort are not passively waiting. They are actively pursuing what they hope to attain. Student activists' orientation is hopeful, because they defer what cannot be attained in the present to the future. Student activists have strategically embodied hope by emphasizing their future potential. They have maximized their youth position in a number of ways to navigate and overcome the very limits that are enforced on them for being youth. They have taken advantage of inter-national agendas that encourage youth empowerment and used them to pitch themselves as a "category of the possible" (Rancière 1999: 129) to the public while protesting on the streets. After they brought their parties back into power, they did their best to keep themselves relevant and garner the influence needed to survive in politics. The age designation they set in the NYP was a response to this political reality. It was an attempt to actualize their aspirations rather than continually defer them into the future. However, by setting the upper age limit of youth to forty, they structurally instituted the misalignment that they themselves have experienced in politics.

As a political category, youth is an inherently relational assemblage that comprises social alliance and reliance, which is grounded in a shared political history. The socio-historical dynamic of political movements fueling Nepal's political process has trained people to look toward tomorrow and wait for things to come. Each generation has something new to contribute; however, the structural realities keep them from fulfilling all that they have promised on the streets. Through their participation, they carry on the political lineage while making it their own. They come to embody political regeneration. And while they may provide the public with hope by offering alternative visions of the future, they simultaneously encourage reproduction of the political status quo.

4 The Organizational Form of Practice, Ideology, and Identity

TO UNDERSTAND THE LINK BETWEEN POLITICS (WITH A CAPITAL P) and the enactment of politics, it is important to identify the link between people's ideological categories and practical categories. The category of organization in Nepali politics provides insight into their shared sense of the Political in the same way that the structural aspects of practice provide a lens into people's worldview (cf. Evans-Pritchard 1940; Leach [1954] 1970). There is a distinct narrative concerning the role of organization in Nepali party politics that at times seems contradictory, but when its different informing factors are deconstructed, what is revealed is an interesting combination of expectation and idealism that is used to place oneself and others in the political playing field. Nepali political actors link political ideology and organizational form as the defining features of their political organizations, which they assess through working styles and lifestyles. In other words, their "organizations (noun) are sustained by organization (verb)" (Harris 2005: 165). Their institutions are manifested through their embodiment and performance and the chronicling of organizational narratives and procedures (cf. Latour 1987, 1994). Ideology, organizational form, working styles, and lifestyles are the "immanent acts of organization" (Harris 2005: 165) that help distinguish institutional cultures from one another in Nepal's political landscape.

Ideology has been described as a political map that positions one in relation to others (Malagodi 2013: 175, citing Breuilly 1993). This definition is illustrative of how ideology works within Nepali party politics; however, political thought is not the only cartographic aggregate of ideology. Ideology is also informed by organization (noun) and organization (verb). One student leader framed it in this way: "Thoughts and theory guide people. Those who are devoid of thoughts and theory are worthless. Man is a social animal and he is associated with one or another philosophy. [This] allows us to group together. This is how we interact in the world and with other people."[1] Conceptions of organizational culture provide a compass. It allows participants to navigate the complicated political terrain that has included exile, civil war, joint political movements, opposition politics, electoral competition, coalition building, and, more recently, state restructuring. Organization dictates both how individuals must conduct themselves in their institutions and how the group conducts itself as an organization while interacting with other organizations.

The shared symbolic associations of organization—what counts as organization and how these associations are rationalized through their everyday practices—create a shared institutional culture between political parties and their student organizations. Four themes have emerged from this discourse: organizational culture; "scientific organization," an ANNISU (R) term; institutional anarchy; and the moral critique of "freedom within control." These elements are referential composites of a complicated number of interrelated factors that people use to define their political organization and frame their political identity.

Many of my interlocutors believe that Nepali political organizations have become weakened because of the discrepancy between their parties' ideology and their internal practices (working styles). There is potent anxiety that the political parties have lost touch with their "master frames" meant to anchor their agenda and maintain organizational cohesion (Snow and Benford 1992: 146). Their explanations allude to the age-old struggle between theory and practice (Djilas 1957; Doolin and Golas 1964; Lenin [1920] 1971). An underpinning assumption of organization is that internal culture and ideology should be recursive (Breines 1989). Organizations may be "autopoietic" (self-regulating and self-reproducing systems), but they are constructed processes that emerge from iterative enactments, and thus organization's recursive nature is loose and unpredictable rather than an evolution from a linear sequence (Weick 1979). Nepali politics demonstrates that. The discrepancies between political ideology and internal practice unintentionally create negative feedback loops, causing unanticipated downfalls and what Nepali political actors call negative political culture.

DIFFERENTIATING: THE PARAMETERS OF POLITICAL CULTURE

Organizational culture allows political actors to distinguish their place and the place of their group in the larger political realm. It creates an inner circle, allowing political actors to differentiate between "us and them" (Bista 1991: 97). Collective identities of any kind rely on such distinction.

Differentiation is an inevitable result of social interaction, "for such differentiation is the very core of their social self-invention" (Wagner 1975: 121).
Anthropology has a long history of identifying such practices (cf. Gellner
and Hirsch 2001; Strathern 1988; Wagner 1975). The shared culture of
Nepali politics is shaped by the interactions between these specific institutional cultures within the socio-historical context of democratic struggle
since the 1950s. The distinctions my interlocutors made between their parties' and unions' internal cultures, political culture, and culture (*sanskriti*)
elucidate how they demarcate belonging in the political terrain and society.[2]

Political organizations' cultures exist in tandem with the subjectivities
and codes of behavior in society in general. A political analyst explained
this dialectical interaction between political culture and general culture in
the following way:

> First of all, political culture encompasses a lot of things. It has an impact
> on everything. Our institutional culture plays the most significant role in
> our varying ideologies and perspectives in politics. But what I do largely
> depends on the society in which I grew up. It depends on the norms and
> culture of my society. In the context of politics, my own culture evolves
> depending on how, where, and with whom I become connected. It is simi-
> lar to the more general concept of culture in the sense that it is accumu-
> lative in the long process of living, and it finally carves the character of
> a person. That is why our diverse views have to be acknowledged and
> respected in the realm of politics.[3]

This analyst's explanation of political culture echoes a general understanding of *sanskriti* within Nepali society. Since the creation of the modern
Nepali nation-state, there has been an acknowledgment of the different
cultures and identities that exist within its borders. In 1854, the Muluki Ain
(legal code) codified social strictures according to assigned caste classification and delineated interactions between people according to Hindu law
(Höfer 1979). Throughout Rana rule, local leaders of the diverse groups of
Nepal had to negotiate expectations of the regime in order to balance varying degrees of local autonomy with central government resource extraction.
In 1964, many of these legal statutes were adjusted to follow the first constitution of King Mahendra's partyless Panchayat system (Höfer 1979).

There is a long-standing tradition of identifying difference and then
figuring out how to relate with one another despite varying hierarchies,
traditions, and worldviews (cf. Gellner and Quigley 1999; Whelpton 2005).

Since the fall of the Rana regime in 1949, politics has been a key venue in which these differences have been contentiously negotiated (Hangen 2010; Hutt 2004; Lawoti 2005). Establishing who is a part of the demos and who is outside it is an essential part of democratic logic (Mouffe 2000: 4, 12). Representative democracy in Nepal has thus required a mutual recognition between actors not only of different social and cultural groups but of different political organizations.

When people talk about culture in Nepali politics, what they are talking about, however, is different from ethnic or religious culture. Institutional political culture is a manifestation of identifiable factors such as ideology, working style and lifestyle, individual characteristics, hierarchical structure, and a particular shared history. These aspects may be components of ethnic or religious culture, yet people do not critically deconstruct them in ethnic and religious culture the way they do when discussing political organizations. Rather, they treat their own and others' ethnic or religious culture, at least conceptually, with reverence as reified tradition—regarded as the essence of tradition, not something that can be extracted, manipulated, or modified. With political organizations, they take an analytic tact that recognizes that organizational culture is constructed within a history and changes along with it and thus can be judged and restructured for the benefit of the institutions. Political culture is mutable. It serves a pragmatic end.

This became apparent in my initial interviews. I noticed that when I asked people about institutional political culture using the Nepali word (*sanskriti*), more often than not people responded using the English word "culture." They would tack back and forth using the word *sanskriti* to describe religious and ethnic traditional ways of life, while using the English word "culture" to describe their institutional culture. If they chose to respond in Nepali, they would use the word *samskār* to distinguish their political culture, which translates more closely to "ritual process," as opposed to *sanskriti*, which is considered more "reified tradition" with its etymological roots based in Sanskrit, the language of the gods. My informants' understanding of culture is informed by their sociology and anthropology courses. The social scientific explanation they learned in the classroom is based on culture as a constructed concept, something that is objective, which can be studied and identified. Thus, the students' understanding of their own and other parties' institutional cultures was, in a sense, academic. Their bifurcated view of culture echoes Roy Wagner's (1975) distinction between convention and invention. They consider their organizational culture within the "'artificial realm' of human manipulation"; they see their political association as an active choice. *Sanskriti*, in contrast, is not chosen and thus is more akin to "'innate' conventions of culture" (103).

Another marked difference between *sanskriti* and institutional culture was articulated in my informants' capacity to be critical of political culture without necessarily believing that those who engaged in it were fundamentally flawed. They objectified the elements of institutional culture by disassociating them from the people who enacted them, whereas being critical of others' *sanskriti* was to be critical of the people and their lineage—for example, judgments of people as "lacking consciousness" because they continue "backward practices." Student politicians engaged critical assessment of their own institutional practices and the practices of other institutions in a morally neutral way. A leader from a small leftist student organization explained: "While our organization is exposed to the society or to other organizations, we have to assess whether others like or dislike our culture [English term spoken]. What I mean by culture is the accumulative form of our working style and interaction with each other and society. If the people outside don't like our styles, we need to change them. For instance, imagine that we are presenting our culture as revolutionaries. But if the people do not support violence, naturally we need to bring changes in our styles."[4] As this quotation demonstrates, political actors engage in detached reflection of their organization in ways that are rarely done when they consider their own or others' *sanskriti*. The constructed nature of their organizations is an obvious attribute; their very survival as organizations is affected by how they present themselves and how they are perceived. Thus, political institutional culture is a reflexive endeavor in which the members are constantly negotiating meaning and struggling over agenda.

Political actors understand their ideology, working style, and lifestyle to be integral to their institutional culture. However, their ideological orientation influences how they prioritize these different aspects in the composition of their own institutional culture and how they think they are prioritized in other student organizations. For the leftist student activists, ideology and working style are the most crucial elements that define their institutional culture. A Maoist student explained to me that "style and culture are more or less sides of the same coin."[5] Working style is the manifestation of the two symbiotic tenets of their institution: their ideology and their political agenda. That is why they define their culture according to their working style. On the opposite end of the political spectrum, Nepal Student Union (NSU) members do not hold their working style in high priority because they do not have a unified style; what binds them is their history of fighting for democracy, a struggle that also occurs internally due to the multiple alignments between the NC and NSU factions.

PARTY IMAGE: CLEAR AND CONSISTENT PARTY LINE

An organization's image hinges on clear ideology and consistent practice. Clarity and consistency lie at the nexus of organization as noun and organization as verb because the very point of organizing is to guide an agenda through to fruition. Yet it is a "complex and inherently ambiguous process of sense-making" (Czarniawska 2005: 269–70). This sense making involves creating party identities that are consistent with their party mission so that they can be recognizable and appealing to citizens. A CPN-UML leader described it in this way: "The ideological base of the party has to be predictable. Even outsiders should be able to know what the party's ideological base is and understand the party's destination. Thus, the party should be committed to a defined ideological base."[6]

A Maoist student leader articulated a similar view about the Prachanda Path: "[It] is not just a slogan or a movement that we do theoretically. We live it both as an organization and as a lifestyle."[7] Party image is assessed based on how consistently party members live according to their party's ideology. The aggregate actions of party members over time is what forms party image. Enacting organization as a lifestyle—organization as verb— resonates with the leftist value of discipline. But in South Asia, it also is rooted in the Gandhian political sensibility of piety in action—one closely linked to politics as social service, as covered in chapter 2. Since politics is a public process, those who engage in it live under public scrutiny, where the actions and lifestyles of party members define a party as much as their party line does.

Most of my informants described other student organizations' culture in stereotypical terms that affirmed their own union of choice. Salini explained that "the internal styles and the culture are a reflection of the character of [an organization's] leaders and cadres."[8] Her reason for choosing to join the ANNFSU highlights this point, making it personal: "Its activities are seen as different than the others' activities. At the school level, one can distinguish the different characteristics among students who belong to different organizations. One group has the honest and studious students, who live simply, whereas the other group has students of opposite characteristics. They have a pompous lifestyle. I was raised to oppose such a lifestyle. The training that I obtained from my family background helped me to choose this organization."[9] As her explanation demonstrates, people are drawn to political affiliations that suit their values and the values of the existing social webs in which they are entrenched. The "character and behaviors" of leaders and cadres mark an organization's niche (cf. Hannan and Freeman 1986) by indicating the values and ideology that distinguish them and maintain social boundaries from other political organizations.

NSU students readily admitted to me that their student members' characteristics and lifestyle, more than their ideology, shape their culture. The majority of NSU students are middle-class and, compared to their leftist peers, not very critical of bourgeois capitalism. For them, politics is about freedom of individual expression and political competition. In the NSU, the sister organization to the NC—which is infamous for being a conglomerate of political fiefdoms—charisma and personality determine how individuals rank in the hierarchy of the union's factional, patronage-based structure. One student explained critically:

> The way the cadres of an organization act determines the overall culture of the organization. We have developed such a culture where one must hold a position, serve one's interest, and create disputes in order to be successful. Of course, this doesn't allow us to conduct our union's activities effectively. Our culture undermines us. For instance, if we passed through the NSU's central committee an edict that we would stop drinking alcohol or smoking, there is a 90 percent chance that we would fail in implementing it. If we decided that we would start wearing simple dress, there is a 95 percent chance that we would fail to implement it. The main reason behind this is the individualistic attitude that has developed among us, although not implementing such measures indicates the tolerance for individual freedom in our organization. That defines us. It helps to attract many students to our organization. But the negative aspect is that, since individuality is prioritized, we cannot reach people in a unified way. Our strength has disintegrated.[10]

This student's critique demonstrates the difficulty of balancing party discipline with individual freedom. From an outside perspective, it is the negative characteristics of individualism and permissiveness that have come to characterize NSU culture.

Discipline and freedom were often-cited values used to describe the differences of the student organizations along the political spectrum. A leftist student leader's response encapsulates this tension:

Of course, it differs on the basis of the culture [English term used] that
a cadre has come from and what has been taught to him. . . . You might
have seen that the style of the student organization affiliated with the
Maoists is different from [that of] other organizations. They are militant.
Their background is that they have taken up arms in the past. . . . In other
organizations, leaders in the high positions of the party abuse others—
they are not disciplined in what they consume and inspire gangsterism.
This obviously has an impact on the lower level of their organization.
These are some of the differences in the working styles of the organiza-
tions. The ideology is one factor, but the behavior changes the ideology.
An organization could not be effective if its ideology and practice don't
match each other.[11]

Militarism was a common identity marker for the Maoists' political culture
in 2006–8. Their cadres and leaders had spent the previous ten years as
rebels leading an armed insurgency against the state and prided themselves
on their dedication to class struggle. From their view, their militarism was
living according to their ideology, and they cherished their consistency as
a strength they had over other parties.

Other student organizations, however, were suspicious of the lack of freedom in the Maoist party. They dismissed the Maoists as militants who opted
for violence over more socially acceptable ways of challenging the state,
particularly the non-violent approach of the multiparty democratic struggle.[12] Other parties highlighted this in their CA election campaigns to cast
the Maoists as pariahs. During his election campaign speeches, Akash
altered Voltaire's liberal democratic maxim in a way that always drew enthu-
siasm from the crowd: "I do not agree with Prachanda's politics, but I will
fight to the death for his right to do politics that I don't agree with."[13] His
point was meant to highlight the NC's commitment to political freedom and
multiparty democracy.

Political freedom may be a lofty ideal, but from an organizational perspective it has been difficult to institute. Freedom in the form of permissiveness has created disorganization and inconsistency. And commitment
to democratic freedom is seen as a rhetorical facade. The general public
recognizes that the democratically oriented political parties thrive on the
ethos of political freedom in competitive politics; however, very few of these
parties have internally instituted democratic freedom in any meaningful
way (Hachhethu 2002). The danger of this disconnect was articulated by an
ANNFSU (Akhil) student leader:

NSU student cadres adorned with student union flags at a CA campaign rally. Bharatpur, Chitwan, 2007.

The most important thing for us to know is how democratic a person's practice is despite the fact that he advocates in favor of democracy. For instance, if I talk loudly on democratic practice, but I am despotic in the internal practices within the organization, how can that organization be democratic? What agendas one advocates in different forums should be an integral part of one's organizational and political life. For instance, in an organization like ours as well, the president assumes more power. But if the president cannot be democratic and cannot accept others' existence, the organization can't be considered democratic. . . . In comparison to other student organizations, our student organization is systematic and practices a collective decision-making process. This is our claim, and this is the truth.[14]

Others have echoed this point that a group's validity hinges on consistency between their actions and ideology.[15] Lack of authenticity will ultimately weaken them in the democratic process they have fought to institute.

Authenticity matters because, despite their different ideologies, all political parties share the same basic platform to justify their political agendas: to serve the people (*janatā*). How they achieve that may differ, from struggling for the people's democratic freedom to fighting for socio-economic justice. The Prachanda Path, for instance, is understood not as one man's manifesto but as a historical materialist agenda based on the needs of the impoverished majority and the socio-political situation. A student's explanation of why the Maoist party would be victorious in the 2008 CA elections nicely articulated the importance of this emphasis on people:

> The ideology of our party is the one that is most closely related to the people. The party has raised the issues of the people. Because of this, the relationship with the party and the people is like that of a nail and the flesh. The party takes the initiative in an organizational form to solve the people's problems. Without the people, the party would not be formed, and the people's problems will not be solved without the party. Therefore, they have a very close relationship. They are complementary. That's why there is no contradiction in the beauty of elevating justice and revolt to revolution; there is a deep and continuous relationship between them, just like the relationship between the party and the people.[16]

For the Maoists, political action is justified as a dialectic between the needs of the people and the party's fulfillment of them. Yet that is not enough. The Maoists must be consistent and organized on the theoretical level, and that must unambiguously translate to the practical level. Maoist cadres explained this to me as "scientific organization" (Snellinger 2010). In their everyday political action, they must demonstrate that they are organized for the people. A student described the uniqueness of the Maoists' revolution: "We don't need to pray to God. Rather, we believe in ourselves and have the faith that we have the support of the people, because all we do is based on their needs."[17] Maoist cadres emphasized the fine balance between being scientifically organized in their political ideology and recognizing that it is the people who inspire their ideology. Although, during the 2013 CA election, the Maoists came to learn the lesson that the other main democratic parties have learned: when parties do not act on their words, then people, as the electorate, question their authenticity and ability to govern.

THE ROLE OF THEORY IN PRACTICE

Political ideology and the role of individual interest influence institutional culture in party politics because they shape practice. In Nepal's context, it is well understood that the degree to which parties are informed by these two elements correlates with their orientation on the political spectrum.[18] The more left parties are, the more their practices, agendas, and internal procedures are informed by political ideology. The more mass-based parties are, the more their practices, agendas, and internal procedures are informed by particular personalities and personal network dynamics. These two factors, however, shape all parties and inform their interactions in the larger arena of interparty competition (Hachhethu 2000; Paramanand 1982). Party activists, students, and general citizens take political ideology, personal charisma, and systems of patronage into consideration when they choose, claim, or reject political affiliation.

The ways in which ideology and personal interest are balanced informs what my interlocutors referred to as "healthy party structure." Maoist students were the most likely to emphasize the strict discipline of their organization when describing the differences between themselves and other political students. One student said party discipline was like "eating iron *chiurā* [beaten rice]."[19] She explained that discipline was as important in maintaining their organization's image as it was in serving its cause. The student sitting alongside her interjected: "If you are truly dedicated to your organization's ideology, then its image and agenda mean more than your own success—this is where sacrifice comes from. We do it because we believe that it is through the ANNISU (R) that we can best fulfill the needs of the country."[20] These two women explained to me the value of scientific organization, translating their ideology and commitment to the party into their lifestyle.

In 2006 and 2007, when I spoke to these women, the Maoists were emerging from the war and still identified as a rebel political group. "Scientific organization" was a simpler concept in those days. But by 2009, things had changed as the Maoists shifted from a revolutionary group (cadre-based) to a political party (mass-based). I returned to Nepal to follow up with the student activists. At that time, Gyanu expressed deep ambivalence over the popularity of the ANNISU (R) on the university campuses. The unexpected result of its CA plurality and dominance in FSU politics, he explained, was that people had begun to join the Maoist party as a professional opportunity, rather than out of commitment to the party's ideology. He lamented that even though the party trained its members, if their intentions were not pure, then they wouldn't enact proper discipline. With increased membership, overseeing the discipline of these new members was harder. He was concerned about the impact it had on the party's image: "Organization is a means of unifying individuals for a common goal. . . . It requires a sense of sacrifice and devotion to solve the issues people are facing"[21]

His concern has a reference point. Both the NC and the CPN-UML acquired new characteristics as they transformed from grassroots movements to contenders for state power: their ideology became diluted, and they became involved in divisive politics (Hachhethu 2002, 2009). These parties that brought multiparty democracy to Nepal twice, in 1950 and 1990, shifted into organizational survival by adapting to the new environment of party politics. Their maneuvering pushed them to the other end of the spectrum from scientific organization, to what I call "institutional anarchy," which is based on the idea of "organized anarchies," wherein organizations calculate their agendas and choices according to what is readily available to them within a given situation rather than on long-term systematic analysis (Minkoff and McCarthy 2005: 300). Many people's view that the ad hoc political fiefdoms of the NC and the NSU lack "long-term vision" (*pāradarshīta chhaina*) reflects this notion. Institutional anarchy, however, expanded to the interparty level during the first and second CAs, wherein both the assembly body itself and the four major parties that guided it were seen as having succumbed to petty immediate dramas, such as leadership appointments, rather than focusing on the long-term process of rebuilding the state.

How a party balances political ideology and individual interest dictates the shape an organization takes through practice. Gyanu's and Akash's thoughts on what guides and shapes organizational practice in their respective organizations are worth comparing because their parties come from opposite ends of the political spectrum, embodying the inherent tension between scientific organization and institutional anarchy. Gyanu explained:

> While talking about the concept of organization in a political party, we
> have to understand the interrelationship between ideology and practice.

When ideology remains just an ideology, without practice, it becomes raw, ideal, and hollow. If it is utilized as a way of life, then it becomes real. . . . Regarding effectiveness, one has to become individually competent in thinking, be creative and have discussions. Then one has to be able to progress from debate on the basis of shared organizational commitment. . . . If this happens in an institution, then it will be an institution in its real sense, and it will drive the political power in an organized way.[22]

Akash's perspective on organization reveals a different balance of how ideology and individual interest determined the NC's and the NSU's institutional practices:

Our party [the NC] was established for a mission—to overthrow the Ranas. An ideology was adopted to attain this mission. People became indoctrinated and invested in that ideology—it involved democratic political freedom. But nowadays, I don't think a person who comes to join our organization understands our organization in this sense. We don't really tell our new member of our mission and ideology when we take him in. We focus on the specific interests of a student during recruitment. For instance, while cultivating new members at Tri-Chandra College, we try to understand the issues, concerns, and interests of the students. It means we focus on local and personal issues. The same thing happens in the case of a constituency area. The people in a particular constituency calculate their benefits and losses, and leaders try to convince the people that they would be more secure if he were their leader. We don't extend our organization by giving members full indoctrination into our party's principles and mission. The continued distortion of our mission for individual purpose has made it seem as if that is the true mission of our organization. We have forgotten why we needed to establish as a party. Slowly, it so happened, and that is what we have become.[23]

Gyanu's and Akash's explanations considered together demonstrate that their organizations comprise the same components, but they are prioritized, weighed, and valued differently. During our discussion, Akash described the NC as an umbrella group of many factions, with a loose ideological basis. In contrast, the Maoists and the leftist parties are more deliberative in how they organize because they have a clear-cut ideology that determines their organizational style, including having ideology departments in their parties to oversee this process. They have an ideological lineage that sets this precedent: Leninism, Stalinism, and Maoism. There were mistakes made that they have learned from, such as those of the Sendero Luminoso and the Khmer Rouge, which the Prachanda Path has taken into consideration.

Political freedom, in contrast, is abstract. The NC grounded it as an agenda in reaction to the autocratic Rana and Panchayat regimes. The agenda was bound to become diluted once the context changed. Since the introduction of multiparty democracy in the 1990s, the NC has become an alternative power structure in which people can further their own ends. That individual pursuit has been respected because the NC values political freedom. This core value keeps the NC united as a party yet internally divided, making the NC's and the NSU's internal structures more radical than is commonly recognized. As radical democratic theory asserts: "For politics, the fact that the people are internally divided is not, actually, a scandal to be deplored. It is the primary condition of the exercise of politics. There is politics from the moment there exists the sphere of appearance of a subject, the people, whose particular attribute is to be different from itself, internally divided" (Rancière 1999: 87). NSU students are quick to contrast themselves with the leftists: "In the communist student organizations the students follow the limitations [agenda] outlined by the party. Thus, their human rights are violated and their freedom of expression is curtailed. In the NSU, one can enjoy the freedom of expression. The NSU regards freedom and every individual's existence."[24]

NSU students, in their embrace of individual freedom as their core value, counter the leftist parties, for whom ideology is the glue that unifies them despite their members' different class, caste, gender, and generational perspectives. Ideology is what erases the differences among them; it keeps internal politics at bay because it does not allow for the disagreements that result when members clash over various subjectivities. A Maoist party leader emphasized this point when explaining what has happened to the UML since it joined party politics in 1990:

> The UML is also heading toward disintegration. The main reason behind this is the lack of ideological development. The Communist Party has to run on the basis of ideology, a lack of which causes the party to become divided. Once the party becomes unable to develop its ideology, it will run according to an individual. His prestige will come to the forefront, rather than cadres giving priority to the organization and ideology. Individual interests will go ahead in a non-restricted way. This is why

splits take place. Political agendas get made according to personal agendas rather than according to ideology that is formed according to the needs of the people. We have seen that this is where some of the biggest social contradictions have been born.[25]

In Nepali political history, dissent created by vying personal agendas has repeatedly factionalized parties. These disputes are often framed as doubts about a person's loyalty to the party line and its political ideology (Baral [1977] 2006; Thapa and Sijapati 2003). That is why so many of my informants embrace party ideology as the key to keeping the party unified and on track. When personal ambition trumps ideology, then parties' agendas unravel and they factionalize.

In 2007 and 2008, it was commonly agreed that the Maoists were able to overcome personal agendas more so than other parties. People cited the structure of their organization as the reason. They had little experience in mass-based democratic politics. As a previous incarnation, Samyukta Jana Morchā (Joint People's Front), the Maoists held nine seats in the first elected multiparty parliament. When they abandoned parliamentary politics in 1996 for armed revolution, they were small, with little influence. They grew into a formidable force as a cadre-based rebel group during the People's War (1996–2006). Until 2008, they had little experience winning elections and none running governments (what they previously dismissed as "bourgeois democracy"). Their appeal was not democratically oriented; they were not interested in convincing voters that their party's ideology catered to them. Rather, their ideology was a truth that they expected to realize by raising the consciousness of the masses.

Similarly, the CPN-UML was a cadre-based party during the Panchayat era, but it shifted to a mass-based system after 1990.[26] This transition occurred during the exercise of parliamentary democracy. The CPN-UML had to win votes. What the Maoist leader diagnosed as the CPN-UML straying from its ideological roots in the previous quotation, democrats viewed as a strategy necessary when mass appeal determined one's place in government. Since then, the CPN-UML has suffered from factional splits caused by personality disputes among its leadership. Its political agenda has become less clear, straying from its original political ideology, which led to the fraying of its constituent base. Many of the Maoists' first supporters in rural areas originally supported the CPN but became frustrated with how they abandoned their commitment to communist ideals (Thapa and Sijapati 2003).

The CPN-UML's transition from a cadre-based to a mass-based party should have been a harbinger of things to come for the Maoists. The Maoists were not invulnerable to these transformations after they came into the mainstream party fold in 2007. Their transition mimicked the NC's and the CPN-UML's in the 1990s, "from a system of solidarity to a system of interest, from adherence to the party's manifest ideology to concentration on organizational survival, from domination of the environment to adaptation to the environment" (Hachhethu 2009: 41–42). In 2012, the Maoists also succumbed to party splits. The most public was when the Mohan Baidya faction split from the UCPN (Maoist) because members thought the party had strayed from its base under the party chairman, Prachanda, and the then prime minister, Baburam Bhattarai, particularly the leaderships' backtracking on identity-based federalism, which caused the first CA to disintegrate (ICG 2012b). This split weakened the UCPN (Maoist). It lost its CA plurality and came in third in both the first-past-the-post and proportional races in the 2013 CA election.

The prevalence of party splits and the resulting erosion of power are why maintaining "healthy party structure" engenders such potent anxiety for political actors. Organization, both as noun and as verb, is the basis on which to judge other parties' abilities. This judgment is two-pronged: the degree to which a party maintains clarity and consistency and whether the party structure is a scientific organization or an institutional anarchy. One Maoist student leader smugly explained: "In the absence of handling political agendas properly, the big organizations will continue disintegrating. Therefore, in the absence of ideology and the proper mechanism to implement that ideology into plans of action, they cannot transform society."[27] People dismissed politics' main weakness as being more talk (*bhanai*) than action (*garai*). As one student explained: "Our movement is concerned with not merely shouting the slogans but enacting those slogans. We don't only do the movements but also foresee where it must end."[28] Mobilizing its members toward the end point is seen as the key to maintaining an effective organization.

THE PRAGMATICS OF ORGANIZATION: STRUCTURE AND WORKING STYLE

Anxiety over organizational cohesion is heightened because Nepali political actors believe that their internal culture should be recursive of larger political ideals and aims. Internal culture is the feedback loop meant to reinforce their political ideals through their practice. Internal culture, however, can inadvertently become a recursive obstacle that keeps parties from achieving their larger political goals and undermine their sense of purpose. Organizational structure influences internal culture because it shapes the working style and practices that enable the parties to enact their political agendas and ideology or hinder them from doing so.

Parties' organizational structures, specifically their internal hierarchy, determine party discipline and the balance between individual autonomy and obedience. The ANNISU (R) secretary best expressed this after he asked me if I saw the knives at the NSU conventions: "This is NSU culture. You would never see this in our culture because we understand the balance between freedom and control. The ANNISU (R) practices a policy of 'freedom within control.' There must be limitations on freedom in the organization. Otherwise, the organization will turn into a chaotic mess."[29] He repeated this sentiment when I asked him if he would allow me to interview him. He did not refuse but rather indicated that there were proper channels by which to gain access to the information I sought. In this case, the freedom to expose the Maoist student unions' inner workings was curtailed by chain of command.

NSU students also believe that working style forms institutional culture, but their notion of working style is different from their leftist peers' because it is not based on ideology. Rather, it relies on the paternalistic pattern of high-caste society in Nepal. As Akash explained:

Our working style created hierarchy in our party and student organization. This type of hierarchy was created since we don't require our cadres to participate in the decision-making process, [but] rather we dictate our decision. The working style in the party, that "I am superior to you," has created hierarchy and become a part of our culture. Again, these actions strengthened the culture of inferiority and superiority. . . . Our union president has never followed the constitution in the decisions he has made so far. But he will blame G. P. Koirala for not following the party constitution or respecting the NSU's constitution. This has become our culture. I'm guilty, too. When I was general secretary, I used to announce to the media that we would protest against the petroleum price hike and then endorse it as the agenda in our central committee meeting. That was not the democratic process, was it? Thus, our working style is shaping our culture, which then re-entrenches our working style. . . . There is a split of big and small people in our party, and that has shaped our culture.[30]

This hierarchy-oriented practice undermines the democratic process mandated in the constitution of the NC and NSU. It is this type of working style that leads outsiders to view NC and NSU members as domineering and casts doubt on their support of democratic process.

The leadership of the ANNISU (R) is also hierarchical. But the union's hierarchical system is incorporated into its scientific organization and is part of its political discipline. A protocol for promotion through the ranks does not create dissent and allows the cadres to respect the leadership. Progression through the party hierarchy is a pyramid system, with the central committee at the top and the regional committees, then the district committees, and finally the area or unit committees below. When I asked a student leader whether people are able to bypass a level or if it mirrors the Cuban style of ascension, he responded:

> There is always a system for everything . . . incompetence will surface when a person who had worked in the organization in 1996 jumps into the organization again in 2002 at a higher level. It happens so, because he would not know what occurred in the course of the student movement in the consecutive years that followed his departure. If he lacked this experience, he would find it really difficult to motivate the people in the movement in the later stages. Only those who have passed through all the levels, accumulating the knowledge obtained in the course of the successive movements, can be effective student leaders. With this calculation in mind, our friends rise, passing through the pyramid structure of the organization.[31]

This explanation illuminates that for Maoist cadres their own experience is an artifact of historical materialism in dialectic with their shared revolution. ANNISU (R) members rise systematically through the ranks in order to acquire proper knowledge and to prove their political dedication to both their superiors and inferiors to gain the confidence of the whole organization. As the student leader continued to emphasize: "It means being an active participant in the process. One's personal experience must be within the context of the unfolding revolution. It is only then that one can claim to have a substantial basis in which to know how to go forward. The personal and the public are one and the same: you must take personal responsibility in orienting yourself to the revolution at every level, most importantly, making the public your personal priority."[32] The ANNISU's hierarchy is accepted because members believe that people's personal experience gained within the revolution allows them to guide their juniors scientifically. Another

ANNISU (R) leader explained, "We make the student cadres understand scientific organization and then they support our directives."[33]

Not every ANNISU (R) member has progressed in this orthodox way, but when promotion is expedited, it is set in a context of what is needed for the progression of the party's overall revolutionary agenda. In 2007 and 2008, the ANNISU (R) students justified swift appointments because they had faith that their party leaders could identify the most capable people to execute what needed to be done. This trust was a result of the ANNISU (R) developing into a student organization during the war. During rebellion, there was no allowance for questioning one's superiors. The ANNISU (R) students prided themselves on what they described as "militant commitment" to their ideology and their party.[34] They viewed the People's War as one part of their revolutionary class struggle. Even after the war was over, they were able to justify irregularities as necessary to further the revolution.

One ANNISU (R) student leader explained: "My organization believes that unity is possible through struggle. Unity achieved through struggle is durable. I am willing to compromise the superficial but won't compromise my devotion to class struggle. This is what is real to us."[35] The Maoists, he explained, understand that power always dictates. People are deluded if they do not recognize that every form of state power enforces a dictatorship on other classes. Therefore, power must be just. The whole point of their class struggle is to negate the capitalists and establish a dictatorship of the proletariat so that the people have power. The ANNISU (R) cadres' belief that all power takes a dictatorial form allows them to suspend their own personal freedom for the form of power they support. Thus, organizational structure for the ANNISU (R) is not about compromise or appeasing all participants through democratic contention, but rather it is about properly indoctrinating cadres with the right sense of discipline and dedication so they follow the orders of their superiors, who they see as the most capable of furthering the ultimate agenda of their shared class struggle.

The way in which leadership is determined further fuels the internal culture and ideology feedback loop. Gyanu explained this process as a difference in priority, with some organizations emphasizing political discussion and creating a road map for leadership formation and others choosing leaders first. Maoist students claim to build their party agenda through deliberation. After they are unanimous on their agenda, then they focus on who will lead the organization. Other student organizations focus more on leadership formation, and those leaders are the ones who decide the agendas and determine how to push them forward.

The student organizations' national conventions in 2007 are a case in point. The two NSU organizations and the ANNFSU (Akhil), on the one hand, took three to eight days to campaign and less than a day to discuss their political proposals. In the mass-based parties, people progress in the party structure by receiving endorsements from political leaders and their networks as well as cultivating their constituents' support. This process causes more intense competition and a lot less stability in how one progresses. The ANNISU (R) and smaller leftist student organizations, on the other hand, spent four days on political discussion and less than half a day on choosing leadership. Gyanu explained, "Our discussions do not end until there is unanimous understanding that our agenda is according to the true spirit of our political ideology."[36] The ANNISU (R) students participate in the discussion on how to craft their agenda; it is through actively participating in this process that they learn ideology, cultivate party dedication, and have a shared sense of ownership.

This discursive space centrally factors into the ANNISU (R) students' sense of how they contribute to their union's agenda. Space is given for people to express various opinions, and they are encouraged to debate with one another. One student quoted Mao's proverb "Let many flowers bloom" to explain their debates. But he was quick to make a distinction between revolutionary and opportunist opinion: "If the opinion emerged from an opportunist line, we have to negate it. But if it comes from the revolutionary line, we have to accept it and institutionalize it in a new way."[37] Thus, there are limitations within the discursive space, but those limitations are not on the opinions themselves but on participants' motivations. If the students are motivated by the revolutionary agenda, then they are encouraged to contribute their ideas. They have freedom, yet only within control. Where the students lack freedom is outside these revolutionary parameters. If they do not align with Maoist doctrine, then there is no place for them. Other student organizations are more flexible in allowing room for personal autonomy. Yet for the ANNISU (R) students, this sort of freedom of opinion runs completely counter to their agenda because their organization is the shared basis through which they will realize their political end.

LIFESTYLE AND PARTY IMAGE

Although power may be inherent within their organization's hierarchal structure, Maoist leaders try to limit that power by making sure that everyone is equal in most contexts. They explained to me that a division of labor is necessary in order to progress in a scientific manner. Therefore, they must accept how their hierarchal structure works. Everyone fulfills a role, but they also understand how their role fits into the overall system of the organization's action plan. Otherwise, there should be no added privilege for a higher position because that would create schisms that would lead people to disassociate their position from the larger agenda. In other words, to avoid political alienation, cadres must feel ownership over the larger process in their everyday activities. The Maoist students attempted to do that by emphasizing equality and uniformity of lifestyle.

Beyond their political and military duties, the leaders' and the cadres' lifestyle should not vary. In 2007 and 2008, they lived together in communes, ate the same food, dressed alike, and rotated duties to maintain the domestic sphere.[38] One student leader admitted that he would be criticized if he took a taxi when his comrades took the bus or if he ate more expensive food or wore more expensive clothes than others did. "I have to refine my thoughts and deeds. . . . A feeling of collective living should prevail in me rather than one of individual living," he explained, because that is what has caused splits and weaknesses in other parties.[39] Nobody struggles for anything but power, and once they have it, they use it to amass wealth and personal prestige. This leads to resentment and cynicism. He asserted that such a political culture is based on a very different lifestyle, a bourgeois way of life premised on individual, private interests.

Student leaders of other organizations are able to leave their offices to go to the private comfort of their homes and families. The discrepancy between their lifestyle and that of their cadres does not bother them, but may even bolster their status in a political environment where material resources and privilege represent prestige and power. Other student activists have competing loyalties. The Maoists, the same student leader explained, communally work and live together to emphasize that the party takes first priority. The party is the reason for the students' involvement; it is what they "struggle and live for."[40] The way the Maoists' describe their lifestyle as collapsing the personal and professional or the family and party demonstrates how they imbue every aspect of their life with the revolutionary cause. Gyanu underscored this point when he asserted, "We have the organizational life, but we have very little personal life."[41]

On the contrary, the NC's original mission was to institute multiparty democracy, and it accomplished that. Afterward, its political mission became abstracted to democratic freedom. Staying true to this ethos became more difficult while governing because the NC's political focus shifted to maintaining its governing power. The NC's influence diminished during the 1990s and 2000s because of its lack of a political agenda beyond maintaining governing power, and its organization weakened because there were no institutional mechanisms in place to live by its democratic ethos with clarity and consistency. The clarity of the NC's and other mainstream parties' political agendas was sharpened after the king dismissed their democratically elected parliament in 2002. The NC again had to fight for political survival, which reinvigorated its original ethos of democratic freedom. The NC's street protests against the state redefined its political mission.

This dynamic explains why so many Nepali politicians and activists embrace their political movements as unfinished and ongoing. Their political agenda is more palpable when they are fighting for their survival. Their movements allow them to continue their struggle for democratic freedom or class struggle. Living their political struggle is embodying politics with a capital *P*. These ideals are obscured in the mundane act of governing.

When an organization's internal culture is no longer recursive of its political ideology, then it can unintentionally push the organization further away from its core values and original tenets. In 2007 and 2008, the ANNISU (R) students were smug about their ability to avoid the weaknesses to which other political parties had succumbed. But even then, there was ambivalence that their leaders had strayed from the party's core discipline of scientific organization. Maoist cadres criticized their leaders for embracing lifestyles that resembled those of other mainstream political leaders. And they did so publicly. At a campaign the ANNISU (R) sponsored demanding equal compensation for the orphaned children of the soldiers of the People's Liberation Army and the Nepal Army, one orphaned female cadre gave a speech railing against the "mobile and motor culture" the Maoist leadership had embraced. She looked directly at party chairman Prachanda in the front row as she declared that her parents did not fight and die for the Maoist leadership to be indistinguishable from that of the other political parties.[43]

The weakening of the UCPN (Maoist), and impending splits after 2012, was fueled by an uneven distribution of influential positions and funds that the party amassed during governing. This, of course, was seen as inconsistent with the Maoists' agenda and harmed their party image. A friend who voted for them in the 2008 CA elections said to me: "They sold out. They are just like the rest of them."[44] The resentment, cynicism, and raw professional ambition for which the ANNISU (R) cadres criticized other student organizations had crept into their own union. This played a key factor in their defeat during the second CA elections. They, too, lost touch with their master frames.

CONCLUSION

During Nepal's state restructuring phase, lethargy took hold in the three largest student unions. When the first CA was dissolved in 2012, neither the ANNFSU (Akhil) nor the NSU had functioning central committees. The CPN-UML dissolved the ANNFSU (Akhil) central committee due to lack of leadership in dealing with financial embezzlement and infighting (Bhusal 2013). The NSU central committee was dissolved in April 2011 after the president resigned because he was unable to establish any centralized leadership between the two previous NSU factions after their 2007 reunification. And the third union, the ANNISU (R), faltered because of the factional split of the UCPN (Maoist) and the CPN-RM (Baidya), which triggered a low-level turf war all the way down to the campus level.

The weakening of student organizations mirrored national politics at the time. The CA had been dissolved and the high-level party commission could not agree on a prime minister, all of which compounded the stagnation of state-restructuring and day-to-day governing. The public consensus was that all the political parties had lost touch with their commitment to rebuild "new Nepal" together. Organizational anarchy had manifested at every level of politics. The opportunistic elements of party politics were overshadowing activists' idealism, specifically enacting their ideology through their organizations. Doing politics (with a small p) had made people lose sight of their Politics (with a capital P). Even the Maoists' scientific organization succumbed to organizational anarchy during their pragmatic transition from a cadre-based to a mass-based party to ensure survival, testing the limits of their "freedom within control" code.

People and their social interaction both within and between organizations are the mechanisms that reproduce the organization. Ideally, political actors reproduce their party organizations by maintaining a party structure and a lifestyle that realize their ideology and party line. The discrepancies between political ideology and internal practice unintentionally fuel a negative feedback loop of unanticipated consequences. These negative feedback loops become an autopoietic factor that affect organizational reproduction. For example, when Akash spoke about his own actions as a student leader, he admitted that his actions were undemocratic and that he did not follow the NSU's constitution, but he was reacting to NC leadership interventions that also defied the NSU's constitution. By publicly announcing street protest to the media, he circumvented NC leadership and ensured his own agenda. His defiance of the rules in order to counter his leaders' defiance of the rules may be seen as justified in the short term. But in the long term, the adoption of such pragmatic tactics ultimately undermines the NC's and the NSU's support of democratic freedom and is perceived as negative political culture. Their inability to institute democracy internally has caused other parties and the general public to dismiss the NSU's and the NC's democratic ethos.

Dismissals of negative political culture fueled my interlocutors' understandings of organization as both noun and verb. Political actors were anxious about maintaining a clear party line that linked their party structure and the lifestyles of their politicians and cadres. That is what identifies them as a distinct group—enactment of their ideological beliefs—and allows them to identify other groups in the playing field.

Nonetheless, student activists' distinction between *sanskriti* and political culture provides the flexibility necessary to alter the momentum of organizational autopoietics. They understand political culture as constructed and mutable. Their contemporary social science understanding of political culture is part of their shared repertoire, influencing how they make claims based on their understanding of how those claims will be received (cf. Tilly 1995). This generation of student activists has a postmodern take on their political culture, which provides them with the awareness to challenge negative feedback loops deliberatively if they choose to do so.

5 Speaking to Be Heard in a Traditionally Elite Enterprise

MY FIRST VISIT BACK TO NEPAL AFTER MY INITIAL ROUND OF fieldwork was in 2009. The Maoist plurality-led government had been in power for over a year. I was curious to know what impact its political agenda to institute secularism, republicanism, and inclusion was having on day-to-day life. My visit coincided with the annual Dasain festival. I was eager to observe the state rituals such as the Phulpati festival, which symbolically reenacts Prithvi Narayan Shah's journey from his homeland in Gorkha to his appointed nation-state capital, Kathmandu.[1] This festival is the quintessential enactment of Hindu territorial sovereignty.

In a torrential downpour that afternoon, crowds gathered around Tundikhel, the army parade grounds, to observe army officers, politicians, and government dignitaries receive the sacred flowers from Gorkha before royal priests offered them to the nine powers (*nava shakti*) of goddess Durga at Hanuman Dhoka temple. In years past, the king was there to receive these nine flowers (*navapatrika*) at Tundikhel and escort them over to Hanuman Dhoka temple for the offering ceremony.

I convinced my cab driver to let me sit in his vehicle alongside the army grounds to observe the ceremony without getting completely drenched. While we watched the ceremony, he asked me what I thought. Dasain in the secular republic of Nepal looked very similar to Dasain during the king's rule, I replied. The Nepal Army served the same function as the Royal Nepal Army had during the monarchy, firing their guns and cannons on point to acoustically mark the arrival of the Phulpati procession. The only major difference was that the president and the deputy prime minister had replaced the king as the figurehead.[2] The taxi driver explained that Dasain was the biggest festival in Nepal and that people felt more connected to their government if the officials were part of the celebration.[3]

As I listened, I thought of the Nepali rupee bill. After the army and state were stripped of the royal designator in 2006, the king's profile was replaced with an image of Mount Everest or a rhododendron, depending on the note's

Army-sponsored buffalo sacrifice during Dasain holiday. Basantapur, Kathmandu, 2007.

denomination. But when you held the banknote up to the light, you could still see the watermark of the king with his crown of peacock feathers. The image had changed, but the underlying stamp was still the same. The bastions of traditional power remained, although they were not apparent at first glance, despite a desire among a cross-section of society for more inclusive institutions.

Nepali democratic activists assert claims in the name of "the people" (*janatā*) as if all citizens are on equal footing. Yet the very act of speaking on behalf of the people obscures the fact that the political actors who have historically challenged the state are, overwhelmingly, from the upper echelons of social order and have better opportunities than the broader population for whom they make claims. Their privilege allows them to collapse multiple identities into one identity—the people—in order to challenge ruling authority. This proves problematic because it eclipses individual and communal experiences in a way that denies the multiple histories of suppression and marginalization.

Gyanu lamented this rhetorical strategy when I visited him in September 2015 right before the new constitution was to be promulgated. "In the name of the people, leaders will do anything," he explained. "I fought in the People's War, and now even the leaders I took orders from are supporting a constitution that does not have popular support."[4] His lament underscores how entrenched the nationalist discourse of speaking for the people is and how the resulting politics has limited marginalized communities' ability to create a space in mainstream politics and alter the political landscape.

By 2006, demands for inclusion, federalism, and secularism were finally becoming mainstream in party politics, a sphere that continues to be dominated by high-caste men of hill origin (Parbatiya) (Hachhethu, Shah, and Kamat 2015). The ways in which these demands were conceptualized and then made by political party activists on behalf of the people mediate social relations by authenticating or disqualifying the different ways Nepali citizenship is experienced. Exploring this process offers insight into the relationship between socio-political change and the perpetuation of the status quo. For people to challenge the status quo—French philosopher Jacques Rancière's (1999) "policing logics"—they must articulate their interventions in a language that the dominant regime can comprehend.[5] In other words, alternatives must resonate within the elite "means of orientation" to disquiet the dominant norms they challenge (Elias 1978, in Shore 2002: 4). Furthermore, the ways that identity claims are both made and understood in Nepali mainstream politics are circumscribed by democratic activists' subject position, wherein they simultaneously make claims on behalf of the people while also trying to assure their future in institutional politics.

Identity politics articulated through inclusion (*samābesikaran*) have been central to state restructuring processes meant to reorder communal relations vis-à-vis the state in the twenty-first century. Demands for inclusion stem in part from the global social justice discourse that asserts that practices and experiences of social inclusion are necessary to produce belonging and a stake in society among different communities (Anthias 2006: 21, in Shneiderman 2015: 108). But the discourse of "social inclusion" in South Asia has fueled a focus on "national indicators" to the degree that endemic practices of local-level exclusion are often overlooked (Shneiderman 2015).

For social inclusion to be successfully instituted, political subjectification at every level is required, as Rancière (1999) outlines: "Political subjectification redefines the field of experience that gave to each their identity with their lot. It decomposes and recomposes the relationships between the ways of *doing*, of *being*, and of *saying* that define the perceptible organization of the community, the relationship between the places where one does one thing and those where one does something else, the capacities associated with this particular *doing* and those required for another" (40; Rancière's emphasis). The peace process and resulting constitution have been a feeble attempt at political subjectification—decomposing and recomposing the "relationships between the ways of *doing*, of *being*, and of *saying* that define the perceptible organization of the community" (40). Unfortunately, localized practices of exclusion, including those within party politics, persist. In fact, the manner in which political subjectification emerged during state restructuring processes has further substantiated the political party structure, ensuring party activists' governing positions and thus maintaining high-caste domination over multiple levels of socio-political organization.

WHERE IS NEW NEPAL?

The intimate spaces and formal self-representations (Herzfeld 2002: 227) within the social order of party politics allow us to understand the veracity of these power dynamics. Yet first it is important to document how the state restructuring process failed to fulfill demands for inclusion.

The debates on inclusion started out hopeful. "Building 'New Nepal'" in 2006 hinged on inclusion and a secular republic. These issues were brought to the forefront of political and social arenas by the decade-long civil war. The Maoists' approach was twofold, to "unmake and remake the state" (Nightingale et al., forthcoming; Ogura 2008). The unmaking entailed delegitimizing the public authority of the Nepali state, in particular the monarchy and the entrenched power elite, by dismantling the physical apparatuses of the state, including village and district development committees. Where the Maoists succeeded in unmaking the state, they established their own people's governments (*jan sarkār*) and people's courts (*jan adālat*) (Ogura 2008). The Maoists' ability to create a parallel state legitimized their political authority, while the political parties became further alienated from the monarchy, ultimately enabling the Maoists and the parties to unite against the monarchy in 2005. The parties and the Maoists' unity expanded the agenda to make "new Nepal" from being driven solely by Maoist ideology to incorporating the multiparty democratic agenda. Despite their coalition, the Maoists and the political parties continue to be "engaged in a struggle over the symbols, practices and institutions through which governance is achieved, albeit this time under the guise of 'democratic politics'" (Nightingale et al., forthcoming).

The Maoists' agenda succeeded because they harnessed frustrations of caste, ethnic, and gender inequality and organized minority fronts (*morchā*) to consolidate various struggles of marginalization under their umbrella of

A Maoist people's government–enforced tollbooth. Annapurna trail range, Kaski, 2006.

revolution.[6] The Maoists' demands "shook Nepali society into thinking in a new way."[7] The 2006–8 Madheshi movement, however, demonstrated that not all minority groups were willing to flatten their experiences to fit within the Maoists' discourse of marginalized class struggle. Madheshi activists doubted that promises of inclusive representation and regional autonomy would be fulfilled no matter which political force emerged from the 2008 CA elections. They believed that the multiple experiences of exclusion, including linguistic and regional exclusion, could only be addressed by devolving power from the central level to local levels (cf. Jha 2014a). They blocked election campaigning until their demands for federalism and a proportional election system were fulfilled. This agreement safeguarded federal state restructuring and proportional political representation in the future constitution.

The April 2008 CA elections were declared healthy and fair both domestically and internationally. Much to everyone's surprise, including their own, the Maoists won both the first-past-the-post and the proportional votes. Things then proceeded slowly, as the Maoists failed to create a coalition to counteract the recalcitrance of the NC and CPN-UML opposition, despite having previously allied with them against the monarchy. Increasing anarchy and lawlessness sans governance in the months after the election led analysts to ask, "How long will the people have to wait for the agenda of a naya [new] Nepal to get off the ground?" (Manchanda 2008: 23).[8] The first CA was eventually dissolved on May 27, 2012, after the Supreme Court refused a fifth extension, because it failed to reach consensus on the federal state structure.

The first CA managed to resolve 199 of 201 disputed issues, with only state restructuring, forms of government, and election setup yet to be addressed. Federal structure and demarcation of states proved to be the most challenging because it was over these issues that the politics of identity and nationalist sentiments were at loggerheads. The UCPN (Maoist), the Madheshi Front, and ethnic activists supported identity-based federalism. They were a politically diverse coalition that lobbied for the federal provinces to be named for historically marginalized communities and policies that would counter the history of ruling high-caste domination. The NC, the CPN-UML, and smaller conservative parties were concerned that identity-based federalism would weaken the state, thinking that devolutionary federalism implied an impending breakup. They argued that poverty and geographical marginalization should be the central focus of federal design. Both sides used scare tactics to rally the public, which proved to be highly divisive, and the debate reverberated onto the streets (cf. Adhikari and Gellner 2016). Ethnic activists and the Madheshi Front were willing to compromise their positions in order to strike this balance between identity and capability; however, the splintered street agitation entrenched the incommensurability among the CA parties that felt pressured not to surrender their position (Snellinger 2015b: 240–41).

The second CA elections were successfully held in November 2013, with voter turnout at 78.34 percent. Many argued that the large turnout was a clear rejection of the election boycott led by the splinter Maoist wing and was therefore a vote to continue the peace process and democratic electoral politics in rejection of any further revolution (Gellner 2014: 255). Only 15 percent of incumbents won their seats, demonstrating the strong anti-incumbency attitude. There was a major swing to the right, with the Maoists losing 157 seats. The Madheshi parties also experienced a defeat, losing 33 seats, due to the splintering of multiple Madheshi parties. The NC and the CPN-UML gained 86 and 72 seats, respectively. In combination, they were just short of the two-thirds plurality needed to promulgate the constitution. The pro-monarchy party RPP-N won 24 proportional seats, making it the fourth-largest party in the CA. The most disappointing outcome for many observers was that the CA was overall less diverse because many of the parties that won proportional seats were below the threshold necessary to abide by the inclusivity quotas when appointing their proportional seats. Representation from Janajāti groups, hill Dalits, the Madheshi community, and women all decreased, with Muslims and Tarai Dalits seeing a small but insignificant increase in seats (Gellner 2014). But the "Khas Aryan and other groups"—comprising the Bahun, Chhetri, Sanyasi, and Thakuri ruling elite— had the largest victory, increasing from 34.9 percent of the 2008 CA to 41 percent of the 2013 CA (Carter Center 2013). For many, this betrayed the spirit of the peace process and indicated the limits of electoral democracy.

Under the leadership of the NC's Sushil Koirala, the second CA began to address the contentious issues that had caused the first CA to dissolve in 2012: the modalities of federal restructuring, specifically, nomenclature, identity- or multi-identity-based federalism, the number of provinces, and boundaries; forms of government; and the election system. Ethnic and regional-based parties protested the dwindling number of proposed provinces being debated. In 2012, the parties had debated between eleven and fourteen provinces. In 2014, the Constitutional Political Dialogue and Consensus Committee declared that the realistic middle ground was seven provinces to garner consensus. The committee's decision attempted to balance out the number of provinces the NC and CPN-UML ruling coalition had proposed, which ranged from three to seven provinces based on administrative and economic feasibility, and the ten provinces the UCPN (Maoist) tabled as a conciliatory downshift after its failure to promulgate a constitution under the first CA and its defeat in the second CA elections. None of the smaller parties were pleased—and for good reason. The fewer the provinces, the more likely the demographic makeup would dilute any one ethnic group's provincial plurality. The tactic appeared to be deliberate because the province map that the NC and CPN-UML alliance proposed comprised upper-caste pluralities in six out of the seven provinces (Jha 2014b).

In the spring of 2015, Nepal was hit by two massive earthquakes.[9] At that point the second CA had missed multiple self-imposed deadlines to resolve the remaining constitutional issues through consensus, further whittling public confidence in the CA process. Since 2008, the central government had done little to devolve governing power to local levels and thus exacerbated the atmosphere of "ad hoc governing" (Byrne, forthcoming) caused by the constitutional impasses and regular government turnovers. The anemic centralized government response to the earthquakes reinforced the limits of top-down governing (Snellinger 2015a), forcing the public to ask, "Where is our government?" (Nelson 2015) as the post-earthquake response became a motley mix of foreign and private interventions. The central government attempted to regain control by regulating relief efforts in a bid to protect Nepal's sovereignty. Such claims are often made both to "(re)define the state-society boundary by insisting that the government is acting for the nation" and to "(re)assert the right of the government to have exclusive domain over public authority" (Nightingale et al., forthcoming).

The CA's effort to reclaim its exclusive domain over governing authority was most apparent in how it promulgated the constitution less than five months after the earthquakes. Regaining its grip on governing, if only to oversee post-earthquake reconstruction, became a matter of urgency. Prime Minister Sushil Koirala and top leaders used the beleaguered post-earthquake atmosphere to expedite the constitution in order to regain some relevancy. The leaders calculated that the post-earthquake national unity and support from international forces made fast-tracking promulgation possible, and they presumed that post-earthquake rebuilding in many hill districts and the monsoon and agricultural season in the south would deter mass protest. The leadership of the top three parties (NC, CPN-UML, and UCPN [Maoist]) relied on their plurality rather than brokering broader consensus, despite deep opposition from ethnic and regional-based parties and women's groups against the citizenship law, political representation, and federal state delineation.

The government grossly miscalculated public sentiment. Protests ensued nationwide, leading to strikes; the government enforced curfews in the Tarai before the promulgation of the constitution and then opposition-enforced border blockades for almost five months afterward. Both the state and the opposition were complicit in the violent escalation, which took a pointed turn after seven policemen and a child were killed during a mass rally in Tikapur, Kailali, on August 24, 2015. Officially, it was declared mob violence, even though Tharu activists claimed that it was an orchestrated event conducted by a small radical faction. After this tragedy, tensions between the security forces and all protesting groups throughout the Tarai became personal. The political establishment did little to dispel the protesters' feelings of being second-class citizens in the south, at times making derogatory remarks and whipping up anti-India, hill nationalism.

Nepal promulgated its constitution on September 20, 2015. The cost was an estimated forty-five lives, including police and security forces, protesters, and innocent bystanders who died in August and September 2015. Over a dozen more were killed post-promulgation during the 135-day protester-enforced border blockades. Many thought that the new constitution was regressive. Some even burned it in protest (M. Thapa 2015). Ethnic minorities

throughout the country believed that the federal boundaries were gerryman-
dered to dilute their political representation. The citizenship provision only
allowed citizenship to be conferred by paternal descent, which signaled gender discrimination to women's groups and another way to disenfranchise the
Madheshi population because of their cross-border affinal ties. This law rendered over 4 million stateless and disqualified many more from the highest
political offices.[10] The constitution's language on secularism was also seen to
fall short of the demand for a secular republic, which had been agreed in 2007.
Judging on the basis of gender, ethnic, caste, and religious inclusion, Nepal's
seventh constitution replicated the patterns of political, social, and legal exclusion that spurred the Maoist civil war, the 2006 public revolt that ousted the
Hindu monarchy, and the federal demands of the 2006–8 Madheshi movement (cf. Malagodi 2013). In the meantime, "new Nepal" was nowhere in sight.

ELITES OF THE STATE: HIGH-CASTE POLITICAL DOMINANCE

People of minority caste, ethnic, and gender status have sacrificed for Nepali
political causes, and even a few reached positions of notoriety. Nonetheless,
their presence has not significantly altered the dominant norms of mainstream political parties. Why the dearth of alternative voices in these parties? People articulated two explanations. The first focused on the inherent
pressures of belonging in caste-based South Asia. A Madheshi leader who
was a Maoist-appointed ambassador framed this dynamic in terms of how
he understood M. N. Srinivas's theory of Sanskritization:

> The problem here is if you are a person belonging to a lower caste or reli-
> gious group, you have to transform yourself into an elite in order to make
> it in politics. It is a big challenge. You were a Dalit leader, but you must
> act like a Brahman. Then you call the person who belongs to your own
> caste and religion dirty or illiterate. Change means imitation in main-
> stream society. Therefore, in regard to caste, the leaders who come from
> the lower caste transform only themselves, and the rest of their commu-
> nity will remain at the same level.[11]

This politician imprecisely represents Srinivas's theory of Sanskritization,
which focuses on group mobility rather than individual mobility.[12] Nevertheless, his point speaks to the pressures generated by the normative value
system that inextricably links caste, class, education, prestige, and awareness in how social distinction is evaluated. Traditionally, only those of

upper-caste status had access to education. With national and global initiatives to universalize education beginning in the 1960s, however, education has become publicly more accessible in South Asia. Nevertheless, certain forms of labor, knowledge, and traditions continue to be connected to low-caste or working-class associations (Channa 2010). This is particularly true in Nepal, where both leftist and conservative ideologies of progress and development take a paternalistic approach of knowing what is best for the "unaware" and "uneducated" (cf. Nightingale 2005; Byrne, forthcoming). Minorities who want to succeed in the hill-based, high-caste-dominated enterprise of party politics internalize the prestige of being "educated" and "raising the consciousness of the people" (*janatā ko chetanā bardne*).

The second explanation given for the lack of alternative voices within mainstream parties relates to internal party dynamics and hegemonic leadership. A central committee member of the Tarai Madhesh Democratic Party (TMDP), who rose through the ranks of the NSU and defected from the NC, bluntly explained:

> Our party organizations are such that nothing beyond the interest of the party leaders can take place. If you want to remain in the party, you have to abide by this. Otherwise, where can you go? If you give up the party, you will suffer more, you have no influence on the outside. Outwardly, the party leaders talk about democracy, but inside their party they favor submissive characters. They create slaves of their cadres and make policy barriers. Of course, this would discourage the minority people from participating in politics. But where else do they have to go?[13]

Nepali politics, he said, is made up of three groups. The first and most prominent comprises the people of elite status fighting for the downtrodden—traditionally as party leaders have done in speaking for "the people" and more recently in the Madheshi movement when the landowning elite spoke for the peasants and laboring masses of the Tarai. The second group contains people from minority groups who conform to the elite system and no longer identify with their roots. The third group is made up of those who work outside the political system to make a change. The TMDP central committee member admitted that he often considered shifting to the third group because he was tired of having to compromise his views and position. But he believed that there was no power or benefit in working outside the party system. During the Madheshi movement, however, he saw a chance to have both influence and a voice when Madheshi parties began, as he put it, "to capture the imagination" of the Tarai.

There is little incentive for minorities to participate in student and party politics, because few minorities "believe they have the capacity to transform the political landscape in ways that might grant them a greater sense of belonging" (Shneiderman 2015: 109). The practices of student politics from the 1990s onward in particular have perpetuated the gap between political and nonpolitical youth (Snellinger 2005). High-caste men rise to leadership and tend to dominate, causing minorities to internalize "psychological hesitation," as Darshan, a student leader, explained, and constantly question their position, wondering whether they merely represent token ethnic diversity.[14] Darshan experienced this "psychological hesitation" firsthand after he was elected president of the NSU (D). He admitted that the NC (D) party leadership had advised him not to nominate more than one ethnic minority to his central committee. Otherwise, he would be viewed as an ethnic activist and would no longer be promoted because both students and party leaders would consider his purview to be too narrow. When I asked why he bothered, he explained: "I have changed Plato's saying. He said, 'If good people don't join in politics, they have to be ready to be ruled by the bad ones.' What I say is, 'If Janajātis, women, Madheshis, and Dalits don't join politics, they have to be ready to be ruled by the Bahuns and Chhetris [Parbatiya high-caste].' There are just two alternatives, to be active or to be ruled. In this sense, my duty is to inspire minorities to join in politics, and I do this as best I can."[15] The majority of women and minorities I spoke to had a similar view, although they tended to see student and party politics as the most effective way to garner the public authority needed to create social change.

Salini's experiences further capture the challenges of being a minority in party politics. The first time we discussed this issue, she provided a long description about how politics has been an exclusive system with little opportunity for minorities and women. She then reiterated all the talking points of political exclusion that people commonly raised regarding women's and minorities' ability to succeed in the party system. What was her personal experience? I asked. How had she managed to get ahead?

> Salini: I am the vice president now. . . . Within a year, I have to compete
>   for the position of president, and for that I have to obtain the ticket. If
>   I speak in favor of women or minorities, leaders won't like that. There-
>   fore, I should not speak in their favor. I have to observe silence. Others

can speak about that, but not me. If I raise this issue, it gives a bad impression that I want to stir things up. It is fine to stir things up on the street in order to point your finger at others, but you should not point your finger at the party.

Amanda: Really, there is no way you are able to raise this issue?

Salini: No, I should not address it. That is the reason why I speak less now than I did before. Even if I raised a trifling issue, I would be blamed for doing it for myself, not the party. Therefore, it is really hard to accept this paradoxical existence. Even now, people don't easily accept my silence. When I was in the junior posts, I was not treated as being as competent as others, so I could say what I wanted. My voice was not influential. But now, since I am competing for the high posts, people see my role as meaningful, [and] therefore I must diminish my voice to maintain my position. It is ironic—I am finally at a place where people expect me to do something, but I can't. Regardless, raising the voice of the voiceless is mere rhetoric—no one raises it in any true sense.

Amanda: One has to observe silence in order to obtain a high post?

Salini: Only those who are powerful are talked about. Even today, women are considered as "sari" [the traditional dress for married women] and not considered capable of taking leadership positions. This is a feudal-istic culture, our Nepali culture. You must prove yourself to be what you are not to get a high post.[16]

Salini's experience captures the double bind of progressing as a minority in Nepali party politics. The party elite dictate the structure of progression, wherein raising minority issues is dismissed as a self-aggrandizing endeavor. For Salini to rise to a prominent position where she is taken seriously, she has needed to erase her minority identity and demonstrate that she can speak for the majority, "the people." As her experience and that of other minority student leaders demonstrate, one may progress as a token minority but only if one is willing to erase any trace of political subjectification. And thus, those who want "to be talked about" must be silent.

GENDERED INTERACTIONS

As I walked with Uma, an ANNFSU (Akhil) student leader, to Minbhawan Campus to attend the prime minister's Dasain commemoration, we ran into a high-level CPN-UML leader.[17] I knew his face, name, and history, but we had met only once, in 2005, during a street protest where he and many other party leaders had been arrested. Uma began to introduce him, telling me that he was a former student activist who was now a CPN-UML central committee member, a position he had held for a long time, and that at the end of the Movement Against Regression he was the minister of sports and education. During this introduction, he looked at her eagerly, waiting to interject. As she paused, he said: "Leader [Nētā], I am a CPN-UML party leader. And this is my daughter." He pointed affectionately to Uma, claiming her as fictive kin. "I have known her for years. She is rising quickly in the ANNFSU." I remarked that he and I had met years earlier on the streets and that it was nice to meet again. He stared at me a bit blankly, trying to recollect. He then asked, "Is my daughter taking care of you?" And then to Uma, he said (Uma is not really his daughter): "Please make our guest feel welcome." Uma nodded and mentioned that she would come to his house before she returned to her village for Dasain. As he drove off toward the commemoration, Uma looked at me and said: "Guest? I think you know too much about us to be our guest." This minister's response captured the gender dynamics I have observed in Nepali politics, where men designate themselves as leaders and incorporate women into their circles by assigning diminutive fictive kin markers.

As this vignette demonstrates, in politics women's positions are depicted as relational; their relationships are with their natal families, their husbands' families, their sons, and, when those are not politically convenient, fictive kin. The late CPN-UML leader Sahana Pradhan, in her capacity as minister of foreign affairs, explained to me:

> For a woman to get ahead in politics, the family environment must
> be conducive. Her husband, son, brothers have to be supportive. In our
> society, the socialization process for a son and a daughter is different. A
> son is taken as one who earns and who performs the parents' funeral ritu-
> als. A daughter, on the other hand, is treated as someone who will go to
> another's home after marriage. A woman has to live within the control of
> her father before she gets married, her husband after she is married, and
> her son after the demise of her husband. She is never free. Women don't
> have their own self-identity. [A woman] is always identified as someone's
> daughter, someone's wife, and someone's mother.[18]

Although she did not make it explicitly clear, the multigenerational injunction she describes is a reference to the Hindu scripture, *Manusmriti*. She used it to illustrate her own political experience, explaining that she entered politics to fight for women's civil rights. She thought that the plight of women and the trials of the average Nepali person were similar but that women had a double layer of servitude.[19] At the time she became politically active, the Nepali citizenry was subject to the king; Nepali women, however, were also subject to their male kin. For her, politics was a way to eliminate both levels of suppression, making all citizens equal. And by doing it as a woman, she hoped she could create space where other women could carve out identities beyond being daughters, sisters, and mothers. When asked what she accomplished in bolstering women's status, she indicated that she saw no difference between her personal political ambition and her fight for women's political rights. Her mere presence in politics was beneficial to women because men were forced to take her seriously in leadership roles. Increases in women's educational opportunities, she believed, would automatically increase their participation in politics and that would bring much-needed change.

In many ways, Sahana's experience was exceptional for her generation, but in other ways she could not escape the limits she described to me. Her rise in politics was due in part to her connection to men in political power. Her family lived outside of Nepal when she was born, and they encouraged her both to study and to be politically active. Reaching higher education during the Panchayat era gave her access to a political life that few Nepali women had. Her marriage to Pushpa Lal Shrestha, a founder of CPN, "attached her to politics for life," she said.[20] This connection was one she could not move past even after he died. Any time I mentioned her to others, they would first ask me if I knew who her husband was. Her experience illustrates the degree to which Nepali politics is a network-based apparatus. Since politics is a public endeavor, kin or affinal connections buttress women's positions, what Risha derisively described as *shrīmatibād* (nepotism by marriage).[21] It is both a benefit and a hindrance. As a social mechanism, it allows women access to a sphere they might otherwise not have. As in Uma's case, fictive kin connections can be manufactured to accommodate and promote women who do not have family in politics.

Although kin connections may provide women entrée into politics, they also can significantly limit women's role, particularly when public perception of these same connections prevents them from representing interests beyond their sponsored connections. A Madheshi student activist articulated this common dismissal, asserting that Sujata Koirala no more represented his mother than her father, G. P. Koirala, had as the NC party president.

> Please tell me how my mother's life will be different if Sujata Koirala becomes a deputy prime minister? It does not matter whether Sujata

is male or female. She is capable enough, of course, because she has everything. Sujata does not need to be empowered. The very direction of women in the name of the feminist movement is wrong in our country. Sujata does not fight to live or for recognition. She fights to maintain her family's wealth and influence, which was established on the premise of democratic rights. That is her family's business. Without it, her family is jeopardized. With it, she is guaranteed to have a leadership role, even if as a minister without portfolio [an official mandate or ministry to lead]. How ridiculous is that?[22]

Such dismissals cause a dilemma for many women. The most influential women are disregarded for the very same reason that they are able to get to an influential position: they embody nepotism. They are a physical manifestation of the networks that fuel Nepali politics. People spurn Sujata Koirala because she represents the reality that she, her family, the NC, and Nepali politics in general are run by an elite few. She is a homologue of her kin connections (Strathern 1991: 212), but these connections also eclipse any individual political project she may undertake.

One of Sujata's political projects has been cultivating her own network by grooming younger women, enabling them to access a political sphere that would otherwise be off limits. The presence of her father, uncles, and nephews has allowed her to attend the political bargaining meetings where real decisions are made. And as a leader, she commands the respect of other men. That Risha was one of the women she groomed seemed promising, since Risha was proactive about supporting women from all sectors and geographic localities. Sujata's support opened doors for Risha.

But Sujata's support was also a double-edged sword that threatened to undermine Risha's own ambitions. That became clear after Prabal, an NSU central committee member, contemptuously dismissed Risha in 2009. Risha and Prabal's relationship always seemed transactional; nevertheless, they coordinated activities for the same causes. She referred to him as an older brother and would leverage her influence for him when she could, and he provided her with material and social support as well as encouraged her mentoring of younger female students. I ran into Prabal at the end of a political program in late 2009. It was early evening, when social gathering points shifted from tea stalls to bars for particular party activists. Prabal invited me and a few other ex–NSU student leaders for a beer. We sat at the bar in hushed silence, focusing on the news headline flashing across the television screen with an update on the talks between the NC, CPN-UML, and

UCPN (Maoist) party leaders to resolve the stalemate of the CA government. Baburam Bhattarai was being considered for the prime ministership, the announcer reported, but G. P. Koirala would agree only if his daughter was appointed deputy prime minister. In footage of leaders exiting the meeting, Sujata Koirala was seen walking to her motorcade with Risha behind her. Prabal pointed toward the screen at Risha, looked at me, and said, "Shadow goddess [*Chāyā devī*]."[23] His dismissal of Risha demonstrated the difficulty women face in their political progression. Risha's attempt to get beyond the limits of male-dominated politics in fact limited her ability to command their respect. In the minds of others, she was unable to transcend her personal connections with Sujata.

By 2015, however, Risha admitted that she no longer visited Sujata. She had begun to keep her distance after Sujata did not endorse her name for the first-past-the-post seat in her home constituency in the 2013 CA elections. The frustration she expressed over Sujata's lack of support was similar to Prabal's. Sujata just wanted women to follow her, she explained, "like a shadow." Risha decided that Sujata's support was a liability, and she was determined to "make it on her own" rather than be subject to political patronage and party factionalism.[24]

Despite the desire to be unencumbered in her political pursuits, Risha, like many other female politicians, utilizes metaphors of family and kin to garner broad-based appeal. In speeches, they claim to represent the mothers and sisters of Nepal. Older women give well wishes to their sons as well as their daughters. Young women encourage their younger sisters to participate in politics both to fulfill the aspirations of their mothers and to pave the future for their daughters. They appeal to men as brothers, fathers, and sons "to assist them in fulfilling their own mothers' aspirations, for both the sons and daughters of Nepal."[25] They use the metaphor of family to streamline their agenda by drawing on the sense of duty that undergirds kinship. A female student pointed to the terms that define the relationship between parties and student organizations, "mother" and "sister" organizations, to explain what inspires this discourse. From her perspective, the mother-sister organization dynamic is a misnomer because women have not played a central role. This is something she intended to change; women must make themselves "more prominent in the political family structure."[26]

Rhetorically mobilizing filial metaphors may allow women's demands to resonate within elite politics; however, it does not challenge the "relationships between the ways of *doing*, of *being*, and of *saying* that define the perceptible organization of the community" (Rancière 1999: 40). In this way, party politics continue to impose a double bind on women.

POLITICAL LIMITS

I often discussed politics with taxi drivers who couriered me to and from political programs and meetings during field research. Taxis provided privacy and intimacy, allowing drivers, who tend to be very politically opinionated, to be frank despite my being a stranger. Their opinions varied quite broadly. I often asked them to help me, as a foreigner, understand Nepali politics. On the return from a program commemorating the reunification of the two NC parties in 2007, a taxi driver's dismissive comment captured public sentiment. "Politics is so-called leaders playing the game of leading," he explained. "Everyone aims to be the leader. Those who are successful have followers and can broker compromise with other party leaders. It's a major distraction—people focus too much on building their own influence and don't really do anything useful."[27] Establishing leadership is indeed central to political progression. Leadership is the bar by which people are assessed and placed in politics. To command influence is part of the habitus of party politics, putting those not empowered to assert themselves in Nepal's social hierarchy at a distinct disadvantage. Thus, leadership capability is not a value-free ability in Nepali politics but rather predetermines who succeeds in politics. Women and minorities face this challenge, albeit in different ways.

I relayed that conversation with the taxi driver to Risha. She chuckled and then chided me for only focusing on this political dimension after three years into research.

> People say that women don't rise in politics because they are limited
> or don't have the capacity or consciousness. They won't say that women
> are incapable, because that sounds discriminating. But what do they
> mean by limited? That they are suppressed and can't enter into poli-
> tics? As you have observed, one must be influential or connected to influ-
> ence to advance politically. What does that involve? It involves either
> having your own following or being relentlessly cunning. Better yet,
> both. Women's connections are usually limited to their families. It is
> also inappropriate for women to be relentlessly cunning. So how do women
> become successful politicians? The thing that limits them most is the
> judgment of others.[28]

What Risha meant by relentlessly cunning was the embodiment of a superior conviction in one's abilities and agendas. She explained to me that high-caste men are raised to behave with such steadfast conviction, but for most others such behavior is socially discouraged.

The dominance of a high-caste male orientation not only dictates the terms of success in politics, but it also determines how exclusion is understood. Because exclusion is understood vis-à-vis the high-caste male elite, the subtle differences between exclusionary experiences are glossed over. Yet the ways women and ethnic minority men experience exclusion is quite different. Minority men can find partial success in politics if they are willing to adopt a high-caste male persona. For high-caste or ethnic women to engage these qualities, however, is considered inappropriate. For them, it is social suicide to act like one of the guys: staying out late to attend critical meetings, hoisting up a glass of whiskey to seal crucial deals, and asserting their own agenda in lieu of others' interests. Instead, women must take advantage of caste and kin affiliations with those already politically established.

The legalization of patriarchy during the Panchayat era further elucidates the limits women face in politics. Patriarchy shifted away from the domestic sphere to the legal sphere, wherein women's rights and roles as daughters, wives, and mothers became legally prescribed. "In Nepal, gendered citizenship must be understood . . . in the maintenance of masculinized Hindu rule; the attempted homogenization of Nepal's diverse population and creation of 'the Nepali woman' (legally and otherwise) as a chief instrument" (S. Tamang 2000: 152). The ideal-type hill-based Brahmin and Chhetri family became the template for all families; Hindu filial duty came to circumscribe women. The Panchayat government instituted development policies to modernize women in a particular way. "The illiterate and 'conscious-less' women of Nepal had to be 'awakened' from their pitiful, superstition-ridden lives and moved forward to help develop the nation" (133). The Hindu filial paradigm that informed the Panchayat regime's construction of the Nepali female citizen continues to determine the obstacles women face in both society and politics.

Metaphors of nature and religion are used to explain why women are cordoned to particular spheres and roles in politics. Proverbs such as *Pothi basna hunna*, or "A hen should not crow," or dismissals of a woman as a "sari" because she is required to cover her head and to avoid eye contact in the presence men are used to identify the obstacles women face. One ethnic female student leader explained:

In Nepali culture, it is said that a hen should not crow. It is taken as ominous. It is taken as a sign of bad luck. The assumption that a hen should not crow establishes the presumption that females—whether they are the daughter, daughter-in-law, mother, sister—should not speak in the presence of males. The society has never encouraged women to speak up. Women with the courage to speak out do not receive compliments. . . . No, rather they are referred to as "bad women" and "characterless women" [spoken in English]. In a society like this, it is really risky to become involved in politics or to speak out. You are judged by your family and your family is judged by others.[29]

This student's explanation captures the social truth that limits women in politics. They may embody multiple social relations, as men do; however, hegemonic prescriptions dictate how they should behave and interact.

This reality is not lost on the female student leaders, who cope with the limits they face in both creative and desperate ways. How Tanuja, an NSU (K) central committee member, dealt with being dismissed was particularly illustrative. Risha and I flew down to Jhapa to attend a few NSU (K) district conventions, and Tanuja hosted us during the Jhapa convention. Afterward, she decided to join a group of us for the Morang convention. For the first two hours of our drive, she frantically sang devotional songs to Shiva. She was frustrated by the election outcome of the Jhapa convention. Like Risha and many other student leaders who rallied for a healthy democratic process, she was disappointed that the NC district leadership had interfered to influence election results. Every time one of our male compatriots tried to rehash the events to ponder what went wrong, Tanuja cut him off with a devotional song. During a pit stop, I asked her if she was all right, and she replied: "No one listened to me throughout the convention. Now they want to discuss all that went wrong. I don't want to hear it. They interrupted me before, but they won't interrupt my songs to Shiva [*mero Shiava bhajan*]." She complained how frustrating it was to be interrupted: "We have a choice—we can be assertive, even though we know no one cares to listen, or we [can] remain silent. Do you think that we like being pushy? No. But there is no way for a woman to be graceful in politics—we must be bullies or be silent."[30] The proverb "A hen should not crow" captures Tanuja's dilemma. Her way of coping was to assert her agency by occupying the traditionally sanctioned space religion provided. It may have been a small case of "foot dragging," but it allowed her to vent her frustration to her male peers (cf. Scott 1985).

Many female students admitted that they were wary when people listened to them or took their opinion into account, doubting whether their interest was a hollow gesture toward inclusion. Salini's experience after becoming the ANNFSU (Akhil) president underscored this situation. She had achieved the most coveted role in student politics. As I congratulated her, a student in her entourage pointed out that she was not only the first female student president but also the first elected female student president. Another student proudly indicated that she was a Janajāti as well, but then he cowered when everyone averted their eyes because it was a crass point. Later, when we were alone, I asked Salini about her experience, and she responded: "You know I had always thought that being politically active was a compulsion. It was for us, especially during the movement. But recently, people have been saying that it is volunteer work. That is the response I hear when I try to give orders to make things happen. It's frustrating. I find it really hard. I have no way to convince people to serve the organization except through ideological conviction and our aim to achieve justice. When people start defining their political duty as volunteer work, I don't know how to direct them."[31] At the time, Salini was too savvy to define her cadres' disobedience as an attempt to undermine her as a woman in authority, but a couple of years later she admitted that was her meaning. Women are not overtly suppressed in politics, she ruefully observed; rather, they are put in positions where they must act beyond the scope of social acceptability to be effective. They must shout over interrupting voices, strictly administer orders, and attend late-night meetings that may involve alcohol or other male indulgences—that is, if they are lucky enough to be invited, which they rarely are because it is not an appropriate atmosphere for a woman of character. These are the limits women experience in trying to achieve the leadership necessary to thrive in politics.

Even attempts at inclusion such as the proportional election system have their limits. The proportional election system was meant to bring into the political process minorities and women who lack the clout, influence, or resources to contest elections directly. In both CA elections, there were 335 proportional seats and 240 first-past-the-post direct election seats. However, the way the parties manipulated the system during the 2013 election created unintended consequences and further obstacles for women to establish themselves in party politics. Those who secure proportional seats are seen as less influential than those who have won direct seats, because they have party support rather than voter support and thus must tote the party line since their seats are contingent on party blessing. Furthermore, since securing a possible seat is determined by the number of proportional seats their party secures, proportionate list candidates are compelled to campaign where the party directs them rather than campaign for themselves in their own constituency. That they are thus cheated out of the opportunity to distinguish themselves as politicians with a voter base perpetuates their dependency on party support.

In 2013, Risha, Salini, and Tanuja rushed around to different parts of the country to sell their party to voters who would not have the opportunity to vote for them directly. Yet despite all their campaign efforts, none of these young women were given proportional seats. Many established female politicians decided not to contest direct elections because either they lost in 2008 or they became unpopular incumbents. Hisila Yami of the UCPN (Maoist) was the only senior woman leader to contest in direct elections as an incumbent, and she lost (Dhital 2013). Other established female leaders chose the safe route to secure CA seats, which pushed their juniors further down the proportional list. It also cost the 2013 CA overall, which was 30 percent women compared to 33 percent in the 2008 CA. Risha and Salini both lamented that this decrease, especially in directly elected women, hindered the creation of a women's caucus to oppose the citizenship law, which did not allow maternal transfer of citizenship.

STATE OF ELITES IN THE SECULAR ERA

The shift toward secularism was another attempt to institute broad-based inclusion. The 2008 and 2013 CAs undertook the task to again "redress historical wrongs by legal means," which the 1991 constitution failed to do (Malagodi 2013: 49). Institutionally restructuring the state into "new Nepal" was a monumental pursuit. It required a shift away from the traditional state paradigm because the three national pillars—the Shah monarchy, Nepal's status as a Hindu nation, and Nepali as the national language—were gone. This changed the nature of the 2008 and 2013 CA debates; however, the concern of "preserving national unity" (143) that shaped the 1991 constitution continued to be the fundamental basis for these new iterations. In 1991, the constitutional drafters' desire to maintain social harmony re-entrenched the political authority of the Hindu monarchy as a necessary foundation to preserve "unity in diversity" (143). Removing the monarchy from the state paradigm became possible because the 2001 palace massacre and King Gyanendra's constitutional overreach undermined the institutional sanctity the monarchy managed to maintain for over two centuries. On a superficial level, devolving the monarchy involved deposing a maligned man who lacked public support. The political discourse of 2007 inextricably linked support for the Hindu state to support for the monarchy, and therefore many politicians were reluctant to oppose secularism for fear of seeming pro-monarchy and thus supporting King Gyanendra. Salini explained: "When we stand in favor of the Hindu state, it supports the underlying cultural existence of the monarchy and a king who can again act against democracy. Hence, we are in favor of secularism."[32]

The king is now gone; yet the religious elements of institutional state-craft have proved more perennial. By 2013, the political parties had taken complete control of institutional power, and thus supporting state pro-tection for Hinduism was no longer seen as pro-monarchy. Rather than eliminate Hindu ritual from state ritual, the parties merely replaced the king (cf. Mocko 2015; Zotter 2016), continuing to rely on the "ontological and ideational foundations of the Nepali state" (Malagodi 2013: 159). The politi-cal subjectification necessary to institute secularism in any substantial man-ner remained absent during state restructuring. Instead, the political elite relied on institutional continuity rather than redefine national unity in a way that foregrounds Nepal's diversity.

Article 4 of the 2007 interim constitution stated that Nepal was *dharma nirapeksha* (autonomous from / indifferent to religion). This declaration neither cemented an absolute separation of church and state—in contrast to the prior Hindu kingdom's dharma-oriented (*dharma sāpeksha*) state— nor set parameters for religious pluralism in the legal code. The 2008 elected CA was tasked with clarifying the legal parameters of secularism. There was public momentum to remove religion from statecraft, particularly fueled by Buddhist, Muslim, and ethnic activists, who failed to establish secular-ism during the drafting of the 1991 constitution (cf. Leve 2007; Malagodi 2013; Letizia 2012). Thereafter, minorities increasingly rallied for a more inclusive atmosphere where their cultural and religious traditions received equal recognition and accommodation from the state (cf. Gellner, Hausner, and Letizia 2016; Hangen 2010). Secularism resonated enough publicly that the Maoists included it in their forty-point demand that precipitated the People's War. Thus by 2007, secularism was viewed as a palpable reform toward instituting socio-cultural inclusion: *hamro bhāshā, dharma, san-skriti* (our language, religion, culture) (Letizia 2012: 82).

By 2015, however, many were not comfortable with the idea of secularism. Tense debates over identity-based federalism and minority accommodation divided the national polity rather than unified it. This was particularly stark in 2012 after the dissolution of the first CA. Polarizing an already divided public, conservatives scapegoated secularism by associating the increasing lack of economic and social opportunity with the assault on people's traditional way of life. Echoing Hindu sentiment in India, pro-Hindu activists linked ethnic politics and Christian missionary activity, collapsing them into an anti-national specter intent on dividing the nation (Jaffrelot 2007; Osuri 2013).

Kamal Thapa and his royalist party, the RPP-N, capitalized on this socioeconomic unease in the 2013 CA elections. Risha explained this tactic as "emotionally blackmailing the Nepali people" in order to win votes for their party.[33] Although it was unrealistic that the monarchy would be reinstituted, Thapa received traction among many constituencies with his insistence that Hinduism remain the state religion. The RPP-N won twenty-four seats in the proportional election while gaining none in the first-past-the-post election, creating a power block that forced the second CA to concede overt secular language. Without Thapa's support, the big three parties would not have been able to promulgate the contentious constitution. Thus, the 2015 constitution maintained the 2007 interim constitution's provision that Nepal remain a secular state; however, it added a clause mandating that the state must protect "sanatana dharma and religious and cultural freedom." Sanatana dharma means the "original dharma," as defined by Hinduism, from which other religions stem (sanatandekhi caliaeka dharma). This definition can be understood to include Buddhism as it stems from Hinduism, and thus traditional Buddhist practice and festivals must be constitutionally protected. However, Christianity and Islam do not fit within this definition and are vulnerable to falling outside the parameters of constitutional protection (Gellner and Letizia 2016). The state's express purpose to protect sanatana dharma and religious freedom may indicate religious tolerance; however, anyone familiar with Hindu doctrine understands that the basis for such tolerance is hierarchy rather than inclusion based on religious equality.

Once again, the constitutional outcome vis-à-vis secularism resulted from a "specific ethnocultural version of the nation" that was previously entrenched by political symbols, institutional choices, and legal language that perpetuated patterns of exclusion (Malagodi 2013: 13). How has this ethno-cultural version endured despite radical shifts in institutional power arrangements since 2006? The nationalist ideology that has historically dictated the unitary vision of the Nepali nation is rooted in hill-based (Parbatiya) high-caste logic. The governing actors may have changed; however, their means of orientation are shared despite differing political ideology. Hill-based, high-caste Hindu logic continues to be the crux of national ideology, which has determined legitimacy in modern Nepal.

An analysis of how two student leaders addressed secularism in their attempts at political transformation helps explain how deeply rooted this logic is. The ways they contended with the limits of dominant nationalist discourse demonstrate the inherent challenges to instituting inclusion based on religious equality in a majority Hindu nation.

The resistance Akash faced when he tried to propose what a secular republic could look like in Nepal demonstrates how entrenched Hindu tradition is in nationalist discourse. His reputation as a compelling orator is undisputed. Yet during the 2007 election campaign, he lacked his typical conviction when addressing the topic of political practice in "new Nepal." He asked the audience to consider what "new Nepal" was and if it included the practices of wearing tōpīs and giving blessings (tikā), or if it included sponsoring the king to go to the Pashupati temple.[34] Were these practices a part of politics, or did they reinforce a different project that went against public interest? His challenge elicited a tepid response from the crowd. I later asked him about his indirect approach and chided him by saying, "You usually get people fired up so they support your radical demands." He admitted that he was struggling to promote secularism. It was much less well received than his demand for a republic during the Movement Against Regression.

Initially, Akash tried to campaign for secular political practice by asserting that political traditions, even through the 1990s, were those based on the superiority of the Hindu monarchy. He stressed that political practice oriented toward a Hindu state further entrenched the monarchy. He wanted to convince people that if they wanted a republic that was not at risk of recapture by the monarchy, then they must remove Hindu symbols and rituals from both the government and political institutions. Crowds saw his provocation as an affront to their values. He gave the example of a village development committee where he raised this issue. In the previous month, a walkathon raising funds for tuberculosis had thirty participants and collected about NR 10,000. A week later, the Pashupati Temple Trust held a rally attended by more than one thousand people and raised over NR 300,000. He asked the audience to consider who benefited from the money raised: the ill or Pashupatinath, the god from which the king derived his ruling mandate. Afterward, he was surprised when people approached him and asked why he was anti-Hindu. After that, he skirted the issue, trying to challenge innocuous political practices to make people understand what needed to be done to remove the monarchy from national politics.

Akash struggled because his audience approached secularism as an either-or binary (cf. Bangstad 2009). Those who resisted his move to create a degree of separation between religion and statecraft saw it as a threat to their identity vis-à-vis the state. In response, Akash gathered quotations and teachings to communicate the Hindu belief that god is in all creatures. He tried to convey that he was interested not in forcing people to choose between Hinduism and no Hinduism but in promoting communal inclusion via the Hindu practice of worshipping the god in others. Using familiar tropes, he attempted to "create a kind of analogue of divine honor within human society" (Parish 1994: 86). He recognized the irony of his approach, using people's Hindu faith to compel inclusion and unity, the same sentiment the monarchy exploited. He wondered, "How do I break the cycle and try to institute a political practice of equality that avoids the king's tactics?"[35] Akash's inability to disassociate certain modes of identity from certain realms of practice highlights the vestiges of Hinduism in the "dialectics of belonging" in national discourse (van der Veer 1994).

Despite his ambivalence, Akash ultimately relied on Hindu references that resonate with dominant norms in his attempt to create a new type of national unity that no longer relied on the three national pillars. His attempt at political subjectification—redefining the relational organization of the community (Rancière 1999)—was unable to remove the residues of Hindu symbolism. Other political actors embraced familiar symbols with less ambivalence to make their demands resonate.

In 2009, a conglomeration of youth groups organized a program in Kathmandu to celebrate Dasain. They protested the CA's delay in drafting the constitution. An ex–student activist, Rajeev, stressed the *pan-yubā* (all-youth) spirit of their program, emphasizing that many participants were from civil society and that student organizations were barred from displaying their flags. The program was a "symbolic protest." Rajeev was confident in the effectiveness of their message, conveyed in a dramatization of a key Dasain ritual that solidified the social interdependence of traditional patronage hierarchy in filial, business, and political spheres. In the skit, a mother gave her son the Dasain blessing and then tried to give the boy a gift. The boy refused to take the gift and retorted: "All I want for Dasain is a constitution. How do you expect me to ensure the prosperity of our family and country without a constitution?" Then the same skit was repeated, but this time a father gave his daughter a blessing and she requested a constitution. The participants then emerged from the crowd and sang a song appealing to citizens not merely to accept their leaders' blessing but to request a constitution so they can invest in their country.

Rajeev was very excited that the media came to cover the program. He urged the television crews to broadcast the skit instead of the speeches. By broadcasting the skit into "homes across Nepal," Rajeev hoped that it would prompt people to think about what their priorities should be. He turned to me and asked what I thought. Was it effective? I mused over whether people, especially those who boycott Dasain, would be troubled to see the leaders of "new Nepal" presented as Hindu patriarchs. Rajeev dismissed my misgivings. He reasoned that everyone celebrates Dasain, so they would identify with the program's sentiment. He paused and then asserted, "We need to make a statement in a way that everyone understands." Then he added: "People understand this—even you understand it. That's why it's effective."[36]

Rajeev's approach differed from that of Akash, who struggled to get beyond the Hindu logic entrenched in nationalist discourse. They shared party affiliation, but Rajeev embraced the familiar "dialectics of belonging" in order to achieve his goal. He perceived a new constitution and traditional forms that resonate with the public as mutually reinforcing, and he utilized them to shape public opinion. He was not critical of his means toward this end, even if that involved referencing traditional symbols that Akash and others viewed as obstructing "new Nepal." By resonating with established norms, Rajeev's approach reinforced a particular ethno-cultural version of public and political life that continued to allow the elites who have historically thrived to maintain their status within the state.

The 2015 constitution effectively substantiated that. After the promulgation, Gyanu admitted that it was lamentable, but secularism was not popular. He believed that if a referendum were to be held, then secularism would lose because people saw it as a threat to their way of life.[37] His explanation, however, did not take into account opinion polls documenting significant differences in the way Janajātis, Khas Aryan, Dalits, and Madheshi communities view secularism (Sharma and Khadka 2011; Sen 2015). Nor did his analysis take into account the referential feedback loop that continually reinforces Hinduism's residual effect in defining the nation and the ways communities are organized within it. Both Akash's and Rajeev's approaches amply demonstrate that effect.

EVOLVING VIEWS ON FEDERALISM AND INCLUSION

The residues of traditional power structures that have institutionalized socio-political marginalization have proved tenacious. Removing two of the three national pillars was seen as the way to make broad-based inclusion possible in 2006. However, the political parties' ability to reestablish their authority as the state's caretaker has ensured the shortfalls of the newly promulgated constitution, because it did not bring the required institutional change needed to alter endemic practices of marginalization in state and political institutions. In particular, the elite "means of orientation" (Elias 1978, in Shore 2002: 4) has continued to limit the ways that people can make demands and address the internal workings of political parties. The evolution of these student leaders' views on federalism and inclusion over the past decade demonstrates the degree to which the nationalistic values of party politics have kept them from fully endorsing inclusionary practice.

All five of these young political leaders have grown ambivalent regarding federalism, worrying that it could undermine national unity. Except for Lagan, who maintained the Workers and Peasants party line against federalism, the other democratic student leaders originally supported federalism but came to find it problematic. Salini explained: "In the beginning, we perceived it as our strength. In fact, we were in favor of a federal structure and were against the center controlling everything. . . . But when we were raising the slogan of federalism, some infiltrated with an intention to divide the Nepali people."[38] Even Gyanu admitted that the demand for "ethnic states" (*jātīya rājya*) was taken as "single ethnic states" (*ekal jātīya rājya*), which "divided the Nepali psychology." He explained: "This was a very dangerous matter. What I mean is the state has to reinstate the rights that were seized. That does not mean to seize other people's rights and chase them away."[39]

Nevertheless, all five thought that decentralization was important. Risha and Lagan supported institutionalized decentralization to tackle issues of social justice. Akash still supported federalism to achieve decentralization, "because decentralizing efforts since the Panchayat era have proved ineffective";[40] however, he thought that federalism should not be decided on the basis of inclusion and identity but rather should be linked to institution building. Salini and Gyanu still supported federalism, too, but as communists, they were frustrated that class was sidelined by ethnicity in the state-restructuring debates. Like many leftists, they prioritize the register of economic marginalization over social marginalization, which many ethnic activists believe continues to perpetuate the social exclusion endemic in state processes (Jha 2014; Lawoti 2005; Malagodi 2013).

Their views on inclusion-based policies such as reservations also demonstrate their reluctance. They were skeptical about reservations in two distinct ways. The first was in effect the "creamy layer" argument, which held that the reservation system may unintentionally perpetuate marginalization by giving benefits to the most prosperous and resourced in each of the marginalized demographic groups and thereby continuing to exclude precisely those who ought to be helped.[41] The left-leaning respondents felt that reservation accommodations should be determined by economic marginalization rather than social marginalization. The second concern was that reservations might undermine quality. All five respondents emphasized that those who receive minority accommodation must be "capable." Some thought that, rather than reservations, a more fruitful approach to equalize opportunity would be investing in capacity building and education. This attitude, however, is problematic because, as with political leadership, "capability" is not a value-free quality. Rather, how capability is defined, who is considered capable, and who is considered in need of capacity building are determined by dominant norms, which in this case are dictated by the criteria of educated distinction. Until these norms and expectations are reworked to value other types of capability and capacity, then Nepal will continue to struggle with socio-economic marginalization.

These ex–student leaders' views ideologically diverge, but ultimately the underlying motivation leading to their evolved opinions is similar, how to maintain national unity. Salini captured this succinctly when she explained, "This is a society that has survived on coexistence."[42] For all of them, coexistence is still best achieved by "unity in diversity" (Malagodi 2013) rather than by establishing unity through inclusion.

CONCLUSION

Salini and I met two days before the new constitution was to be promulgated in September 2015. I peppered her with questions on what she thought of this constitution, which she and her cohort had fought to institute for over a decade. My questions were not easy for her or any of the ex–student leaders to answer because they felt compelled to defend their parties and the legitimacy of the political process against the mounting criticism that this constitution was more regressive than the 2007 interim constitution, particularly in terms of the federal structure, citizenship laws, political representation, and secularism. Salini's immediate response was to quote the proverb *Chāmal mā biya hunchha*, or "Even hulled rice contains a few unhusked grains." She explained that it means nothing is 100 percent perfect. But, she added hopefully, nothing is 100 percent imperfect, either.

Her sentiment echoed the way all five ex–student leaders processed this critical juncture. They all articulated the realization that the big institutional ruptures they achieved did not bring the change they had hoped for.

Salini lamented: "During the *āndolan* we thought *ganatantra* [republicanism] would change things, but we realize that changes must be addressed in the experience of life. . . . We were thinking on the macro level, but now we are thinking about things on a micro level to affect the larger whole."[43]

Akash explained that their altered perspective was due in part to their shift from the demand-side of politics to the supply-side of politics: "Yesterday, I was not bothered about changing institutions. We wanted to demolish institutions we saw as obstacles. I had thought that after the demolition of the monarchy, new institutions would develop on their own. But what I've observed is that some changes may have taken place in the superstructure of society. For instance, the president was elected in place of the monarch, but really it just amounted to someone replacing another in a similar seat of power. Since we have not built new institutions from the base, due to cultural aspects, new results have not come."[44]

Gyanu articulated a similar sentiment from a Marxist viewpoint that there was no attempt to change the economic base and that this has maintained continuity regardless of any superstructural changes. Republicanism was supposed to replace the monarchy and change traditions and "working culture," but since the new leadership has not changed things at the base level, he explained, "old traditions and culture remain—we can call it status quo."[45]

Political regeneration engenders the status quo as much as it engenders socio-political transformation. The politically active students whom I worked with are mainly from socially or economically privileged backgrounds. Nevertheless, they are enmeshed in the political context that motivated demands for socio-economic justice. They understand the local, national, and international discourses that have shaped these demands and the resulting political formations. Their desire to achieve socio-economic justice is genuine. However, their attempts are curtailed both by their subject position and by their political motivations. They are invested in maintaining the political parties' stronghold to ensure their political futures and achieve their political demands. The social and political transformations they hope to achieve are negotiated by dominant political norms. This dynamic is not abstract but is mediated by social relations. The interactions between political generations within the party structure dictate the terms of this dynamic.

As these ex–student leaders have come of age, they have come to realize that large-scale transformations are hard to achieve while trying to maintain national unity. But at the same time, they are acutely aware that this is an ongoing process. Akash articulated that during a conversation dissecting public disappointment over the recently promulgated constitution. He replied: "Look, the constitution is a living process. If we see it merely as a document, then we'd have to admit defeat. As a process, it will change according to circumstances and with time."[46]

As he made that assertion, I thought back to something Salini had said to me in 2005, after she was arrested and jailed during the state of emergency. In her comment from a decade earlier were some of the first seeds of empirical data affirming political regeneration:

> I've come to realize the struggle for democracy is not complete in one struggle. . . . On the one hand, the students are rallying for a republican setup and full democracy, while our political parties are still maintaining the agenda of parliamentary reinstatement. Since the political parties united for a common agenda, it should be the agenda of the people. The students recognize that, so we, as party wings, are demanding a republic despite our parties' settling for mere parliament reinstatement. . . . Therefore, the struggle for democracy has to be fought continuously. . . . To move toward betterment and development is the lifestyle of our generation. It should be the lifestyle of every generation. . . . The struggle will become more refined as the issues become clearer. It seems to me that this is a continuous process. The struggle for democracy is a way of life. . . . Today we are fighting for the basic things of democracy [political rights], but tomorrow's struggle may be for prosperity [socio-economic rights].[47]

She was alluding to their democratic struggle's generative progressive form. Interpreting Akash's emphasis on the constitution as a living process, in light of Salini's explanation, underscores the stakes of political subjectification—decomposing and recomposing the "relationships between the ways of *doing*, of *being*, and of *saying* that define the perceptible organization of the community" (Rancière 1999: 40). Maintaining that this is an iterative process is a hopeful coping measure for these ex–student leaders, allowing them to avoid closure and remain open to future possibilities (Snellinger 2016a).

6 Accumulating Influence through Scalar Politics

DESPITE BEING ONE OF THE MOST SUCCESSFUL STUDENT LEADERS of his generation, Akash was never the president of his student union. Party leaders discouraged his early ambitions and stymied his active bid twice. The first time was in 2005 during the failed Pokhara convention, leading to what became known as the "Pokhara scandal" because it disintegrated into chaos and vandalism following widespread rumors that voter lists had been rigged to defeat Akash's chances.[1] The second time was when G. P. Koirala offered Akash a proportional CA seat if he agreed not to run for president at the 2007 Chitwan convention.

Between 2005 and 2007, Akash toyed with the idea of starting his own party to represent the youth demographic. He first considered this political move in 2005 after he was forced by the NC leadership to sign a "consensus agreement" to dissolve the NSU (K) central committee and appoint an interim committee.[2] He mulled the idea over as he departed for Germany to attend an INGO governance program. He decided not to pursue it after he returned, explaining that his meetings with the Nepali diaspora in Europe made him confident that he had a future in the NC because people wanted him to change things inside the party. In 2007, he decided to take the CA proportional seat deal rather than pursue his youth party idea (Snellinger 2016a). Akash's ability to transition from a student leader to an influential NC central committee member and parliamentarian without having held an elected position on his student union's central committee has little precedent.[3]

Akash, however, is not an outlier. Student leaders, especially those who challenge the party status quo, are often marginalized by their leaders. His story of political progression elucidates both old and new political trends. His political luck had much to do with timing—the Movement Against Regression provided him with a public platform to establish broad-based political support. Nevertheless, his tactic to reach out and garner influence beyond the party to ensure his political future is not new. Rather, this strategy has been central to overcoming domestic political repression since the first democratic movement in the 1950s. There were, however, structural factors that played a part in Akash's and his peers' success that were not present during previous political movements. In addition to mobilizing their youth position discursively to counter their leaders' dominance, student activists employed techniques of scalar politics to circumvent the political limits they faced within their party hierarchies.

Danny MacKinnon (2010) developed the concept of scalar politics to reconcile the political-economic and post-structural approaches to scale, both of which he thought had merit but erred too much on the side of fixity and fluidity, respectively. The scalar politics paradigm addresses post-structural concerns of how scales are socially constructed through practice and discourse and the ways they map onto social landscapes, but not at the expense of a material consideration of how they are socially reproduced and transformed over time (31). Scalar politics allow us to focus "attention on the ability of particular social actors, organizations and movements to harness and manipulate the discursive and material dimensions of scale effectively in pursuit of their agendas" (30). Scalar politics reveal the struggle between powerful actors and subaltern groups and how they leverage associations at the local, domestic, regional, and international levels either to secure the reproduction of socio-political relations or alter them (Cox and Mair 1988; Huber and Emel 2009).

Out of necessity, Nepali student activists develop networks beyond their parties to earn recognition and support. This bottom-up mobilization bypasses party hierarchy and appeals to external actors in the hopes to leverage top-down and lateral pressure on their party hierarchy. In this regard, Nepali student activists' techniques of "scale jumping" (Smith 2004) replicate what Margaret E. Keck and Kathryn Sikkink (1998) coined the "boomerang effect" that transnational advocacy networks have generated in the era of late capitalism. Student activist may have reached outside of Nepal to regional and international forces to compel them to pressure their government and party leaders; however, their techniques of scalar politics do not merely mimic the boomerang pattern (Keck and Sikkink 1998: 13). They also scale laterally within other domestic sectors to garner influence, which they leverage to pressure their party leaders. The students engage a range of overlapping political and social networks that span territorial boundaries, taking advantage of the practical entanglements networks and scales provide (cf. Allen and Cochrane 2007).

HISTORY OF POLITICAL PROGRESS
THROUGH SCALAR POLITICS

When Akash and his fellow student leaders demanded a republic during the Movement Against Regression, they were branded as anti-nationalists by the king's government and even arrested for sedition. The Maoists were branded as terrorists whose actions undermined national sovereignty, paving the way for King Gyanendra to enact article 127 to dismiss the democratically elected parliament. In the summer of 2015, Tarai and Madheshi activists who opposed the proposed constitution were also branded as anti-nationalists and dismissed as Indian infiltrators. The latter accusation was further cemented in the public imaginary after Madheshi activists enforced a 135-day border blockade to protest the constitution's promulgation. The government and much of Kathmandu's media establishment declared that the blockade had been orchestrated by the Indian government, collapsing any oppositional voice with an anti-nationalistic agenda to ignore the political demands of Tarai-dwelling citizens.

Branding opposition as anti-national is not merely a twenty-first-century trend but dates back to the Rana regime. The paradox underlying this trend is that all political progress in Nepal has been a result of marginalized political opposition leveraging external forces to disrupt the ruling stronghold in Kathmandu. Such maneuvers are not just realpolitik; they also engender the dialogical relationship between the external and internal political values that Nepali politics comprises. Dating back to the 1816 Treaty of Sagauli, and the demarcation of an autonomous boundary between sovereign Nepal and the British occupied territory, negotiations over sovereignty and rights claims have developed in a field of "intercultural relations" (Burghart 1984), which challenges normative notions of nationalism and sovereignty.

Due to the repressive environment in Nepal during the Rana regime, many of Nepal's early democratic organizers were born or studied in India, mainly in Patna, Banaras, and Calcutta. While Tanka Prasad Acharya and other Kathmandu intellectuals established the Praja Parishad (People's Council) in 1936 (the anti-Rana organization that was the precursor to the Nepali National Congress), many of its members were arrested or fled to India after their anti-Rana leaflet campaign in 1940. Ganesh Man Singh was one of those arrested and sentenced to death, but he managed to escape in 1944 and fled to Banaras to organize Nepali students and exiles in India.

The cross-fertilization of political principles was already under way by the time Ganesh Man Singh arrived in Banaras.

Many Nepali expatriates were taken with the Indian National Congress's fight for autonomy from the British and participated in the Quit India movement. Inspired by Mahatma Gandhi, B. P. Koirala began working for the Indian National Congress party in 1934 while at Banaras Hindu University, establishing close links with its subsidiary party, the Congress Socialist Party.[4] He was arrested a number of times and jailed by the British from 1942 to 1945 for attempting to recruit Nepali expatriates into the Quit India movement. After meeting with Ganesh Man Singh in Banaras, B. P. Koirala published an appeal in different Indian newspapers declaring that a political party must be created to bring democracy to Nepal. In October 1945, the All India Nepalese Congress was formed in Banaras. Due to urging from Indian Socialist Party leaders, Ram Manohar Lohia and Jaya Prakash Narayan, Nepali political workers throughout India and Nepal, met in Calcutta to transform the party into the Nepali National Congress on January 26, 1947 (Ojha 2012: 48–52).

The Nepali National Congress's establishment was due in part to students' organizing in Banaras and Calcutta. The Nepali Chhatra Sangha consolidated itself as the NSU at Banaras Hindu University in 1946 with the support of Prakash Gupta of the Indian National Congress and Ram Manohar Lohia of the Socialist Party India. And the Himanchal Vidyārthī Sangh (Hill Student Union) was revived in Calcutta in 1946, after students were inspired by speeches given by Ram Manohar Lohia and B. P. Koirala at a program in 1945 (Ojha 2012: 90–100). These political organizations' anti-Rana regime message had a direct effect on the students who led the Jayatu Sanskritam movement. While taking their exams in Banaras in 1947, they became acquainted with their Nepali peers' oppositional efforts, and when they returned to Kathmandu, they undertook what is sighted as the first successful political movement against the Rana regime.

Nepal's communist party was organized, in Calcutta in 1949. Ayodya Singh and Ratan Lal Brahman of the Communist Party India (CPI) greatly influenced Pushpa Lal Shrestha and the other founding members of the Nepal communist party who were active both in Calcutta and Banaras. After Indian independence, high-level Indian independence activists encouraged the Nepali National Congress to revolt against the Rana government, which was seen to be flotsam of British rule. It was India's first independence government led by Jawaharlal Nehru that gave King Tribhuvan political refuge in 1950, leading to disintegration of the Rana government and Nepal's first attempt at multiparty democracy.

Nepali students studying in India continued to organize for Nepal's democratic progress throughout the 1950s and through the Panchayat era. The All India Nepalese Students' Union (AINSU) was established in 1955 to unite Nepali students throughout India to counter the increasing partisanship of politically oriented organizations within both Nepal and India (Ojha 2012: 123–29). Nevertheless, it was heavily inspired by Gandhian socialism and the leadership of the Indian Socialist Party, and its organizational activities were centered in Banaras. B. P. Koirala inaugurated the AINSU's second conference in Bombay in October 1960, in a speech outlining his plans for a general election, land reform, and industrialization. King Mahendra also sent a letter of felicitation, although less than two months later he banned political parties. The AINSU continued its activities, maintaining strong ideological ties to the Indian Socialist Party.

Nepali activists who came of age during the early Panchayat era fled to Banaras and Patna to either escape or avoid being jailed for underground political activities. Pradip Giri, an NC member, explained to me: "In those days, India was the only window we had to the rest of the world. Most often we saw things from the Indian angle."[5] While studying, Pradip and his peers engaged anti-Panchayat opposition through the AINSU as well as participated in Ram Manohar Lohia's Angreji Hatāu āndolan (Remove English movement) (1966) and Jaya Prakash Narayan's Sampurna Krānti āndolan (Total Revolution movement) opposing Indira Gandhi's overreach (1974–75). A sociology professor at Banaras Hindu University, who was active in Jaya Prakash Narayan's movement and continues to be in the Janata Party, praised his fellow Nepali cadres in the AINSU as very dedicated to the Sampurna Krānti āndolan. He said: "Ideologically, we were aligned, and they saw fighting against Indira Gandhi's autocracy as furthering their struggle in Nepal. We benefited a lot from their dedication, and we've continued to support them in their struggle in Nepal."[6]

Through the 1970s and 1980s, the AINSU attracted burgeoning Nepali politicians into its ranks, including Baburam Bhattarai and Hisila Yami, top Maoist politburo leaders, who served key leadership positions in the AINSU while studying at Jawaharlal Nehru University in the early 1980s. Both Nepali and Indian student activists from those times recollected that they were ideologically and personally kindred because they struggled together during their formative years. Pradip Giri emphasized this, saying,

"These are not only relationships between school friends; they are relationships of political ideology and commitment."[7] These relationships and networks are deep and long-lasting and continue to shape the political circles Nepali activists move within as well as their political perspectives.

Different communist parties have also cultivated other political networks and ideological linkages, all of which derive their lineage from Marx and Lenin, and some, in particular the Maoists, extend it to Stalin, Mao, and Abimael Guzman, the commander of Peru's Shining Path insurgency. The Communist Party of Nepal (CPN) split over ideology multiple times during the Panchayat era, including a split over support for Soviet-style communism or Chinese-style communism. Nevertheless, the left-leaning parties—particularly the CPN in all its iterations—are known to be staunchly nationalist and anti-Indian (Hachhethu 2002). Their connections to transnational networks are not at odds with their nationalism because the basis of their ideology is a universalistic commitment against class inequity. An ANNFSU (Akhil) ex–student leader emphasized this after returning from a post in Budapest, where he served as the Asia-Pacific region vice president of the World Federation of Democratic Youth.[8] He explained that the CPN-UML and ANNFSU (Akhil) commitment to fight exploitation in Nepal was part of a larger project to decrease exploitation in the world. Participating in INGOs like the World Federation of Democratic Youth allowed them to "connect with comrades" who were "fighting for the same goal in different countries." He stated, "We [gave] them support and we receive[d] support," mainly moral, through advocacy and lobbying. As he explained, "The World Federation of Democratic Youth backed us in our fight against autocracy and imperialism domestically and regionally because that is part of the organization's mission."[9] His emphasis on domestic and regional autocracy and imperialism is notable because it intimates that they used these connections to counter Indian regional interference as much as domestic political obstacles.

Another left-leaning political network is the connection of the CPN (Maoist) to the Revolutionary Internationalist Movement (RIM). The Communist Party Nepal (Masal) was a founding member of RIM when it was established in 1984, and many of its leaders, including Mohan Baidya and Baburam Bhattarai, established the CPN (Maoist). The Maoists ideologically embedded their People's War in the world revolution, in which the CPN (Maoist) people's army is a counterpart of RIM's international proletariat army. In May 1996, RIM issued a May Day statement supporting the People's War in Nepal as furthering the embryonic struggle of the international proletariat.

It claimed that this initiation of war had transformed Nepal from a "backward oppressed country to an advanced outpost of the world proletarian revolution" (*A World to Win* 1996).

The CPN (Maoist) has been transparent about RIM's theoretical and practical contributions to its party agenda (A. Adhikari 2014). The Prachanda Path echoes RIM's revolutionary mission: "This synthesis of Nepalese experience is based upon the indivisible dialectical relationship between international essence and national expression, universality and particularity, the whole and the part, the general and the particular, and it objectively serves the world proletarian revolution and proletarian internationalism" (*Revolutionary Worker* 2000). In May 2001, RIM applauded the Prachanda Path as forging the correct strategy for the revolution in Nepal and pledged its allegiance to the revolution in Nepal as part of RIM's political agenda (RIM Committee 2001). The CPN (Maoist) also learned from other wars, including that of the Communist Party of Peru (PCP), and from the experiences in Turkey, Iran, the Philippines, Bangladesh, and Sri Lanka. At the same time, members of the CPN (Maoist) attribute their understanding of the whole process of their own people's war to the direct and continuous debate with their Indian communist comrades, mainly with the People's War Group (PWG), Maoist Communist Centre (MCC), Revolutionary Communist Centre of India (MLM), and Revolutionary Communist Centre of India (Maoist).

As this history demonstrates, scalar politics have been central to Nepali ideological and socio-political development. Yet, it is also a specter undermining Nepal's sovereignty. Pradip Giri underscored this point when analyzing the connection between anti-Indian sentiment and Nepali nationalism.[10] He explained that there are three things all political actors in Nepal have in common: first, when they oppose the established power, they are branded as anti-national; second, when they become the established power, they brand the opposition as anti-national; and, third, while in power, they all bargain with Delhi (the Indian state) and try to leverage whatever influence through their Indian political networks when they are out of power. A report by the International Crisis Group analyzing the 2015 constitutional promulgation echoes this as well: "There is undoubtedly Indian influence in Nepal's politics, but the outcry over sovereignty can be specious. The media regularly reports on politicians' visits to New Delhi to seek support ahead of government changes in Kathmandu. Politicians and commentators are pleased to use Indian influence if New Delhi agrees with their position or can help their political fortunes" (ICG 2016: 24). Nepal's history of scalar politics challenges the liberal assumption that there has ever been a separation between domestic and foreign politics (cf. Keck and Sikkink 1998: 214–15). National-istic fears of Nepal's sovereignty being eroded by interventions resulting from scalar politics speak to Nepal's structurally weak position in both regional and global politics. Indian, donor, and INGO presence pose an existential threat, personifying geopolitical structural inequalities (ICG 2016) while also playing a dialogical role in Nepal's political progress.

SOCIO-POLITICAL SHIFTS AFFECTING SCALAR POLITICS IN THE TWENTY-FIRST CENTURY

"In those days, India was the only window we had to the rest of the world," Pradip Giri asserted, comparing the difference between politics during the Panchayat era and afterward. He continued, "These days Nepal is open."[11] The country's being open—politically, economically, and socially—was the most distinct difference between the experience of the twenty-first-century student activists and that of previous generations. The 1990 People's Move-ment marked this shift. The movement's main demands were the right to competitive politics, the right to public gathering, a free press, and the right to consume. All four were achieved during the last decade of the twentieth century. Democratic competitive politics opened up to alternative forms of oppositional politics, including ethnic and identity politics (Hangen 2007, 2010; Gellner 2009). The right to consume translated into liberal market reform that opened Nepal's domestic market to foreign consumer goods and relaxed restrictions on international investment (Rankin 2004). Thus, Nepal's economic and political opening to the world in the 1990s and early 2000s increased the student activists' ability to mobilize scalar politics beyond India, and they became adept at leveraging these networking oppor-tunities to their political advantage.

The presence of bilateral and multilateral donors and diplomatic entities in multiparty Nepal greatly enabled the transnational component of the student activists' scalar politics. Donors and international agencies have had increasing influence in Nepal since the 1960s, focusing on infrastruc-ture, education, and poverty alleviation as well as humanitarian and con-flict interventions. Nepal received increasing amounts of aid from both the United States and the Soviet Union through the 1980s due to its non-alignment policy during the Cold War (Khadka 2000). Foreign aid covered 20 percent of government expenditure from 1960 to 1992, incrementally increasing to 80 percent by 1992 and then steadily dropping to a little less than 50 percent by the turn of the century (Bhattarai 2005).

The main factor that amplified Nepal's aid dependency was the way that donor and INGO aid distribution shifted in the 1990s after multiparty democracy was instituted. During the Panchayat era, aid was channeled through the central government to district and local village development committees according to the government's national development plans. In the 1990s and 2000s, the model for foreign aid investment distribution was increasingly scale dependent; large-scale national policy initiatives involved coordination between donors and INGOs and government ministries and agencies, and programmatic work at the local level required services provided by local partners. NGOs rapidly spawned as a result, from 221 NGOs in 1990 to 30,000 by 2011 (Yogi 2012). By 2014, 40,000 NGOs and 189 INGOs representing twenty-five countries were registered with the Social Welfare Council (*Himalayan Times* 2014). NGOs typically fall within the rubric of civil society organizations; however, this particular aid-driven model created a mushrooming of politically aligned NGOs (Ismail 2014) that competed for aid resources to bolster the parties' authority as resource distributors. Thus, NGOs, particularly in rural Nepal, became a central node in the party patronage-based networks within which student activists were intimately entangled.

Nepal's increasing political volatility from the mid-1990s onward opened the country up to ever more donor and diplomatic intervention. Unstable politics resulting from the civil war, the palace massacre, the 2002 dismissal of parliament, and increasing human rights violations and disappearances gave cause for concern. The International Red Cross, the Office of the United Nations High Commissioner for Human Rights (OHCHR), Amnesty International, and the International Crisis Group became investigative fixtures in war-torn Nepal, tracking the Maoists' and national security forces' violations of UN declarations and international law. Nevertheless, accusations over the donor and aid agencies' track record of co-constructing governance in Nepal and then pathologizing Nepal's "state fragility" in an ahistorical manner to justify ever-increasing intervention are appropriately salient (S. Tamang 2012).

This dynamic was unfolding during the students' Movement Against Regression protests. The UN and many embassies—namely, the Indian, US, and British embassies—played a central role in army training to minimize human rights violations, interfacing with a range of political actors as well as diplomatic back-channeling to manufacture a peaceful political situation. After King Gyanendra's second declared state of emergency in February 2005 and the mass arrests of high-profile political, civil society, media, and public intellectual advocates, there was a growing consensus that the king needed to be removed from the equation. Different Indian government agencies helped coordinate the Maoists' and the political parties' 2005 liaison in Delhi, which led to a twelve-point agreement (A. Adhikari 2014; Jha 2014a; von Einsiedel, Malone, and Pradhan 2012).

The culmination of transnational governing occurred during Nepal's post-conflict transition after King Gyanendra stepped down and the political parties and Maoists engaged in peace talks (Shneiderman and Snellinger 2014). From 2006 to 2010, the United Nations Mission in Nepal (UNMIN) played a mediating role in the peace talks between the political parties and the Maoists, overseeing the CA elections, monitoring the Maoist cantonments, and integrating the Maoist army into the Nepal Army. UN governance took a more central role in Nepal's post-conflict agenda after 2006, which drastically altered the dynamics of aid distribution and bilateral and multilateral cooperation. INGOs and donors bypassed the government to work directly with NGOs and create parallel aid structures (Subedi 2009). Foreign donor and diplomatic interventions with the intention of saving Nepal from itself for the past decade and a half have institutionalized "govern[ing] beyond the state" (Pierre and Peters 2000: 12).

The student activists were an explicit focus of donors and diplomatic interventions. Foreign analysts sought out student leaders to gather alternative perspectives on the volatile political situation. The main reason that embassies and donors sought out these young people, however, was to cultivate them. These foreign entities were interested in courting the coming generation of political leaders and promoting particular values: respect for social, political, and human rights; non-contentious political action; rule of law; transparency; and minority empowerment. That they recognized their political potential is demonstrated by diplomatic cables that were sent during US ambassador James Moriarty's tenure and later released on WikiLeaks.[12] These cables recount the historic role that student politics has played in Nepal, provide bibliographic summaries of high-profile student leaders in the Movement Against Regression, and speak of student activism's potential to counter autocracy and Maoism and deepen Nepal's democracy.

The US embassy made a conscious effort to connect with youth activists and encourage them to "advocate for democratic values and freedom peacefully."[13] I became familiar with the embassy's agenda to court student activists after I met the US Mission in Nepal's communications director during my research on a Fulbright IIE grant. She asked me to introduce her team

Student sit-in held in front of the United Nations Mission in Nepal's headquarters, Naya Baneshwor, Kathmandu, 2006.

to promising student leaders. In particular, she was interested in promoting locally influential women, inviting them over to her house once a month to network and discuss solutions to Nepal's problems. She invited me to attend along with female students, so I brought Risha. I also attended informal gatherings hosted by junior foreign officers to bring civil society and student youth leaders together to exchange ideas in an "open environment."[14] The US Mission also recruited me to help organize a networking conference that brought together youth activists from member countries of the South Asian Association for Regional Cooperation (SAARC) to encourage cross-fertilization of ideas.[15]

The US Mission in Nepal organized the "South Asian Regional Student Leader Conference: Establishing an Agenda for Change through Dialogue," which was scheduled for the week after King Gyanendra's 2005 state of emergency. Over one hundred youth activists from Afghanistan, Pakistan, India, Bangladesh, and Sri Lanka, as well as the US diplomatic teams from those countries, were expected to attend. The king's government granted authorization to hold the conference; however, the embassy was warned not to raise issues that would disrupt "social harmony." There was concern whether any of the Nepali student activists would participate. Many had already been arrested, and a number of others were in hiding to avoid arrest. The US Mission staff reached out to the invited students and offered them a diplomatic escort to the resort where the conference was being held. Some agreed and attended. For others, it was too risky. Akash, for instance, had credible information that plainclothes officers were planted outside the resort's gates, waiting to arrest him. Salini attended but declined a diplomatic escort. She surreptitiously entered through a back entrance and stayed on-site the entire conference. She explained that she had worked closely with the US Mission's director to organize the conference, and she thought that it was important to make contacts with the student leaders from other countries so they knew the threats Nepali activists were facing.

While attending the conference, I managed to meet Akash a few times during his time in hiding. At one point, he noted that those who were at the US Mission's conference and those who were not indicated who was influential and who was trying to gain influence. He explained: "Those who didn't go because they've been arrested or they're at risk already are influential enough to threaten the king's regime. Those who went don't have any clout, so they are taking advantage of the opportunity to amass influence with foreigners."[16] His observation points to the factors motivating activists' scalar politics. However, even at that time, Akash was not willing to eschew foreign connections. He admitted that he would have attended if doing so did not put him in danger. He was interested in meeting the other SAARC activists. They must have had connections if the US embassy invited them, he reckoned, although they were probably "establishment" activists.

Akash's international connections provided him with a modicum of safety when he finally was arrested in April 2005. A Nepali acquaintance, who worked for the International Crisis Group, went to the jail where Akash was purportedly being held. As he arrived, the Red Cross International's delegation team had just received official confirmation that Akash was being detained there. The sub-inspector refused my friend's visit request, and in response my friend warned him: "Remember, the world is watching. You can't disappear him."[17] The following July, the International Commission of Jurists sent representatives to attend Akash's habeas corpus hearing. Having attained international exposure on the streets during the Movement Against Regression, Akash and others were afforded this privilege, which protected them from being among the disappeared, unlike the hundreds of suspected Maoist combatants or informants who did not have relationships with the international media, human rights organizations, donors, and diplomats.

Another notable opportunity that allowed these activists to scale their influence was international junkets. Typically, these junkets were focused on governance and democracy training, hosted by INGOs, donors, or embassies. All five of the former student leaders had visited countries on political or diplomatic-related programs. Lagan's only visit was to China, on an invitation from the international relations department of the Chinese Communist Party. The rest had gone to multiple countries. Risha, Salini, and Akash had circumnavigated the globe, including stops in the United States under the auspices of the International Visitor Leadership Program. Salini even visited North Korea.

The main benefit they attributed to their travel was the opportunity to see how other political and economic systems work and better understand Nepal's geopolitical position. As Salini succinctly noted: "Seeing things with your eyes makes them more durable in your memory than the things you learn and read in books. And through interaction you come to see things from others' viewpoint."[18] Gyanu and Akash also emphasized that traveling broadened their perspectives and allowed them to develop a critical view of society beyond the Nepali context. Gyanu explained that during the war their interactions with all sectors of Nepali society really allowed them to understand the country's external form (*rup*) and essence (*sār*). While traveling in different countries, he endeavored to identify these mechanisms to understand how different societies operate: "Some places seem so developed and progressed. They have clean roads and tall modern buildings. But how are their education systems and health provisions? Are people happy? What's the impact of the economy on people's lives?"[19] Finland, he noted, was the country with the least contradiction between its form and essence. He believed that he had become a more rigorous intellectual by engaging in these assessments during his travels.

Salini, Risha, Gyanu, and Akash thought that the exchanges and interactions they had on junkets also provided them with experience and confidence and broadened their networks. Risha admitted that going to the United States on the leadership program groomed her by providing "quality leadership training, exposure, and recognition."[20] They advocated for women's and youth issues and at times persuaded donors or political representatives to make these issues a central part of their Nepal-related policy. Akash expressly noted that he used these travel opportunities to meet with members of the Nepali diaspora. Nepali organizations exist worldwide; some are politically affiliated and others are non-partisan. He prioritized their invitations because, he explained: "Many are first-generation living abroad.

They care what happens in Nepal, and they can influence their friends and families back home. To win the support of one family in the United Kingdom can lead to the support of ten families in Nepal." Gaining the support of diaspora organizations is wise because they are able to compel party leaders by expressing their support or exerting political pressure through donations, "which is something party leaders listen to."[21] Thus, Akash's scalar politics unsettle Keck and Sikkink's boomerang pattern by demonstrating that it is not merely transnational activist networks that apply domestic pressure, but due to increasing global migration, networks that once were local are now transnational and can be leveraged to pressure the political status quo in new ways.

SCALAR POLITICS THROUGH TRADITIONAL AND ALTERNATIVE MEDIA

A burgeoning free press through the 1990s also influenced how students negotiated scalar politics in the twenty-first century. While media opened up Nepal in significant ways, there were legal, social, and other structural factors that limited many activists' ability to use the newly freed press to amplify their voices. Thus, marginalized voices relied on alternative media outlets beyond the national press. The Maoists in particular faced strident censorship measures, which led them to be some of the earliest politicos to adopt cyber media. The student activists on the streets during the Movement Against Regression were keen to connect with journalists both domestic and international to garner political capital beyond their parties. Those who were able to make such inroads benefited greatly from the positive feedback loop that international coverage provided. Those who were not as lucky readily embraced social media such as Facebook and Twitter to sidestep what they saw were limitations of traditional media.

All media was state controlled during the Panchayat era. Activists of the 1990 People's Movement were convinced that a free press was a necessary component to a liberal democratic system. To institute media as a productive mainstay of democratic freedom, the 1990 constitution included the right to freedom (article 12), the press and publication right (article 13), the right to privacy (article 22), and the Civil Rights Act of 1955. In 1991, parliament passed the Press and Publications Act, which allowed no pre-censorship (section 12) and included the No Cancellation of Registration Act (section 13). In the same year, the government also enforced the Press and Publication

Regulation and the Working Journalist Act (CEHURDES 2001: 8–9). These bills were passed amid a number of bills ensuring and promoting press freedom, safety of journalists and media workers, human rights, and individual freedom of expression, including the Universal Declaration of Human Rights and the International Covenant on Civil and Political Rights.

Despite the constitutional measures taken to ensure freedom of the press, there were legal obstacles installed to curtail the press's wholesale freedom. In the 1991 Press and Publications Act, section 14 declared a prohibition on publications, in which the state retained the right to prohibit publications that disrespected the monarchy, undermined the nation's sovereignty, breached national security, promoted communal and ethnic conflict, or "adversely affected the ethics, morals, and social mores of the public" (CEHURDES 2001: 10). This section put broad but vague limitations on the press, leaving many actions and statements vulnerable to misinterpretation and state censorship. The Restriction on Publication (section 15 of the same act) put limitations on the private press, stating that the state-run press could make the private press accountable to whatever authority it designates. The Treason Act (section 4) of the constitution was also used to censor a number of journalists and activists for challenging the king or the sovereignty of Nepal, either directly or indirectly. The vague wording of these ordinances allowed the government flexibility to tighten the grips on media when needed.

A number of social factors also limited Nepali media from being inclusive and balanced. Less than ten years into Nepal's free press experiment, a prominent political columnist, C. K. Lal, determined that "media is politics" (Rayamajhi and Subedi 1999: 46). It was a common criticism leveled against Nepal's mainstream media. Commercial investments in private media were not diverse enough to encourage a non-partisan press. Advertising was unable to generate large revenues for newspapers because consumer patterns were not steady enough at the time. Therefore, the media options were hyper-local dailies, the political parties' mouthpieces (*mukh patra*), or a few Nepali and English national dailies supported by a handful of tycoons who had both economic and political interests for investing. Corporate media houses supported by Kathmandu's power centers had to play it safe to avoid offending various camps (Onta 2002: 263). Another structural limitation in the burgeoning mediascape was that the majority of journalists were educated high-caste or Kathmandu Newar males (265). The demographic makeup of media mirrored that of political parties and bureaucracy through the 1990s and into the 2000s. Thus, rather than broaden coverage, socio-political bias created a media focused on Kathmandu and party politics, allowing little room for voices of women and minorities or news from the countryside.

Alternative voices instead found outlets through small presses and radio stations. By the end of 2000, 1,536 newspapers were registered with the district administration offices throughout the country, many of them politics-, religious-, gender-, caste-, or ethnic-issue-based publications (CEHURDES 2001: 11). Through the 1990s, radio was slowly becoming a popular medium for alternative press, too, but it was more difficult to secure licenses and was expensive to operate (cf. Kunreuther 2014). Thus, the degree to which alternative media outlets were able to disseminate news and information depended on money, connections, and support. There were no restrictions on Internet media, but it was not a common format at the turn of the century because most citizens did not have regular access. At the time, alternative media used the Internet to broaden its readership beyond Nepal.

Like all Nepali political parties, the Maoists developed their own mouth-pieces to publicize their ideas and programs that the mainstream media refused or failed to cover. These publications, however, did not bring them from the margins into mainstream discourse. In 2000, foreign journalists were invited to Dolakha and Sindhupalchok to observe their strongholds. The Maoists courted the mainstream international press to project them-selves as a viable alternative to the monarchy's constitutional democracy. Their contact with international journalists, however, was brief. The state blocked journalists' access to the Maoists by blacklisting them as terrorists. As of August 2000, all police forces were to report information only to police headquarters in Kathmandu for dissemination; this resulted in an immedi-ate embargo of media in Maoist stronghold areas. The Maoists were then compelled to turn to the Internet as an alternative media outlet, making them the first political force to embrace Internet technology as a central medium of information dissemination.

The Maoists' embrace of cyber media was further precipitated by the 2001 state of emergency. On November 26, 2001—five days after official peace talks failed, NR 225 million were stolen and sixty-four police and national soldiers and sixty Maoist rebels died in skirmishes—the House of Representatives voted by a two-thirds majority to allow the king to declare a state of emergency under the authority of article 115 of the constitution. This government suspended the right to freedom of opinion and expression, the press and publication right, the right to information, the right to privacy, and access to judicial remedy (apart from habeas corpus) provided by article 23. The state of emergency's impact on press, radio, and television was sweeping. Papers were seized and censored, including the shuttering of ten radical-left newspapers (CEHURDES 2001). One hundred and thirty journalists were arrested, some held on ninety-day charges and others detained for much longer without having been officially charged (CEHURDES 2001). Zones of silence expanded in war-torn rural areas because news collection and dissemination was nearly impossible.

Soon after the state of emergency, the Ministry of Information came out with a list of dos and don'ts to establish parameters for the media (CEHURDES 2001). Everything—words, expressions, actions, non-action—became hypercharged and suspect, creating cultural and social dislocation that was both structural and symbolic. It perpetuated a sense of chaos and fear to curb dissent. Most mainstream journalists were able to keep themselves safe through self-censorship and avoiding investigative journalism. An editor at the *Kathmandu Post* explained that there were no specific parameters set on the newspaper by its editorial board. People knew to follow the Ministry of Information guidelines and not to ask about the lack of information. He recollected that there were fewer disputes with editors over wording and details during the state of emergency. "We just used common sense and kept safe."[22] This situation changed, however, on June 6, 2001, after *Kantipur* published an opinion article by Maoist leader Baburam Bhattarai outlining the conspiracy behind the palace massacre. *Kantipur*'s managing director, Yubaraj Ghimire, and directors, Kailash Sirohiya and Binod Raj Gyawali, were arrested for sedition—a charge that carried up to three years' imprisonment.

The state used all the means at its disposal to obstruct Maoists' efforts to report their version of the People's War. At the turn of the century, the Internet was largely unregulated in Nepal and thus became an ideal outlet for the Maoists to bypass state-enforced censorship. The website Humans Rights and People's War in Nepal became the online mouthpiece for the Maoist movement in Nepal. It hosted a number of articles, official statements, conference notes, and Maoist political journals, including the *Worker*, a monthly dedicated solely to the documentation of the events of the Maoist movement. It also maintained an updated list of martyrs of the People's War. This documentation simultaneously informed human rights organizations of loss of life when the Nepali security forces' reporting was suspect, memorialized these individuals, and demonized the security forces while legitimizing the People's War.

The Maoist movement also benefited from its connection with RIM to bring its activism online. Web journals such as *A World to Win* and *Dispatches* documented Nepal's Maoist movement. Li Onesto, an American journalist who spent time in Maoist stronghold areas, regularly reported the Maoists' progress and contribution to the international socialist struggle. She viewed her reporting as fueling a dialectic between Nepali Maoists and their international comrades.[23] Consequently, the international support provided legitimacy to the Maoist insurgency when it was being dismissed by the Kathmandu establishment. When discussing the role of the Internet during the People's War, Gyanu explained to me that the Internet was able to protect and propagate their story.[24]

By the time the students were protesting in the Movement Against Regression, the state of emergency that had squelched oppositional media, as well as the parliament that approved it, was disbanded. A *Nepali Times* article at the time refuted suppression of the press by asserting that currently "free press is oxygen for democracy" and documenting the following:

> There is so much free expression that not a day goes by without multiple rallies on the streets of the capital. And Nepali media is freer today than it has ever been. The pro-Maoist papers have restarted, the political mouth-pieces of the various parties are at the vanguard of their pro-democracy agitation, the private corporate media is vibrant and growing, news and current affairs on community FM stations have transformed the way many Nepalis receive information, and soon private television will change the media landscape beyond recognition. In fact, we can say without brag-ging that in the post-emergency and post-ceasefire months, Nepal has enjoyed one of the freest media in the world. (*Nepali Times* 2003)

While this statement is overblown, it is true that student activists benefited from both the domestic and international presses' ability to cover their street protests. The media spotlight gave them a platform to establish them-selves as public figures beyond their parties. Mainstream journalists were happy to publicize the students' transgressive protests because they were sensational: violating sedition laws, committing vandalism, burning effigies of the king, establishing campuses as republican zones, felicitating dogs in lieu of the king (cf. Snellinger 2016a). Mainstream press coverage of the students framed them as political alternatives to the king and their party leadership while still promoting multiparty democracy.

Many of the journalists who covered these protests were schoolmates or were socially connected to the student activists and either tacitly or overtly supported their opposition against the king and party leadership. These personal connections reverberated when foreign journalists came to cover the street protests. Foreign journalists relied on local journalists and analysts for contacts, which benefited the student leaders who were linked into domestic media and intelligentsia networks. International and domestic media publicity bolstered particular activists' political careers. When I met Akash in hiding during the 2005 state of emergency, I asked him why he thought he was on the security forces' list of highest priority arrests, and he replied: "Because they know I inspire people and can get them to mobilize. Plus, the local media may be gagged right now, but the foreign media still publicizes my cause."[25]

This positive feedback loop may have benefited certain activists, but it served as yet another gatekeeping measure for others. I recall that being an issue for Darshan, a student from the NC (D). He and his fellow NSU (D) students did not participate in the Movement Against Regression because their leader, Sher Bahadur Deuba, was blamed for enabling the king's takeover. The two NC parties' reunification before the 2008 CA elections affected both NSU factions as well. Both had recently held their union conventions. Darshan had secured a high-level position on the NSU (D) central committee, but he was worried that he would not retain his position after reunification because he had less clout than many NSU (K) student leaders. He attributed that to their street credibility and explained with frustration: "These days nobody is known for their political abilities. They are known for burning tires, getting arrested, or [getting] injured on the streets." He cited the infamous picture of Salini bloodied from a rock police pelted at her head; the picture had become synonymous with the students' struggles against the king. He asked rhetorically, "Do you think people know her political strengths? No, they know that picture. The media has made them famous based on their protests."[26] His observations were astute. Those whom the media promoted as the future leaders of the country had more experience vandalizing property, chanting slogans, and delivering fiery speeches, rather than proficiently running an organization. They were valorized for qualities not suitable to governing. But Darshan's complaint was more about not having the opportunity to establish his own media platform since he did not participate in contentious politics at the time. That put him at a disadvantage during the NC's reunification. His position had eroded after he was appointed one of five vice presidents on the NSU's reunified central committee.

Media photographing a student activist defying the government-enforced protest ban. Bāg Bazār, Kathmandu, 2004.

Social media such as Facebook and Twitter have provided people like Darshan in particular with a disseminating outlet despite lack of access to traditional media. The same is true for organizations and causes. Lagan admitted to me that social media has been a useful platform for small parties like his, which have never been a part of the power center that media "naturally focuses on."[27] But since it is a technology available to everyone, the

Media documenting arrest of activists during the government-enforced protest ban. Bāg Bazār, Kathmandu, 2004

effects of such access are negligible. The Workers and Peasants Party may have a Facebook page and Twitter feed, but so does every political outfit ranging down to the campus and village levels. In this regard, social media has merely extended the reach of party mouthpieces, allowing them to become paperless and amass a following beyond geographic locality.

Every politician and activists, big and small, must maintain a social media presence. Established political leaders, including Akash, have media assistance to help maintain their profiles and update their message. Nevertheless, social media allows people like Akash or Salini to speak directly to their audience rather than be filtered through a media lens, which they say gives them more control over their image. Risha uses her own Facebook page and her women's network's to showcase her social and political work. She explained to me: "I post pictures of programs I organize to show who attends. It allows me to show my sponsors, party members, and the women I serve the influential reach I have. It gives them confidence in my work and they support me to keep doing it."[28]

For Gyanu, social media became useful after he defected from the UCPN (Maoist). He heavily relied on Facebook to broadcast his criticism when the first CA dissolved and to encourage people to boycott the second CA election.

He must wear two hats now that he is in an opposition splinter party: he is an intellectual who writes books and op-eds on socio-political critique, and he is an online activist who informs people about programs and his opinions on everyday matters. These two roles are necessary, he believes, because he has two different audiences to reach, engaged intellectuals and the masses. Facebook allows him to maintain his relevancy by interacting with general people and fellow cadres. He noted that he tried to promote debate on Facebook, but "nobody is interested in engaging substantial issues on social media." For this reason, he thinks the potential of the technology is being squandered and many just use it as "timepass."[29]

All five of the ex–student leaders use social media to broadcast, connect, gauge public opinion, and derive support. Salini said that it keeps her grounded because people's comments allow her to "self-examine and hear if what we [her party] are doing is working." She also added that it provides her with a perspective beyond the party, particularly when her party disappoints her expectations: "They [Facebook friends] console me, saying the party might have chosen to do something else due to its own provisions, but it is injustice to me. Thus, they move the debate forward about how I am treated. It forces party leaders to answer challenging questions. Sometimes it makes such a stir that it becomes a news topic. People online also advise me on how [I] should proceed."[30] Risha echoed this sentiment, explaining that the leaders are afraid of social media because they cannot control it the way they control other things. She said social media has kept the current leaders from being dictatorial like the Ranas or the Panchayat leaders.[31] Akash admitted that social media has chipped away at traditional media's ability to craft public opinion or political leadership's ability to control the narrative, but he was dubious about its structural impact. He asked whether things have really changed in politics or society.[32]

Except for Akash, who does not manage his own Facebook page, the rest of these individuals use Facebook beyond broadcasting themselves to maintain relationships both local and afar. Facebook is a key way for Risha to stay in touch with women she meets at international and local workshops. For me as well, when I am outside of Nepal, Facebook, Twitter, and Viber are the lines of communication I use with all of my interlocutors. It allows me to stay updated on their lives, their achievements and disappointments, and the day-to-day goings-on of politics. Social media enables us to participate in each other's lives. This is a central component of their scalar politics. It is as much about the forging and maintenance of personal relationships as it is about the extended support or influence gained.

SCALING LATERALLY

Risha's national network of women's organizations is a multifaceted example of scalar politics. As a product, the network demonstrates how she has harnessed resources and connections to pursue her own agenda. From the moment I met Risha, she has engaged a range of overlapping political and social networks, continually cultivating local, national, international, and transnational connections. She leveraged these associations to secure her position and ensure that her influence is continually replicated. Risha also mobilized her burgeoning transnational connections to scale her endeavors laterally, which has allowed her to avoid relying on party leaders to achieve her goals. She is now in a position to provide opportunities and cultivate her own following. Her story demonstrates how transnational networks transform the individuals who participate in them (Keck and Sikkink 1998).

Risha's network resulted from a series of workshops in 2007, hosted by the Centre for Development and Population Activities (CEDPA), a women's empowerment INGO, which brought together women activists and social entrepreneurs to discuss advocacy to ensure women's rights in the new constitution. It comprises thirty-six women's NGOs throughout the country, and it runs programs in forty-five districts. Risha realized that to truly change women's lives they needed to address laws and policies. Thus, the initial aim of the network was to lobby the CA on women's issues, including distributing the Charter for Women's Rights to all 601 CA members and registering it with the National Women's Commission. The network also lobbied the Truth and Reconciliation Commission to maintain international treaties on gender sensitivity.

By 2009, the network expanded its work to include training and awareness programs, which allowed it to sustain its advocacy work. It secured contracts from the Asia Foundation and the UNDP's Support to Participatory Constitution Building in Nepal to run interaction programs between CA members and different citizen stakeholders in various districts. I attended its programs in Gorkha and Mugling in 2011 to get a sense of how it was pursuing its mission, "fostering collaboration between government authorities and grassroots communities."[33] The notable thing about the network's programming model is that it provides training and opportunity to the women who work in the network-affiliated NGOs to run the programs in their localities and other districts. For each program, Risha and her team work with the network's local NGOs as well as Risha's other connections in the area, which are contracted to oversee logistics, including inviting local attendees, securing the venue, printing programs, and providing meals. Risha and her team come to work alongside the local women facilitating the program. From what I observed, much of the two-day program was an educational session on the CA body, its mandate, and different amendments, culminating with a brainstorming session compiling suggestions and priorities the CA should undertake.

The network has branched out since 2013, also running programs to coordinate zero-waste zones and recycling initiatives. Like many other organizations with deep local networks, it mobilized quickly after the 2015 earthquakes to provide on-the-ground support through local contacts. They set up hotlines, providing guidance on getting government earthquake support, and focused on distributing material support to single women who lost their homes. The network secured a five-year contract from the Asia Foundation to ensure gender and social inclusion in post-earthquake rebuilding.

When I asked Risha what inspired her to make this network her main priority, she said it had a lot to do with her transition from the *āndolan*:

> I was examining my role in the party. There should have been a chance for me to implement some of the demands I was raising. But it was not happening. It felt narrowed down—there were a lot of limitations and hooks. Then I had a realization that, ultimately, I grew up from a mass of activists on the streets. Nothing was given to our generation who had contributed so much through our activism. This happened after party politics became mainstream again. There was no role for my generation. I felt we had to search for a role. Plus, I am a woman. I looked around, and some of my fellow activists had gotten opportunit[ies]. Why didn't I? This is because I am a woman and a youth. Both positions are marginal. Instead of remaining inactive or going abroad, I realized I must struggle here by changing my role. So I worked to establish this women's network.[34]

Since I first met Risha, she was very clear that her motivation was to be a leader because the country needed female leaders. She was disappointed with the direction national politics had taken. She bitterly expressed frustration over political nepotism. Finally, she realized that she could accomplish what she wanted to do through social activism instead, and, as a woman, there was support and a venue to address the issues that mattered to her rather than being, as she put it, "the token woman at the table."

Risha was forthcoming about the benefits her foreign connections had yielded. She thanked me for opening doors by introducing her to the US

Mission's director. It allowed her to help organize the South Asia youth activist conference and demonstrate her ability to lead. She was then invited to visit the United States through the international leadership program. Later, the US embassy sponsored her to go to the Women Lead in Peace and Stability conference in Washington, DC, hosted by CEDPA, where she met women from twenty-two war-affected countries and got to "hear their stories and learn from them." After she returned to Nepal, she received a number of invitations, including the South Asian youth donors' conference in the United Kingdom and a transitional justice workshop in Germany.

These opportunities helped her in her private, political, and professional life. They made her realize that she had a voice as she advocated to donors to invest in youth and women's programming, and she learned practical skills such as program management, facilitation skills, and how to design program proposals. These experiences taught her how to be the NGO service provider that the donors want to fund. She once noted that she is always "on time because she is on donors' time." I looked at her a little puzzled, and she said she is successful and keeps getting project support because she has learned to be "prompt, transparent, and organized."[35] I asked her if it was difficult to change her working style, because politics does not work that way. She shook her head and said no because, as she explained, "[the donors] saved my activism"; they believed in her by supporting her programs and motivating her. She said that with their contributions she has had the opportunity to travel throughout the country and disseminate her ideas; plus, it has given her confidence, knowledge, and a bit of financial security.

Risha's perseverance has paid off on multiple fronts as she has established herself as an influential social activist and deepened her political network. She was proud to tell me that people, both big and small, vouch for her abilities. When I joined her on programs in Gorkha and Mugling, I observed how she maximizes her time to connect with an array of different groups. While we were there we met with the NC district committee, the NSU district committee, and local campus students, local female activists and others known for their social service as well as a family of an NSU martyr killed during the war. Risha interfaced with multiple strands of Gorkha bazaar's social and political web through these external meetings as well as the meetings she had with the local headmaster, parent-teacher association leaders, and forest resource committee members who arranged for their students and members to attend her program. As we traveled back from Gorkha to Mugling, I noted that the number of people she knows must be incalculable. She matter-of-factly quipped that she has built up a network that covers the whole nation. To acknowledge the power of that, she then noted: "When your network is strong, the leaders call you."[36]

There is pragmatism to Risha's approach; her current work is laying the ground for her political future. Hers is a long-term strategy to be a true leader, a big person (*thulo manchhe*) par excellence. That became apparent after I pushed her on the youth network I overheard her discussing with some of the NSU students in Gorkha. She explained that a youth network would provide support so people were not beholden to one particular leader. She said, "I use my network to give opportunities to youth in different districts." She supports her connections for positions in their districts and guides them as they progress. Eventually, the people she has groomed "throughout the nation will come to the center" (Kathmandu).[37] Cultivating people at the "grass roots" is as much a reaction as it is a strategy. Political patronage did not play out in her favor, as party leaders failed to provide opportunities she thought she deserved. But now she is not limited. She can sit and collaborate with anyone in the party because, she claims, she owes allegiance to no one. Ultimately, Risha is working to shore up enough political capital to avoid relying on party leaders for her advancement and is cultivating her own courtiers whose support will hopefully propel her into party leadership. She is using scalar politics to turn the top-down party hierarchy dynamic on its head to her advantage, yet without unsettling the structure completely.

CONCLUSION

Students' scalar politics highlight the connection between their personal struggles to establish themselves in politics and how political values, ideas, and practices circulate among local, national, and transnational levels. Their scalar politics demonstrate political regeneration (Cole and Durham 2007) rather than vernacularization (Merry 2006) because these young activists are not merely translating universal concepts into a local vernacular. Yet, at the same time, the historicity of their rights claims has never been wholly native in form (cf. Subramanian 2009). Local idioms are not derivative of, or independent from, external political concepts but are instead dialogic, resulting from the social relations Nepali activists have fostered on multiple scales since the Rana regime. It is worth recalling Pradip Giri's point that "these are not only relationships between school friends; they are relationships of political ideology and commitment."[38] My interlocutors mediate this socio-political heritage through the networks they have cultivated in order to craft a political horizon that ensures their place in politics. In doing so, they have introduced new rights claims that refine previous rights claims.

Thus, their scalar politics undermine the liberal assumption that domestic and foreign politics are separate (Keck and Sikkink 1998: 214). Nevertheless, scalar politics exacerbate nationalistic anxieties regarding the erosion of Nepali sovereignty due to the structural inequalities embedded in the regional and transnational relational dynamic. Unfortunately, this anxiety is used to dismiss oppositional rights claims as anti-national rather than seeing them as an investment in Nepal, albeit through contentious claim making meant to disrupt the status quo. This indeed has been the case since Nepal's first *āndolan.*

Conclusion

Dissensus and Political Regeneration

I RETURNED TO NEPAL IN THE SUMMER OF 2015, EAGER TO CON-
nect with friends and interlocutors who were still reeling from the previous
spring's massive earthquakes. I came for follow-up research on a project I
had been conducting since 2013 in southern Nepal looking at the social
practices, livelihood strategies, and the politics of educated, unemployed
youth. A year of research along the Nepal-India border had broadened my
views of Nepali politics significantly. I observed the 2013 CA elections in
Parsa district, interviewed district and local administrators on government
intervention programs, and discussed issues of economy and politics with
villagers and urbanites. I observed how party politics and governance operates at the local and district levels beyond party headquarters, campuses,
and parliament in Kathmandu, the state capital. Working with Madheshi,
Tharu, and migrated hill populations also provided insight into various
socio-political grievances and how diversity is accommodated in city and
village life in southern Nepal.

I returned to collect feedback on a 2,800-household survey on education,
employment, and migration our team conducted in three Parsa villages. I
initially managed to return to all three villages, although with difficulty,
traveling by *tāngā* (horse-drawn carriage) because of region-wide strikes
enforced by Madheshi and Tharu activists. They were protesting the proposed citizenship law, political representation system, and federal-state
delineation in the recently released constitutional draft that was being fast-
tracked toward promulgation.[1] My research agenda was eclipsed by the inten-
sifying political situation. Instead of discussing survey results, I witnessed
rallies, strikes, and blockades protesting promulgation of the proposed
constitution. The security situation quickly deteriorated after seven policemen and a child were killed in the southwest town of Tikapur during a
protest rally. In response, the government clamped down on protests across
the south.

I was in Birganj when the citywide curfews began in response to activists
defying the no-protest zone prohibitions along the India-Nepal highway.

After a few days confined to my hotel—hearing gunshots, inhaling smoke fumes, and trying to stay informed through Twitter and Facebook, phone calls, and conversations with hotel staff and neighboring residents as they yelled from their rooftops—it became clear I should return to Kathmandu. I managed a stealthy departure via village roads on the back of a motorbike. A few kilometers outside Birganj's city limits in the neighboring district of Bara, we blazed past a vandalized police post. A felled tree obstructed the intersection, a tire was smoldering, and the post itself had been knocked over, its corrugated metal door barely holding onto rusty hinges. The motor-bike driver pointed to the police residence, and I could see that the windows had been smashed. He said the police had fled the village. As I wondered if police posts across the area had been targeted, my driver reported that two of the young men who died the previous day, shot for violating the curfew, were apparently brothers from this village.

I waited in Kathmandu for tensions to subside, maintaining close com-munication with my contacts for updates. This of course included my politi-cal party contacts. Considering their own previous political struggles, I found their general lack of empathy disconcerting. Many found the situa-tion problematic, but it was obviously not their battle. Some dismissed the protesters as infiltrators; others lamented the identity-based federalism agenda, saying it had divided the country; and still others dismissed the protesters as lackeys doing the bidding of corrupt leaders who were merely consolidating power through their state delineation demands.

They listened as I told them what I witnessed. It was the process by which the constitution was being fast-tracked that alienated Parsa residents, I asserted. First their political leaders and CA members were ignored and pressured to fall in line with the NC, CPN-UML, and Maoists plurality. Then their activists dissented through the time-honored tactics of strikes (*bandh*) and street protest (*julus*), all to no avail. When protesters defied no-protest zones, the army clamped down rapidly, announcing a curfew with less than three hours warning and using live ammunition against curfew violators. When we had been on the streets together between 2003 and 2006, I explained, no one warned me to "stay inside, because bullets don't have eyes." I never heard mothers shriek with utter terror at their sons playing in the gullies, as I had heard during the curfew in Birganj.

Many were unconvinced. National anxiety increased after the Tikapur incident, following which army mobilization in the south seemed justified. Demands for inclusive enfranchisement and citizenship across the Tarai now rang as anti-national affronts. My inability to compel a number of my long-standing interlocutors to realize the severity of the situation and to convince them that their leadership should delay constitutional promulgation and negotiate a political solution was disheartening. The ultra-nationalist rhetoric coming from some of their party leaders was even more chilling.

I was eager to return to Parsa. I wanted to connect with my many friends and acquaintances as they endured this hardship. And I wanted to personally deliver our final survey reports to the villages. Things calmed down enough the week before the constitution's scheduled promulgation. The curfew was lifted for a couple of hours in the morning and evening each day. Members of an NGO with whom I worked had obtained curfew passes and offered to ferry me around. It seemed we could coordinate our coming and going with the curfew schedule to visit the three villages over a few days. Two NGO workers and my research assistant met me on motorbikes at the Simara airport, about twenty kilometers north of Birganj. We went to the northern-most village to deliver the surveys since it was en route to Birganj. Although people received the reports appreciatively, they were distracted. An elder Tharu leader was visibly upset about what happened in Tikapur, particularly how the national media was framing it to invalidate their demands for a plurality Tharu state. He said it was a targeted attack by a small rebel faction that does not represent the majority view. It was not in the government's interest to publicize that, he surmised, because they wanted to suppress all opposition. The village cooperative workers with whom I coordinated research were worried about communal relations in the village since it is a mix of Tharu, Madheshi, and high-caste and ethnic hill migrants. They had weathered the Maoist war and the 2006–8 Madheshi movement with little intercommunal tension. Nevertheless, the anxiety that such antagonistic politics could disrupt local social cohesion was palpable to these service workers who had dedicated themselves to bettering their village.

I was unable to visit the other two villages. The day after I arrived, the constitution was promulgated. Hundreds of urban and rural residents poured into Birganj to protest. That day I visited the central Narayani hospital and morgue. A young man who was shot during the protest died from bullet wounds to his head and throat. He had just returned from Delhi, having finished a tailor training program. He planned to open a shop in his village. His village neighbored the one in central Parsa where we conducted research. We were unable to return to there and to the southern-most village to deliver our survey reports because of road blockades protesting this young man's death. Among the many protesters who defied the curfews in

Birganj from August 31 to September 20, over two hundred were treated for severe injuries, including gunshot wounds all above the waist, flaunting the United Nations Basic Principles on the Use of Force and Firearms by Law Enforcement Officials, and six young men lost their lives. At least forty-five people across the country, including policemen, protesters, and civilians, died in clashes in August and September 2015.

The protests in Birganj were tamped out by early evening, before the CA gathered in Kathmandu to promulgate the constitution. The streets were desolate. Few but the police in riot gear remained, lingering in the shade of shuttered stores. Those with press and curfew passes whipped on motor-bikes through streets littered with rocks and shattered glass, spent tear-gas shells, and sandals people lost in stampedes fleeing security forces. I chatted with a few local journalists covering the events for Al Jazeera; they were filing their report and uploading video footage at the local TV station.

The clock tower in the center of the bazaar rang out to commemorate promulgation. I snapped a photograph of the clock tower with a crew of exhausted police hunkered below and the sun setting behind it, a lurid pink from the day's heat. I then went into the TV station to watch the live broad-cast of the CA speeches. President Ram Baran Yadav's speech commenced the promulgation process. Two minutes into it, he honored the martyrs who fought for this "inclusive, proportional, and representative constitution." I sighed. All six men in the room shook their heads in disappointment. One said: "Let's get out of here. I can't watch this."[2] As we exited, it struck me that I had spent three years on the streets with the student activists who fought to get these leaders back into power, and now they were claiming to have instituted an inclusive constitution despite widespread discontent, which they were suppressing through alarming means. This further underscored the close-knit relationship between contentious politics and governance in Nepal's political history.

POLITICAL PATHWAYS

The varying paths and evolving political perspectives of Akash, Lagan, Gyanu, Risha, and Salini elucidate the ways that Nepali politics has changed and remained the same through Nepal's political transition. Their paths encapsulate political regeneration as a discursive dynamic between party ideologies, the history of claim making in Nepal's democratic struggle, and new political configurations shaped by their coming-of-age experiences. The themes of this book—the sociality of politics, politics as service and profession, youth as a politically discursive category, organization as noun and verb, political limits and gendered interactions, and scalar politics—emerge as salient elements of their personal narratives, demonstrating that for them the political is personal as much as the personal is political.

Among Akash's peers, his political progression has been exemplary. His rise through the ranks would be enviable to anyone with political ambition. His broad popularity beyond NC supporters has forced his party leaders to ensure his place in government. He was a CA member twice. After serving his appointment to a proportional seat representing the youth demographic in the 2008 CA, he was given a direct election ticket in 2013, which he handily won, securing with over 50 percent of his constituency's vote. Within the NC, he was voted in as member of the central working committee by the twelfth national convention, and in 2015's thirteenth convention he ran for general secretary, even though he was at least twenty years younger than every other candidate. He lost. Some dismissed his running while so junior as hubris, but he claimed he felt compelled to do it for his supporters. The point of running, he explained, was not merely to gain power but to take advantage of the campaign platform to raise issues that mattered to his generation and to press the party leadership for internal change.

Akash's rise has not been without obstacles. These obstacles are by-products of factionalism, patronage, and ageism that structure Nepali party politics. Akash has at times had to embrace these elements to his advantage. But he continues to challenge the NC's party ageist hierarchy by setting himself apart as a marginalized youth leader and counterpoint to the political guard. Thirteen years since my first meeting with Akash, he still deploys youth as a political category to make claims against his party's establishment. During the Movement Against Regression, he cast the monarchy as an antiquated institution of the twentieth century and he encouraged the public to invest in his generation to lead Nepal into the twenty-first century. Now Akash and a few of his cohort are pressing the NC to create more decision-making positions for young leaders. In a declaration to overhaul NC ideology, they asserted that the party has become ossified and will become defunct if his generation is not allowed to transform the party platform. Their line of argumentation has not changed: the young generation of leaders is better positioned to institute new Nepal because they are more in touch with the pressing needs of the country. They claim to be the ones who can develop a new national unity while promoting development. Akash has gone so far to say that such transformations are the agenda of his generation, and only people like him can execute it.[3] The difference between

Akash's and his cohort's current claims as youth and those of yesterday is that during the Movement Against Regression they encouraged the public to reinvest in party politics so they could be leaders tomorrow. This time they are demanding to be leaders today to ensure the NC's political future.

Lagan's path has been the most modest by choice. He embodies the conviction that politics is service. I asked him when we met in 2015 if he was satisfied with his political progression since the movement. He responded: "Some of the friends who worked with us during the movement have reached the CA. Others have been active in party politics. Some others have become frustrated. In my case, I don't have any reason to be frustrated. . . . I have been able to earn social capital by helping people."[4] Lagan's father invested his life in being a devoted cadre, traveling to Jumla, Kalikot, and Dailekh to strengthen their party organization and was even imprisoned for eight years during the Panchayat. The "political culture" Lagan was exposed to at home, he explained, taught him that one entered politics to bring social change. His student days during the Movement Against Regression brought him into politics beyond his community, and then later he worked in the sectors where his party gave him responsibility.

These areas were education and journalism. He has opened schools to serve poor communities in Kavre, Bhaktapur, Sarlahi, Rautahat, and Kailali. He has actively protested the practice of politically appointing seats in university administration in the Teachers' Association of the Colleges. And he is an editor of two newspapers engaged in "mission journalism." He explained, "In the past, we used to spread the revolutionary ideals through our speeches, but nowadays I do so through my writing."

After stating that he has derived satisfaction from serving his party and community, he insisted: "Our protest is meaningful."[5] I thought I misheard him and asked, "You mean your service?" He reasserted that his service and protest are one in the same because, he reasoned, "I am part of a community, so I work to improve everyone's living conditions in my community." This is how service is protest, he explained: his actions change his community. His continued work as a party cadre underscores the sociality that party politics offers people. For many of Lagan's peers, ambition may be ambivalently intertwined with politics, but at the heart of it their political interventions are motivated by the desire to nurture and be nurtured by party, community, and family, whether they call it service or protest.

Gyanu's sentiments also point to the sociality politics engenders; however, he expressed his position through resignation. He described himself to me in 2015 as unemployed. Factionalism had weakened the Maoist cause, and thus there were no tasks for cadres like him. He lamented: "I'm the kind of man who does not like to give much time to my own individual work. Rather, I prefer investing in the organization. But currently, there's not much for me to do in the organization. Therefore, I don't have enough work."[6] Gyanu has always been ambitious, but his ambition is grounded in instituting Maoist ideology through the party. Unfortunately, "the old has been reestablished despite our revolution"; without his party, he has lost his compass and has had difficulty directing his efforts effectively. So he serves as a political commentator, writing op-eds for a mainstream daily, appearing on news shows, and writing books on Maoist ideology. He sees his public role as that of an intellectual (*buddhijībī*), reminding people what the Maoist mission was meant to be, how it has strayed, and how it should progress.

Gyanu's path is an analogue for the Maoist shift from revolutionary politics to mainstream politics. He admitted feeling defeated. He lost his first wife and friends in the People's War. He has sacrificed a lot for the party, which has accomplished little. He sighed, looked at me, and, after a few moments, blankly noted: "We brought the party to the people but not politics to the people."[7] The Maoist party had indeed lost touch with its "master frames" (Snow and Benford 1992: 146). Politicking and personal ambition has muddled the strong link between party ideology and scientific organization, pushing the party further away from its core values and original tenets.

It was why he left the UCPN (Maoist) with Baidya's faction. The terms and theories he used to identify what happened to his party were the same ones he had used to critique other parties vis-à-vis ideology and organization in the past. He explained that the UCPN (Maoist) has a form (*rup*) but internally has lost its essence (*sār*); it has become hollow because members no longer live their ideology. Much of his frustration is with the leadership because of the top-down nature of their party structure. He spoke as a jilted member whose leaders abandoned the organizational contract that gave the party cohesion. He warned: "The party movement can't be led alone. I can't lead it alone nor can the leaders." I asked if there is any solution. Whatever the solution, he said, it has to involve the coming generation: "My experience has been such that the older we get, the less honest we become. When young, people are idealistic and hopeful, but young people don't become leaders." He was not sure how the next generation would emerge, particularly with the languishing of student union politics. But, he concluded, people were frustrated by the lack of development, and eventually that anger would translate into action, leaving "a chance of rebellion in the days to come."[8]

Risha's handling of her transition into mainstream politics epitomizes scalar politics. Nevertheless, the obstacles she has faced encapsulate a number of the challenges party politics engender, namely, factionalism, patronage, and lack of internal democracy. During the 2008 and 2013 CA elections, she was disappointed that her name appeared on the proportional list but she was not appointed a proportional seat. She was particularly frustrated in 2013 for not securing the NC's direct election ticket in her constituency after having established the grassroots support needed to defeat the Maoist incumbent. Instead, a male septuagenarian party loyalist was given the ticket and was defeated. Nevertheless, on a few occasions she admitted relief that she never ended up in the CA. She thought the process made all the CA members look bad, and she was saved from having to compromise her beliefs by toting the party line for this problematic constitution. From the sidelines, she voiced her opposition, and, as she explained, she was able to pitch herself as an "alternative voice," especially on the issue of citizenship.[9]

In 2015, she informed me of her plans to run for a central committee seat from her district constituency at the coming party convention. She had been investing in her constituency by building schools and promoting the rights of marginalized minorities. She explained that in order to be a political leader you must first be a social leader by going into the communities and working for them. Her political and social networking and her support from her constituents made her confident that she had the support necessary to win the seat: "I will compete and win based on my own capability. I will show them I've built my capacity on my own."[10] She did not win the seat. Despite her feeling of confidence that she had the support from all sectors of the party, factionalism and patronage kept many junior party members from voting freely, because they felt pressured to vote according to their party leader's directive. On Facebook, Risha noted voting irregularities and interference at the general convention. Nevertheless, she is not one to give up. She thanked all her supporters and declared that they inspire her desire to work hard. In the meantime, she explained, she will continue to dedicate herself to her mission through her social work.

Salini was hesitant in 2015, as her progression into mainstream politics had been a mix of successes and disappointments. Balancing life proved difficult, since she had "dedicated a lot to public life at the expense of private life."[11] After serving as student union president, Salini married and had a son. Her peers in other student unions dismissed her as having left politics to become a daughter-in-law. I knew that wasn't true, as I had observed her continual political service; nevertheless, these presumptive remarks demonstrated the difficulty women face in balancing political and personal transitions. Men are not subject to such aspersions but rather are lauded for settling down and becoming family men. Salini has remained a dedicated party member, working in the ideology department and cultivating her juniors. She currently works for the Sahana Pradhan Memorial Foundation, which publishes books to educate youth cadres. Similar to Risha, her party leadership has not propelled her into appointed seats in the party hierarchy or through its CA proportional list. After the 2013 CA elections, she spoke out quite critically against youth activists like her not being given opportunity to participate more centrally. But when I asked her about it in 2015, she demurred, saying it was the media that raised the issue. Her recently attained central committee seat may have influenced her less critical stance toward her party leadership.

Despite her frustrations with party leadership not giving her and her cohort more opportunity, Salini has benefited from the democratization of internal party procedure. Since 2007, CPN-UML central committee members are directly elected by party representatives in both the CPN-UML and ANNFSU (Akhil) national conventions. Previously, party representatives selected national council members for the election commission. Through consensus, the election commission would choose the central committee leadership. The CPN-UML consciously instituted these procedural revisions after the 2006 People's Movement as a way to distinguish itself from its newest competitors, the Maoists (Snellinger 2009a).

Salini's peers voted for her, rather than her leaders appointing her. She won the ANNFSU (Akhil) presidency through direct elections in 2008, and at the CPN-UML's ninth convention in 2014 she obtained the most votes for a central committee member seat. She proudly explained: "My party members know me for my activism and my political dedication. They've shown their support for youth like me with their votes."[12] Her case demonstrates how internal democratic practices can allow people to progress despite political patronage and party leaders' interference.

Salini was quite straightforward that the accomplishments of the past decade have not been as sweeping as they hoped. She echoed Gyanu, asserting that "politics may have changed, but society has not." "The process of development has failed," she admitted, and blamed the "first-generation leaders who have been working to serve their petty interests." She said some of the youth who made the movement successful might have come into satisfactory positions in the CA or their party's central committees, but "the ball is not in our court—we don't play decisive roles." She then turned and said, "Well, as you know, retirement is not common among politicians." Her frustration echoed a comment that Risha made back in 2014: "During the *āndolan*, we the youths were the deciders. Whenever we were in the streets, we were treated as kingmakers. . . . Once the movement came to an end, the leaders who were hiding grabbed all the power and made politics about securing their own positions."[13] All five of these young leaders see their generation as the forward-looking generation that can solve today's problems. But instead of poising themselves as the political future, they now assert that it is their time to govern and lead because their generation brought Nepal into the twenty-first century through the *āndolan*. The temporal shift from tomorrow to today is the most distinct difference between the way they asserted themselves in 2015 and how they had in 2004–5. They no longer cope with their socio-political status by employing a "not-yet" mode of being (E. Bloch [1959] 1986); however, they must continue to maximize the contingencies at their disposal to get ahead.

POLITICAL REGENERATION THROUGH DISSENSUS

It was difficult for these young leaders to square the optimism they had in 2006 when the country embarked on building "new Nepal" with the constitution that was promulgated. Many Nepali citizens believe that this new document is more regressive than the 2007 interim constitution. Akash's emphasis on the constitution as a living document, which should be amended according to circumstance, highlights the iterative nature of political process. All of them, except perhaps Gyanu, are invested in this process of democratic governance via party politics no matter how flawed it might be. Critics may say they have become a part of the status quo establishment. They would rebut that, saying they are not their leaders and should be given the chance to do things differently. This is indeed true; their subject position is oriented to the world differently than for previous generations, and they have altered their ideologies and agendas for what they see are the needs of the time. Nevertheless, they are still addressing those needs through party politics, which continue to prioritize national unity over diversity and devolution of power. When it comes to understanding the grievances of marginalized demographics, the political parties still frame the problem in terms of safeguarding national sovereignty and social harmony. This is something their generation must come to terms with.

The ways in which political events have unfolded in post-earthquake Nepal demonstrate that those in establishment politics and their dissenters continue to talk past one another because they have not figured out how to bridge the ontological divide between them. In keeping with Nepal's radical democratic tradition, this divide will eventually be bridged. A new generation has come of age in post-conflict Nepal, in which the socio-political landscape is extremely different from that before 2006. They were able to convince the public to support republicanism when their leaders were merely asking for full democracy. They cannot avoid the calls for inclusion that resonate with much of the Nepali populace. If they want to lead the country and safeguard democratic party politics, this generation must contend with the new claims being asserted and the new subjectivities that emerged as the constitution was drafted over the decade after 2006.

The Sanghiya Gathbandhan (Federal Alliance) is the newest alliance to articulate demands in response to these new political configurations. This federal alliance of Madheshi and ethnic (*janajāti*) forces has led Kathmandu-centric protests since 2016 to pressure parliament to amend the constitution to address their grievance. This alliance is a game changer in the political equation.

Upon my return from curfew-stricken Birganj in 2015, a noted Madheshi public intellectual reassured me that there was a silver lining: Madheshi, Tharu, and *janajāti* activists finally realized they must unite against their common rival, the high-caste hill (Khas Aryan Pahadi) ruling elite. While drawing a diagram for illustration, he explained: "For centuries, the Khas rulers divided and conquered the different ethnic groups in Nepal—first the Shahs, then Ranas, and then mainstream political parties. They pinned us against one another so they could continue to rule. They were in the majority if they kept all the minorities separate. But now minorities are realizing their political goals are not at odds. If they unite, they outnumber the ruling elite."[14] The way the federal map was delineated to ensure a high-caste hill plurality in all seven states, except state number 2 which has a Madheshi majority, is the most recent evidence of this divide-and-rule tactic. The Sanghiya Gathbandhan is restructuring the political dynamic, aligning a diverse plurality to uproot the historically entrenched Khas Aryan plurality. Such alliances have the potential to shift the nationalist paradigm from "unity in diversity" (Malagodi 2013) to unity out of diversity.

Again, it is through *āndolan* that the core elements of dissensus—new political subjects, demands, and meanings—are emerging. How integral the *āndolan* is to the generative process of politics became evident when I was observing protests in Birganj. The Kathmandu establishment dismissed the dissent as Madheshi party leaders' orchestrations to undermine the CA for their own political gain. These dismissals were tone-deaf to the genuine grievances of alienation among the general population in the south. Many—Tarai residents, Madheshi, Tharus, and those of hill origin—were as frustrated with their own political leaders as they were with the Kathmandu political elite. A young NGO activist expressed hope that new leadership would arise through their *āndolan*. New leaders, he explained, could simultaneously galvanize the base, distance the struggle from corrupt politicians engaging in power politics, and convince outsiders they merely want a voice in building new Nepal.

His hope encapsulates political reconfiguration through dissensus. Leaders emerge through the *āndolan*. New political subjects are recognized through the *āndolan*. New political paradigms are introduced through the *āndolan*. And yet it is through governance and restructuring that all these elements become instituted. Institutionalization has always been partial and incomplete. But a new generation will emerge, shaped by Nepal's accumulated socio-political heritage, which they will mediate to shape a livable present and future for themselves and their country, perhaps by continuing the movement.

Appendix

Overview of Featured Political Parties

I made it a priority to understand how student activists participated in both contentious and organized politic across the political spectrum.[1] I interviewed members of all participating parties in the Movement Against Regression and their student organizations as well as the Unified Communist Party of Nepal (Maoist) (UCPN [Maoist]) and the Nepali Congress (Democratic) (NC [D]). Most of these parties are small, and their leadership role is subsumed by the three largest parties, the Nepali Congress (NC), Communist Party of Nepal–Unified Marxist Leninist (CPN-UML), and UCPN (Maoist).[2] I also interviewed members of the pro-monarchy Panchayat party that had transformed itself into the National Democratic Party (Rāstriya Prajātantra Parishad [RPP]) in order to compete in the multiparty democratic process after 1991.[3]

Nepali Congress

The NC is historically known for championing democratic rights. The party has had its share of charismatic leaders. However, the Koirala family, of which three members have held the position of prime minister eight times, has consistently dictated its legacy. B. P. Koirala is nostalgically referred to as "the father of Nepali democracy." The NC originally identified as a socialist democratic party; however, since multiparty democracy was reestablished in the 1990s, it has promoted market-driven neoliberal policies. The party held the prime minister position fifteen times between 1950 and 2013. Its eleventh tenure under Sher Bahadur Deuba led to a split in the party, which factionalized into the Nepali Congress (Koirala) (NC [K]) faction and the NC (D) faction from 2002 to 2007. As I began my research, the NC (K) and its affiliated student organization were participating in the Movement Against Regression, and the NC (D) and its affiliated student organization acquiesced to the king's active rule and were in and out of his government. The NC (D) did not join the agitating political parties until 2006, in the Second People's Movement. The two NC parties reunited in 2007 to maximize their advantage in the 2008 Constituent Assembly (CA) elections. The split and merger of the Nepal Student Union (Democratic) (NSU [D]) and the Nepal Student Union (Koirala) (NSU [K]) and its impact on their organization at the central committee and cadre levels is evident in this analysis of student activism.

Communist Party of Nepal–Unified Marxist Leninist

The CPN-UML was the largest mass-based communist party before the Maoists returned to the mainstream in 2006. It traces its lineage to the Communist Party of Nepal (CPN). Organizationally, the CPN has been quite fluid due to ongoing splits and mergers since its creation in 1949.[4] The CPN-UML is the only communist party to have an elected prime minister during the years of multiparty democracy under the constitutional monarchy (1990–2006). Politically, the CPN-UML is considered to be to the right of the UCPN (Maoist), because it supported multiparty democracy with a socialist structure without the use of violence at a time when the Maoists were leading an insurgency against the state. During the late 1990s, the Maoists gained a lot of support from people who were previously loyal to the CPN. Many CPN-UML supporters, especially in the rural areas, had become disillusioned with the party's inability to influence the state structure in any progressive way while in government in the 1990s. The UCPN (Maoist) offered this frustrated constituency a more radical alternative after the many compromises the CPN-UML made in the day-to-day of parliamentary politics (Hachhethu 2009).

Communist Party of Nepal (Maoist)

The history of the CPN (Maoist) stems from a unity of small radical parties that formed the Communist Party of Nepal (Unity Centre) soon after the 1990 People's Movement (A. Adhikari 2014; D. Thapa 2004; Thapa and Sijapati 2003). The Unity Centre's front organization, Samyukta Jana Morchā (Joint People's Front; SJM), contested the 1991 elections, winning nine parliamentary seats. In 1994, the CPN (Unity Centre) and the SJM split due to a dispute over whether or not to proceed with the People's War. The election commission refused to recognize the more radical faction of the SJM, led by Baburam Bhattarai, forcing members to boycott the elections. In 1995, the radical faction led by Pushpa Kamal Dahal (also known as Prachanda) and Bhattarai renamed its party the CPN (Maoist) to distinguish itself from the moderate Unity Centre faction. It began preparing for armed insurgency in the districts of Rolpa and Rukum. The government launched Operation Romeo to crackdown on the Maoists' targeting of "class enemies," namely, government workers and NC party members. In early February 1996, the Maoists presented NC prime minister Sher Bahadur Deuba with a list of forty demands, threatening armed insurgency against the state if they were not satisfied. On February 13, the Maoists launched their revolution with coordinated attacks on police posts in the districts of Rukum, Rolpa, and Sindhuli and destroyed loan documents of a Kavre district money lender and the Agricultural Development Bank in Gorkha district.

When I began my research in 2003, the Maoists had been underground for seven years and were engaged in a full-scale civil war with the king's government.[5] In 2005, the Maoists pursued talks in Delhi with the seven parties that were leading to the Movement Against Regression. Together they drafted an official agreement to undertake a joint movement to establish a secular, multiparty democratic federal republic. The CPN (Maoist) was credited with pressuring the political parties toward the more radical stance of a secular, federal republic by agreeing to peace talks and multiparty democracy. It won the majority of the first-past-the-post and proportional seats in the 2008 CA elections. After 2008, the party became the UCPN (Maoist) as it merged with smaller radical factions. It struggled to transition from a revolutionary force to a governing political party (Hachhethu 2009). It held the seat of prime minister twice during the first CA government and was blamed for the breakdown of the first CA because it could not broker an agreement over federalism (Adhikari and Gellner 2016; ICG 2012a; Snellinger 2015b). Politburo leader Mohan Baidya defected from the party, blaming party leaders Pushpa Kamal Dahal and Baburam Bhattarai for abandoning the party's agenda of identity-based federalism and causing the collapse of the CA. Baidya established the Communist Party of Nepal–Revolutionary Maoist (CPN-RM [Baidya]) party and unsuccessfully led a thirty-three-party opposition against the interim government and the second CA elections in 2013.

Nepal Workers and Peasants Party (Nepal Majdūr Kisān Dal)

The Majdūr Kisān party is a small communist party that adopted the Chinese communist line, splitting from Pushpa Lal Shrestha's CPN in 1975. Narayan Man Bijukchhe, also known as Comrade Rohit, has been the party's president since its inception; this non-rotation is now recognized to be a major weakness, causing many to wonder if the party will survive past

Bijukchhe. During the Panchayat government, the party rallied around laborers' and farmers' rights issues in the Kathmandu Valley, drawing early support from the ethnic Newar community. It was integral in organizing ethnic Newar enclaves there during the 1990 People's Movement, and it has participated in multiparty democracy since 1991 (Ogura 2001). Its traditional stronghold is in the city of Bhaktapur, among the ethnic Newar population, but it has also won parliamentary seats in both Jumla and Dailekh districts and has an organizational presence in Kalikot (Hoftun, Raeper, and Whelpton 1999).

Nepal Sadbhavana Party

The Nepal Sadbhavana party was the first Tarai-based regional party, founded in 1985. In the 1990s, it was the most vocal democratic party championing for the rights of Madheshi people, advocating to make Hindi the second national language and increasing Madheshi representation in all public sectors. Ideologically, it is a social democratic party. In 2003, the party split after the chairman, Badri Prasad Mandal, decided to join King Gyanendra's government. Anandidevi Singh created the Sadbhavana (Anandidevi) faction and joined the Movement Against Regression. In 2007, the two factions merged again to contest in the CA elections but then suffered from infighting and further fracturing of the party. Since the 2006–8 Madheshi movement, the Nepal Sadbhavana party has become one of over thirty-three regionally based parties championing for the rights of Madheshi people (cf. Jha 2014a).

Notes

Preface

1   See Amnesty International's report (ASA 31/155/2004) on the tally of disappearances and deaths from 1998 to 2004: www.univie.ac.at/bimtor/dateien/nepal_ai_2004_esca lating_disappearances.pdf.

2   Based on an interaction I had with students from Shankar Dev Campus, February 6, 2004.

3   Due to splits and mergers, the number of student organizations ranged from seven to ten. Despite my interacting with all the key players, this research is informed by some organizations more than others due to the varying degrees of access I received. Certain interlocutors opened up to me more deeply because of the relationships we developed during their political agitation, and I found it easier to access the three largest parties (NC, CPN-UML, and UCPN [Maoist]) because they had more members, programs, and regular publicity. Another factor was the student organizations' internal working styles and discipline. Nevertheless, I strove to gain adequate understanding of all participating organizations to identify the general trends and organizational differences in student politics.

Note on Terminology and Transliteration

1   For a detailed history of this debate, see Chalmers (2003: chap. 5); Gellner (2003a); Hutt (1997: 113–16); Shneiderman (2009b: 13–21).

Introduction: Political Opportunity through Activism

1   Translation of an interaction with a CPN-UML central committee member, April 3, 2004.

2   Translation of an interaction with a NSU cadre, affiliated with the NC (K), April 9, 2004.

3   The student organizations are not the only sister organizations of political parties: the Tarun Dal (Youth Wing), the professional unions, youth and ethnic wings, and the women's organizations have become institutionalized in the past forty years and are mobilized at the parties' behest (Hachhethu 2002).

4   Translation of an interview with a NSU (K) central committee leader, January 24, 2004.

5   Translation of an interview with an NSU (K) campus president, May 17, 2004.

6   Translation of an interview with the Ratna Rajya Laxmi Campus chief, May 19, 2004.

7   A "norm-oriented" movement is concerned with specific goals and generally the product of a specific limited issue. A "value-oriented" movement is concerned with broad, ideological issues (Altbach 1967: 87).

8   Translation of an interview with an NSU (K) central committee member, December 4, 2004.
9   For more in-depth studies of party politics, see A. Adhikari 2014; R. Gautam 2005; Hachhethu 2002; Hoftun, Raeper, and Whelpton 1999; Joshi and Rose (1966) 2004; K.C. 1999; Lawoti 2005; Paramanand 1982; Thapa and Sijapati 2003.
10 I have given these five people pseudonyms and blurred personal details; however, I have not obscured their political affiliations or positions. For this reason, their identity will be known to those familiar with Nepali politics. I have received permission from all five to provide these details in my analysis.
11 Translation of an interview with a former Nepal Revolutionary Student Union and Workers and Peasants party member, September 10, 2015.
12 Translation of an interview with a former ANNISU (R) student leader and CPN-RM (Baidya) member, April 24, 2014.
13 See Chua 2011; Jeffrey 2010; Johnson-Hanks 2002; Katz 2004; Mains 2007; Masquelier 2005.
14 See Bista 1991; Gellner 2009; Miller 1990; Sharrock 2013.
15 See Asad 1993, 2003; Chakrabarty 1992; Chatterjee 2004; Ferguson 2006; Povinelli 2002; Sivaramakrishnan and Agrawal 2003; Spencer 2007; Subramanian 2009.

Chapter 1: Manufacturing the State, Politics, and Politicians

1   Translation of an interaction with a police captain, July 2, 2005.
2   See Dahal 2006; Des Chene 1996; Forbes 1999; Gaenszle 2000; Gellner 2003b; Gellner, Pfaff-Czarnecka, and Whelpton 1997; Guneratne 2002; Hangen 2007; Holmberg 2000; Jha 2014a; Lecomte-Tilouine and Dolfus 2003; Levine 1987; Onta 1996; P. Sharma 2007; Shneiderman 2015; M. Tamang 2008; Turin 2000.
3   Although Nepal was not colonized by foreign powers, its construction could be likened to that of colonial states because it was the project of a small group of elites not representative of the larger citizenry and with influence from the international world, mainly Britain and India (Burghart 1984). Therefore, the postcolonial studies approach of tracking the establishment of colonies to understand how the postcolonial nation-state developed allows us to understand how the power consolidation process in Nepal pushed the nation to become a nation-state (Chatterjee [1986] 1993; Cohn 1996; Corrigan and Sayer 1985; Guha 1989; Mehta 1999; Memmi 1965; Mitchell 1991).
4   The distinction here between nation and nation-state involves the process of taking national "unity" (what is contained within its sovereign borders) and organizing it through government, administration, infrastructure, and education. These institutions organize the nation as a nation-state, which has been how countries interact and negotiate with each other in the modern era (Burghart 1984: 101).
5   See the map of the Gorkhali conquest of Nepal in Malagodi (2013: 70).
6   See Burghart 1996; Lecomte-Tilouine 2005; Malagodi 2013; Whelpton 1997.
7   For a map of Greater Nepal before the Treaty of Sagauli (1806–16), see Aryal and Inchley (2005: 23).
8   Until 2008, thirteen of the nineteen state holidays were Hindu (S. Sharma 2002: 29).

9   Dasain is a nationwide celebration of the triumph of good over evil, commemorating the gods' victory over demons. The main celebration honors goddess Durga's slaying of the demon Mahisasur, who terrorized the earth as a water buffalo.

10 There is much scholarship that illustrates how ethnic groups' terms of surrender to Prithvi Narayan Shah, and their subsequent relationships with the central government, determined how these groups' identities as citizens developed vis-à-vis the Nepali democratic state (Adams 1995; Burghart 1984; Des Chene 1996; Fisher 2001; Gellner, Pfaff-Czarnecka, and Whelpton 1997; Guneratne 2002; Höfer 1979; Holmberg 1989; Levine 1987; Ortner 1989; Parish 1994; Pignède [1966] 1993; Shneiderman 2015; Whelpton 1997).

11 Similar to the Shah dynasty and the Rana regime's attempts to classify Nepal's diversity, anthropology in Nepal began as a cartographic enterprise that attempted to place Nepal's diversity within its remote geography and relation to the state. This occurred despite the fact that close study of political subjects was strongly discouraged by the Panchayat government (Gellner 2003a: 12). See Holmberg 1989; Gellner and Quigley 1999; Guneratne 2002; Levine 1987; Ortner 1989; Whelpton 1997.

12 David N. Gellner (2003a: 9) contrasts peoples' refusal to accept state aid after the 1934 earthquake because it was a sin to take the king's patrimony (*rājasva*) with the growing dependence on the state through the Panchayat era to demonstrate how development and social services affected peoples' conceptions of state responsibility.

13 Nepal's nationalism has been to some degree based on the fear of Indian imperialism, especially after Sikkim was annexed by way of referendum in 1975. Nevertheless, Nepal depends on India for economic support, port access, and political legitimacy. Nepali politicians must carefully balance courting India to their advantage without seeming like lackeys serving Indian interests.

14 This policy publicized Nepal as a Himalayan Shangri-la, attracting many Western travelers as Nepal slowly began opening up to tourism in the late 1970s. Diplomats (J. Bloch 2005) and mainstream journalists (Dubin 2004) have lamented the end of Nepal as a Shangri-la since the Maoist People's War, whereas other public intellectuals and political scientists have debunked the myth of Nepal as a Shangri-la (Bohara, Mitchell, and Nepal 2006; Dixit 2002).

15 See S. Tamang (2012) for analysis problematizing foreign pathologizing of Nepal's state fragility.

16 The governments during both Panchayat rule and after the 2005 coup have been more diverse than during multiparty democracy in the 1990s.

17 In 1999, 8,547 of Nepal's 25,599 schools were private (see Ministry of Education and Sports 1999).

18 The UN peace-building commission codified this intervention as a six-stage process: (1) negotiate settlement to end conflict; (2) establish a peacekeeping presence; (3) "pump-prime democracy" by encouraging a constitution that promotes democratizing governing institutions; (4) maintain a "light footprint" of intervention to shepherd the state through post-conflict fragility; (5) hold post-conflict elections, which are meant to give legitimacy to the peace process and the newly elected government, otherwise known as "prime pumping durable peace"; and (6) coordinate international withdrawal (Collier, Hoeffler, and Söderborn 2008: 463).

19 Many Nepali students studying in exile in Banaras and Patna during the mid-1970s also participated in Jaya Prakash Narayan's movement (Sampurna Krānti [Total Revolution]).

20 See Hoftun, Raeper, and Whelpton (1999) for descriptions of small-scale protests carried out by individuals during the Rana regime.

21 For details on this policy plan, see Hayes (1976) and Carney and Bista (2009).

22 Birendra's rule began in 1972, and his style was quite different from his father's. Even though he planned to enforce his father's constitution of 1962, he was open to reform and working with liberal Panchayat ministers and at times with illegal political parties.

23 See Ojha (2012: 239–46) for the entire list of demands made and granted.

24 In the context of the political struggle for democracy, black is equated with regression. As a political tactic, protesters will often hold black flags, particularly on April 8, which marks King Mahendra's dissolution of democracy in 1960, and October 14, when his son Gyanendra dissolved parliament in 2002.

25 Of the 7,111,000 registered voters, 2.4 million voted for the Panchayat system and 2 million voted for the multiparty system (Hoftun, Raeper, and Whelpton 1999: 93).

26 Students also bore the brunt of police violence. Some were captured and brutally tortured, which did not happen as routinely to party leaders; of the approximately fifty people who died during the movement, two-thirds were students (Ogura 2001).

27 According to my interview with the ANNFSU president who led the campaign, the area under dispute was Nepali land that King Mahendra had allowed Indian soldiers to occupy during their retreat from the India-China border dispute in 1967. The ANNFSU students marched to the border to publicize the Indian government's action of exiling Nepali residents from the Kalapani region in 1998.

28 After the 2006 People's Movement, Akash admitted to me that he had permission from G. P. Koirala to rally the students to make the demand for a republic because Koirala wanted to test public sentiment without sacrificing the parties' bargaining power with the king.

29 For more details on the history of education policy in Nepal, see Carney and Bista (2009) and Onta (1996).

30 In Nepal, the literacy rate for men is 72 percent and for women 51 percent; for the urban population the literacy rate is 77 percent and for the rural population 57 percent (Central Bureau of Statistics 2011). The mean number of years of schooling for adults in urban areas is 9.6 and in rural areas 7.5.

31 See tables 5.1, "Caste/Ethnic Composition of Parties' Central Committees in 2001," and 5.2, "Caste and Ethnic Composition of Legislators," in Malagodi (2013: 196–99); table 2, "Integrated National Index of Governance, 1999," in Hangen (2007: 10); and table 1, "Over- and Underrepresented Groups in Higher Education," in P. Bhatta et al. (2008: 242).

32 P. Bhatta 2011; Carney and Bista 2009; Rappleye 2011; Winther-Schmidt 2011.

33 Fifteen percent of Nepali schools are private (4,388 of the 28,026 schools), a ratio of 3:10 (Ministry of Education and Sports 2004). The Living Standards Survey of 2003 documents that 6 percent of primary, 7.6 percent of lower secondary, and 9.7 percent of higher-secondary students are privately educated (cited in Shakya and Hatakeyama 2008: 8). The Ministry of Education documented in 2005 that 15 percent of primary

students and 27 percent of secondary students attend private school (cited in Mathema 2007; Shields and Rappleye 2008). In 2011, total private education attendance reached 26.8 percent of the school-age population (Central Bureau of Statistics 2011).

34 Students in private schools have much better education outcomes, with a pass rate on the School Leaving Certificate (SLC) examination of 85 percent in 2004, compared to 38 percent for students in public schools. Also, the average SLC score was 17 percent higher in private schools (S. Bhatta 2004).

35 See P. Bhatta et al. 2008; Caddell 2005; Liechty 2003; Mathema 2007; Shakya and Hatakeyama 2008; Shields and Rappleye 2008; Valentin 2011.

36 Translation of an interview with an arrested NSU central committee member, August 8, 2005.

37 CPN-UML minister on the differences between student movements of the different generations, February 4, 2007.

38 Translation of an interview with the Nepal Revolutionary Students Union president, June 10, 2005.

39 Translation of an interaction with an ANNISU (R) district leader, November 24, 2006.

Chapter 2: Discipline and Sacrifice in the Dirty Game of Politics

1 Translation from an interaction with the president of the Nepal Revolutionary Student Union, August 9, 2006.

2 See Burghart 1984, 1994; Heaton Shrestha 2010; Miller 1990; Mines 1994; Ollieuz 2011; Ramirez 2000; Suykens and Stein 2014.

3 Translation from an interview with the ANNFSU (Ekikrit) student union of CPN (Unity Centre–Masal) People's Front, May 19, 2004.

4 Pajeros are Indian sports utility vehicles that are associated with the corrupt political culture of the mid-1990s, known as the Pajero era. As prime minister beginning in 1995, Sher Bahadur Deuba increased the pensions of all parliamentarians by tenfold and repealed import taxes on vehicles for all parliamentarians.

5 Translation from an interview with a CPN-UML central committee member, May 13, 2004.

6 Interview with a Pashupati Campus NSU (K) vice president, December 8, 2003.

7 Interview with a Pashupati Campus ANNFSU (Akhil) president, December 4, 2003.

8 See Byrne and Shrestha 2014; Gellner 2014; Sharrock 2013; Snellinger 2015b.

9 Translation from an interview with an NSU (K) campus president, May 17, 2004.

10 Mark Liechty, in his book *Suitably Modern: Making Middle-Class Culture in a New Consumer Society* (2003), translates *ijjat* as "respectability" or "status." For his informants, modern middle-class Nepali citizens, it has less to do with impressing people through gaining prestige, as this student leader describes, and more to do with ensuring that one's actions do not jeopardize family honor.

11 Translation from an interview with an NSU (D) central committee leader, November 15, 2003.

12 See Hangen 2007; Guneratne 2002; Gellner 2003a; Lawoti 2005; Shneiderman 2015.

13 Gellner and Karki (2010: 136) note in their survey analysis of Nepali activists that the most common word for "party activist" is *kāryakarta* (cadre) and that *āndolankāri*,

literally translated as "movement-ist," is less common. That, however, is not the case for student activists whose entrée into politics and claims of legitimacy are based on the experience of being an *āndolankāri*.

14 In 2004, Deuba was appointed prime minister by the king and was then ousted again in 2005 by the king-led military coup. The CPN-UML also decided to join the king's 2004 government after participating in the Movement Against Regression. Its student organization was actively against this move, yet it did not have enough control or influence and as a result had to withdraw from the joint seven-student-union movement in 2004.

15 Translation of an interaction with an ANNFSU (Akhil) student cadre, May 13, 2005. Democracy Wall was at a Ratna Park intersection and commemorated the protest of the 1990 People's Movement and the ongoing Movement Against Regression. The office of ANNFSU (Akhil), known as the "red house" (*rātō ghar*), had been at that intersection since the 1970s. Its office served as a logistical hub for both movements from 2001 to 2004. After 2004, when the Movement Against Regression protests intensified, public gatherings were banned in particular areas, including Ratna Park. After the king's takeover in 2005, the ANNFSU (Akhil) was evicted from the *rātō ghar* and the building was torn down. The king's government destroyed Democracy Wall and built a pedestrian bridge, removing this historic space from the built environment in order to curb protest. After 2006, Democracy Wall was rebuilt, and the ANNFSU (Akhil) erected a garden called Republican park, dedicated to the political struggle and containing a statue of one of its fallen leaders. In 2006, the ANNISU (R) opened its first central committee office since it went underground during the People's War, locating it in the Ratna Park intersection to stake its claim on this political landscape.

16 *Mandale* is the term for someone who is considered a lackey of the king and the Panchayat government. See chapter 1 for details on its etymology.

17 Translation of interaction between student leaders and police in the police chief's office, June 3, 2005.

18 Based on an interaction with an NSU (K) student leader, August 15, 2005.

19 I thank David N. Gellner for illuminating this point.

20 For a comprehensive visual of the history of splits and mergers of the communist parties, see Thapa and Sijapati (2003: 44).

21 Translation of an ANNISU (R) central committee member's interview, November 12, 2007.

22 From an ANNISU (R) central committee member's interview, October 12, 2007.

23 Translation from a speech of an NSU (D) central committee member at the Nepalganj national convention, July 13, 2007.

24 Translation of a speech of an NC parliamentarian in Gorkha district headquarters, July 25, 2011.

25 Translation of an interview with an ANNFSU (Akhil) student leader, July 19, 2011.

26 This point was made by ANNISU (R) student leaders and activists in conversations and during interviews on October 12, 2007; November 12, 2007; December 4, 2007; January 8, 2008; and July 7, 2008. However, it must be noted that personal biographies have become an increasing post-conflict trend, (see Hutt 2012; Lecomte-Tilouine 2006).

27 Translation of an ANNISU (R) central committee member's interview, October 12, 2007.

28 Translation of an ANNISU (R) central committee member's interview, December 4, 2007.

29 The roots of these two words, *āsha*, translates as "hope," and the suffix, *bādī*, indicates "ideology of hope" or "ideology of hopelessness," and thus "optimism" and "cynicism" capture the meaning in this context more closely than "hopeful" and "hopelessness."

30 Translation of an interaction with an ANNISU (R) student cadre, at the Sitapaila commune in Kathmandu, November 30, 2007.

31 Translation of an ANNISU (R) central committee member's interview, November 4, 2007.

32 Translation of an ANNFSU (Ekikrit) central committee member's interview, November 10, 2007.

33 Translation of a former NSU (K) central committee member's interview, November 16, 2007.

34 Translation of an ANNISU (R) central committee member's interview, July 23, 2011.

35 Translation of an interaction with an ANNFSU (Akhil) student cadre, at the central committee office, November 25, 2007.

Chapter 3: The Political Category of Youth

1 Translation of a conversation with an NC cadre, August 15, 2007.

2 This description is based on conversations I had with NC and NSU activists in 2007 during the CA campaigns.

3 For a more detailed overview of anthropology's analytic approach to youth, see Bucholtz (2002); for a review of youth studies in Nepal, see Snellinger (2013).

4 The Hindu life cycle is a traditional life path that high-caste males are expected to follow to fulfill all the socially prescribed functions a man should embody, taking first from parents and then from society (mainly through education), giving to society through work and raising a family, and finally giving to the gods by retracting from society and focusing on spirituality.

5 This notion of youth as a discreet life stage has only become more common in the general population over the past few decades as access to education has become mass-based (Skinner and Holland 1996; Liechty 1995).

6 NC leader G. P. Koirala, an octogenarian, died in 2009. Ram Chandra Paudel, an NC central committee member, is in his mid-sixties.

7 Translation from an interview with a central committee member of the CPN-UML, January 14, 2007. This translation is modified from the original translation quoted in Snellinger (2009b: 49–50).

8 See *The Ninth Plan (1997–2002)*, 143, table 5 (National Planning Commission 1998).

9 The notion of *vikās*, however, was determined not by abstract means but in measurable outcomes. Daman Nath Dhungana, a drafter of the 1990 constitution, observed that people equated democracy with physical development; democracy to them meant an airport or a road that reaches their district headquarters rather than rights (Malagodi 2013: 118).

10 As Hachhethu documents (2009: 60), Prachanda admitted that his ideology, as out-lined in the Prachanda Path, shares many similarities with Mandan Bhandari's ideol-ogy of *bahudalīya janbad* (multiparty democracy).

11 Discussion with an NSU student leader, April 5, 2004.

12 *Himalayan Times*, May 13, 2004; *Kathmandu Post*, May 11, 2004.

13 Conversation with a former NSU student leader, September 19, 2009.

14 Translation of an interaction with a police inspector, July 2, 2005.

15 Excerpt translated from an interview with an ANNFSU (Akhil) student leader, June 15, 2005.

16 The king's state of emergency proved to be bad timing for the conference. A number of Nepali student activists would not attend due to the threat posed by the police standing outside the resort compound where the conference was held. But the US embassy decided to hold it anyway to demonstrate its support for democracy.

17 Translation from an interaction with an ANNFSU (Akhil) central committee leader, April 28, 2007.

18 Translation from an interview with a central committee member of the CPN-UML, January 14, 2007.

19 Translation based on a conversation with an NSU (K) female student leader, February 15, 2007.

20 Translation from an interview with a central committee member of the CPN (Maoist), January 18, 2007.

21 Translation from a conversation with an NC (D) central committee member and min-ister, September 16, 2007.

22 Translation from an interview with a former ANNISU (R) student leader, April 25, 2014.

23 Translation from a conversation with a woman from the Women Act network, July 13, 2011.

24 The Ministry of Youth and Sports was established in 2010, although it is considered a backwater ministry with little influence. The National Youth Council was finally established in 2016.

25 Interview with a Tarun Dal member on the NYP drafting committee, March 31, 2013.

26 The NYP drafting committee was successful in having female and ethnic representa-tion, but not at a proportionate level. However, there were no members from the Dalit community, from the lower economic classes, or from the far west.

27 Interview with a drafting committee member, April 28, 2013.

28 During the debate of the age limit, many different national and international sources were identified as precedents in advocating for different age caps. The National Plan-ning Commission defines youth as fifteen to twenty-nine years of age for budgeting purposes. The limit for recruitment in the Nepal army, police, and armed forces varies from twenty-two to twenty-five years of age. The upper age limit to appear for the Public Service Commission and Education Service exams is thirty-five years old. Some drafting committee members cited the national youth policies of India, China, and Sri Lanka, where the upper age limit is thirty-five, to advocate for an international prec-edent. But the political youth-wing affiliates rebutted their assertions by citing Japan's NYP, which extends the upper limit to forty-five years of age.

29 These were the youth wings affiliated with the NC, CPN-UML, CPN (Maoist), Nepal Workers and Peasants Party, and CPN (Unity Centre–Masal) People's Front.

30 That the NYP was not presented to parliament to be voted into law was a major issue of contention for the drafting committee members (Snellinger 2014).

31 Interview with a Ministry of Youth and Sports representative on the NYP drafting committee, May 2, 2013.

32 Translation from an interview with a drafting committee member, April 28, 2013.

33 Interview with a leftist youth-wing-affiliated drafting committee member, March 27, 2013.

34 Translated from an interview with a former youth-wing president who served on the NYP drafting committee, April 10, 2013.

35 Interview with a Ministry of Youth and Sports representative on the NYP drafting committee, May 2, 2013.

36 Interview with a former youth-wing president who served on the NYP drafting committee, April 1, 2013.

37 Interview with a leftist youth-wing-affiliated drafting committee member, March 27, 2013.

Chapter 4: The Organizational Form of Practice, Ideology, and Identity

1 Translation from an ANNFSU (Akhil) central committee member's interview, November 25, 2007.

2 I asked various student activists, party cadres, and political leaders a series of questions in order to understand the complexity of organization as noun and verb. Based on advice from some key informants, I did not use the word "culture" (*sanskriti* or *samskār*) until the end of my series of questions, to avoid leading people. I began by asking people about organization and the role it plays in their student unions and political parties, and that led into a question about the role of ideology and the impact that ideology has on the character of their organization. Then I inquired about their organization's internal working styles and what influences it. I then asked them to consider the lifestyles of their members. My penultimate question asked them to compare their own political organization to others. The final question was about the culture of their organization, specifically what informs it and how it plays a role in their organizational identity.

3 Excerpt from an interview with an independent political analyst who was serving as a Maoist-appointed minister, November 19, 2007.

4 Translation from an ANNFSU (Ekikrit) student leader's interview, November 10, 2007.

5 Translation from an ANNISU (R) central committee member's interview, November 12, 2007.

6 Translation from a CPN-UML central committee member's interview, January 14, 2007.

7 Translation from an ANNISU (R) central committee member's interview, January 8, 2007. Prachanda, the chairman of the Maoist party, came out with a declaration in 1998 called the Prachanda Path, which adopts Mao's political philosophies for the cultural, social, and economic conditions of Nepal.

8 Translation from an ANNFSU (Akhil) central committee member's interview, November 25, 2007.

9   Translation from an ANNFSU (Akhil) central committee member's interview, November 25, 2007.

10 Translation from an NSU (D) central committee president's interview, November 28, 2007.

11 Translation from an ANNFSU (Ekikrit) student leader's interview, November 10, 2007.

12 They do not describe them as revolutionaries, because all student activists consider themselves revolutionaries since they all have struggled for their political existence. As I demonstrated in chapter 2, this claim is rhetorically mobilized in political speeches by those of all political stripes to unite their cadres with their history of fighting against the status quo.

13 Translated excerpt from a CA speech given by a former NSU (K) student leader and current CA member, February 23, 2008.

14 Translation from an ANNFSU (Akhil) central committee member's interview, November 26, 2007.

15 Translation from an ANNFSU (Akhil) central committee member's interview, November 25, 2007: "The internal styles and the culture are reflected in the character of its leaders and the cadres. If the [student] organization has a good working style and internal culture, it helps the cadres and leaders win the election and vice versa."

16 Translation from an ANNISU (R) campus leader's interview, April 18, 2007.

17 Translation from an ANNISU (R) central committee member's interview, November 12, 2007.

18 See Baral 1995; Borre, Panday, and Tiwari 1994; Hachhethu 2002, 2009; Hoftun, Raeper, and Whelpton 1999; Shrestha 1996.

19 Translation from an ANNISU (R) female campus leader's interview, June 28, 2007.

20 From an ANNISU (R) Padma Kanya Campus leader's interview, July 7, 2007.

21 Translation from an ANNISU (R) ex-president's interview, September 20, 2009.

22 Translation from an ANNISU (R) central committee leader's interview, October 12, 2007.

23 Translation from an NSU (K) former central committee leader's interview, November 16, 2007.

24 Translation from an NSU (D) central committee student leader's interview, November 28, 2007.

25 Translation from an ANNISU (R) central committee member's interview, November 4, 2007.

26 For more details on this history, see Hachhethu (2009).

27 Translation from an ANNISU (R) central committee member's interview, November 12, 2007.

28 Translation from an ANNISU (R) central committee member's interview, January 8, 2007.

29 Interaction with ANNISU (R) activists at their main office, July 14, 2007.

30 Translation from an NSU (K) former central committee leader's interview, November 16, 2007.

31 Translation from an ANNISU (R) central committee member's interview, January 8, 2007.

32 Translation from an ANNISU (R) central committee member's interview, January 8, 2007.

33 Translation from an ANNISU (R) central committee member's interview, December 4, 2007.

34 The term was used by an ANNISU (R) central committee member in an interview, December 4, 2007.

35 Translation from an ANNISU (R) central committee member's interview, December 4, 2007.

36 Translation from an ANNISU (R) central committee member's interview, January 8, 2007.

37 Translation from an ANNISU (R) central committee member's interview, November 12, 2007.

38 For an ethnographic description of life in the communes, see Dan Hirslund's (2012) dissertation on the life of Youth Communist League members.

39 Translation from an ANNISU (R) central committee member's interview, December 4, 2007.

40 Excerpt based on notes from an interaction with an ANNISU (R) student, July 9, 2007.

41 Translation from an ANNISU (R) central committee member's interview, November 12, 2007.

42 Translation of a speech given at the ANNISU (R) "Let Us Study and Survive" campaign, June 13, 2007.

43 Discussion with Kathmandu-based friend, July 2, 2011.

Chapter 5: Speaking to Be Heard in a Traditionally Elite Enterprise

1 For analysis of this ritual's evolution as political process, see Mocko (2015) and Zotter (2016).

2 The prime minister was abroad at the United Nations Security Council meeting in New York, so the deputy prime minister attended. In 2008, the NC president attended. But the Maoist prime minister, Prachanda, announced that he was refusing to give or take *tikā* and did not attend (Gellner and Letizia 2016: 12).

3 Translation based on an interaction with a cab driver in Kathmandu, September 25, 2009.

4 Translation of a conversation with a former ANNISU (R) leader and CPN-RM (Baidya) member, September 6, 2015.

5 Rancière (1999) defines "policing logics" as dictating the way things are structurally distributed among social groups; this logic determines the possible ways public space is configured and who has a voice in it. Politics questions the hegemony of policing logics by demonstrating how goods and privileges are distributed within it; "the essential work of politics . . . is to get the world of its subjects and its operations to be seen" (Rancière 2010: 37). Thus, calling into question the order of things makes politics a contentious act. Political action unveils the social by highlighting the controversial distribution of places and roles that the social comprises (Rancière 1999: 18).

6 See A. Adhikari 2014; Hutt 2004; Lawoti and Pahari 2010; Lecomte-Tilouine 2013; Pettigrew 2014.

7 Based on a conversation with a former NSU (K) and NC central committee member, May 4, 2014.

8   Such articulations were not novel. Governing in Nepal was a "permanent transition" as early as 1977 (Baral [1977] 2006). More recently, others have described Nepal's political situation as one of "long-term provisionality" (Hindman 2014b) involving "ad hoc governing" (Byrne, forthcoming) because a "political economy of transition serves the 'power polygon,' comprising the ruling elite, oppositional parties, civil society, business groups, and international agencies" (Nightingale et al., forthcoming). Kul Gautam's book *Lost in Transition* (2015) documents Nepal's difficulty to develop economically amid transnational donors' shifting policy in Nepal vis-à-vis the Maoist war, the peace process, and then earthquakes.

9   Nepal was struck by earthquakes on April 25 and May 12, 2015, with magnitudes of 7.8 and 7.6, respectively, and over four hundred aftershocks of 4.0 or higher, which triggered an ongoing series of landslides, affecting thirty-one districts in central Nepal, with fourteen districts rendered crisis-hit. Over 740,000 buildings were destroyed along with historical monuments and infrastructure, such as dams, roads, and bridges. Around nine thousand people died in the initial aftermath, another twenty-four thousand were injured, and millions were left homeless.

10   For an overview of the citizenship issue, see Latschan (2015) and Desouza (2015).

11   Translation of an interview with a Maoist-appointed ambassador and Madheshi activist, April 15, 2008.

12   I thank David N. Gellner for this observation.

13   Translation of an interview with a central committee member of TMDP, April 18, 2008.

14   Based on an interaction with an NSU (D) ethnic student leader, November 28, 2007.

15   Translation from an interview with an NSU (D) president, November 28, 2007.

16   Translation of an interaction with an ANNFSU (Akhil) vice president, November 26, 2007.

17   Interaction at Minbhawan Campus, Naya Baneshwor, Kathmandu, September 27, 2009.

18   Translation based on an interview with a CPN-UML central committee leader, December 3, 2007.

19   Sahana's description of a typical high-caste female experience does not necessarily capture the multitude of female experiences in Nepal's diverse socio-cultural landscape (cf. March 2002). However, the tendency to collapse female experience within high-caste female experience is in line with the Panchayat government's legal policy to homogenize Nepal's diverse population within high-caste, hill-based cultural norms (cf. S. Tamang 2000).

20   Translation based on an interview with a CPN-UML central committee leader, December 3, 2007.

21   The Nepali word for "nepotism" is *natabād*. The root *nata* means "relative" or "kin." Risha replaced *nata* with *shrīmatī*, which means "wife," to capture the trend of women rising in politics due to the nepotism their husbands extend to them. Translation of a conversation with a former NSU leader and NC member, July 17, 2015.

22   Translation of an interview with a Nepal Student Forum (Sadbhavana) central committee member, April 15, 2008.

23   Translation of a conversation with NSU students, October 10, 2009.

24 Translation of a conversation with a former NSU leader and NC member, July 17, 2015.

25 Analysis of political speeches given by female student and party leaders at the Dhading NSU (K) district convention, February 19, 2007; an NSU (D) political program, March 7, 2007; and the NSU (D) Tri-Chandra campus convention, Kathmandu, March 21, 2007.

26 Observation and comment based on a conversation with an NSU (K) female student leader, February 15, 2007.

27 Translation of a conversation with a Kathmandu taxi driver, October 24, 2007.

28 Translation of an interaction with an NSU central committee member, November 2, 2007.

29 Translation from an interview with an ANNFSU (Akhil) central committee member, November 26, 2007.

30 Translation of a conversation with an NSU central committee member, February 11, 2007.

31 Translation of an interaction with an ANNFSU (Akhil) president, October 6, 2009.

32 Translation of a conversation with a CPN-UML party member, September 10, 2015.

33 Translation of an interview with a former NSU (K) student leader, April 27, 2014.

34 *Tōpīs* are hats that were part of the state uniform for bureaucrats and politicians alike during the Panchayat era.

35 Translation of an interaction with a former NSU (K) student leader, November 30, 2006.

36 Based on an interaction with a former NSU (K) student activist at a political program, September 19, 2009.

37 Translation of an interaction with a former ANNISU (R) student leader and CPN-RM (Baidya) member, September 21, 2015.

38 Translation of a conversation with a former ANNFSU (Akhil) leader and UML member, April 28, 2014.

39 Translation of a conversation with a former ANNISU (R) student leader and CPN-RM (Baidya) member, April 24, 2014.

40 Translation of an interview with an NC CA member, May 4, 2014.

41 The term was coined in India's reservation political debates, referring to wealthy and influential Other Backward Classes (OBC) communities that unfairly benefit from positive discrimination schemes. For earlier debates on this issue, consult Béteille (1983, 1991, 1992) for the key issues and Parry (1999) for an ethnographic-based counterargument. For an updated overview of this issue in India and Nepal, see the *Focaal* special issue "Towards an Anthropology of Affirmative Action" (Shah and Shneiderman 2013b).

42 Translation of a conversation with a former ANNFSU (Akhil) leader and UML member, April 28, 2014.

43 Translation of a conversation with a former ANNFSU (Akhil) leader and UML member, September 7, 2015.

44 Translation of a conversation with a former NSU (K) leader and NC central committee member, May 4, 2014.

45 Translation of a conversation with a former ANNISU (R) student leader and CPN-RM (Baidya) member, May 16, 2015.

46 Translation of a conversation with a former NSU (K) leader and NC central committee member, September 22, 2015.

47 Translation of a conversation with an ANNFSU (Akhil) leader, June 15, 2005.

Chapter 6: Accumulating Influence through Scalar Politics

1   During the NSU (K) national conference in 2005, NSU (K) students clashed over irregularities. The then appointed president, who was a candidate, was blamed for manipulating the list of voting representatives with the blessing of NC leaders. The clashes resulted in serious injuries, vandalism of public property, and the torching of the convention hall, with damages of over NR 8 million. The NC canceled the national convention and appointed a new NSU panel, further postponing the national convention that had been overdue since 2004. During the 2006 FSU elections—a nationwide campus competition among all the student organizations—the NSU lost many of its campus strongholds, in part, because its central committee lacked a democratic mandate.

2   The NSU's constitution explicitly states that the NC will not appoint student leaders. But it is well known that the NC often appoints the leadership in the NSU, by pressuring the elected student leaders to agree to the NC's directives. Akash explained to me: "I signed two of those consensus agreements for their appointed leaderships, once when they dissolved my committee during my general secretary tenure and the second time after I tried to run for president." Translation of a conversation with an NSU (K) student leader, March 5, 2007.

3   Akash was general secretary, a position appointed by the president. He was offered this position as an incentive for not running for president in the 2002 general convention, because there was worry that if he did, he would undermine the chances of the student who was in line for the presidency. This is just one case demonstrating that political progression is a rank-and-file process rather than a competitive democratic process (Snellinger 2017).

4   His closest political ally was Devendra Prasad Singh, an Indian National Congress activist of the Socialist Congress Party from Patna who provided logistical, financial, and moral support, during B. P. Koirala's years underground and in exile. Pradip Giri explained their relationship to me: "Like Marx and Engels, Devendra Prasad Singh was just like Friedrich Engels in the life of B. P. Koirala." Translation of an interview with an NC member, February 27, 2008.

5   Translation of an interview with an NC member, February 27, 2008.

6   Interview with a sociology professor at Banaras Hindu University, Varanasi, December 13, 2007.

7   Translation of an interview with an NC member, February 27, 2008.

8   The World Federation for Democratic Youth, a left-leaning organization, was established in London in 1945 to fight against fascism, exploitation, and imperialism and later expanded to include apartheid, racism, and autocracy. Three of Nepal's leftist youth organizations are members: the Democratic National Youth Federation, Nepal (CPN-UML), from which two ANNFSU leaders served as Asia-Pacific vice president at the Budapest headquarters, and the Nepal National Federation of Students and the National Youth Federation, Nepal, which are both affiliated with CPN (United).

9 Translation of a conversation with an ANNFSU (Akhil) student leader, September 23, 2009.

10 Translation of an interview with an NC member, February 27, 2008.

11 Translation of an interview with an NC member, February 27, 2008.

12 For details, see the diplomatic cable titled "Student Politics in Nepal: Not Your College Council" (www.wikileaks.org/plusd/cables/06KATHMANDU2518_a.html), which provides a summary of the history and contemporary key actors in Nepali student politics, sent on September 15, 2006.

13 Discussion with the US Mission to Nepal director, May 13, 2004.

14 Discussion with a US foreign officer, August 7, 2005.

15 I advised the consular officers to invite students from all the different party factions, since they were united in the Movement Against Regression at the time. They expressed interest in being politically inclusive, with the exception of the Maoists, since Maoist-affiliated organizations were on the US terrorist list. Nevertheless, the left-leaning leaders I suggested were absent. When I inquired about this, the consular officers said their calls were not returned, explaining that the leftist parties tend to be less receptive to the US embassy's overtures. Salini, Lagan, and a few other leaders said they were not contacted. This dynamic speaks to the fact that certain embassies are better able to make inroads with certain political affiliations than with others. For instance, the Norwegian embassy heavily courted the ANNISU (R) and the Youth Communist League after 2006, particularly during the drafting of the National Youth Policy, and other politically affiliated youth activists complained that the Norwegian embassy favored the Maoists at the time (cf. Snellinger, forthcoming).

16 Translation of a conversation with an NSU (K) student leader, February 23, 2005.

17 Account recounted to me by a friend in an email received April 21, 2005.

18 Translation of an interview with a former ANNFSU (Akhil) student leader and CPN-UML member, April 28, 2014.

19 Translation of an interview with a former ANNISU (R) student leader and CPN-RM (Baidya) member, April 24, 2014.

20 Translation of an interaction with a former NSU (K) student leader and NC member, August 22, 2011.

21 Translation of an interview with a former NSU (K) student leader and NC member, May 14, 2014.

22 Conversation with a *Kathmandu Post* editor, September 13, 2003.

23 Conversation with a journalist at the Annual Conference on South Asia, University of Wisconsin–Madison, October 2005.

24 Translation of an interview with a former ANNISU (R) student leader and CPN-RM (Baidya) member, April 24, 2014.

25 Translation of a conversation with an NSU (K) student leader, February 23, 2005.

26 Translation of a conversation with a former NSU student leader, October 9, 2007.

27 Translation of an interview with a former Nepal Revolutionary Student Union and Workers and Peasants party member, April 25, 2014.

28 Translation of an interaction with a former NSU (K) student leader and NC member, August 10, 2015.

29 Translation of an interview with a former ANNISU (R) student leader and CPN-RM (Baidya) member, April 24, 2014.

30 Translation of an interview with a former ANNFSU (Akhil) student leader and CPN-UML member, April 28, 2014.

31 Translation of an interaction with a former NSU (K) student leader and NC member, April 27, 2014.

32 Translation of an interaction with a former NSU (K) student leader and NC member, May 4, 2014.

33 From the network's mission statement: Women Act, "About WA," http://womenact .org.np/about-wa.

34 Translation of an interaction with a former NSU (K) student leader and NC member, April 27, 2014.

35 She made this point to me in English. Based on a conversation with a former NSU (K) student leader and NC member, August 26, 2015.

36 Translation of an interaction with a former NSU (K) student leader and NC member, July 15, 2011.

37 Translation of an interaction with a former NSU (K) student leader and NC member, August 22, 2011.

38 Translation of an interview with an NC member, February 27, 2008.

Conclusion: Dissensus and Political Regeneration

1 For more details on the grievances and how the protests unfolded, see ICG (2016) and Snellinger (2016b).

2 Based on field notes from September 20, 2015.

3 Translation of an interview with a former NSU student leader and NC central committee member, February 7, 2016.

4 Translation of an interview with a former Nepal Revolutionary Student Union and Workers and Peasants party member, September 10, 2015.

5 Translation of an interview with a former Nepal Revolutionary Student Union and Workers and Peasants party member, September 10, 2015.

6 Translated from a conversation with a former ANNISU (R) student leader and CPN-RM (Baidya) member, September 7, 2015.

7 Translated from a conversation with a former ANNISU (R) student leader and CPN-RM (Baidya) member, September 7, 2015.

8 Translated from a conversation with a former ANNISU (R) student leader and CPN-RM (Baidya) member, September 7, 2015.

9 Translation of a conversation with a former NSU (K) student leader and NC member, August 26, 2015.

10 Translation of a conversation with a former NSU (K) student leader and NC member, August 26, 2015.

11 Translated from a conversation with a former ANNFSU (Akhil) student leader and CPN-UML member, September 7, 2015.

12 Translated from a conversation with a former ANNFSU (Akhil) student leader and CPN-UML member, September 7, 2015.

13 Translated from a conversation with a former NSU (K) student leader and NC member, April 27, 2014.

14 Translation of a conversation with a Madheshi public intellectual, September 7, 2015.

Appendix

1 Ethnic and regional parties were beyond the scope of this project, although I did query my interlocutors on ethnic and regional parties and issues of diversity and inclusion in Nepal's mainstream politics. For more in-depth studies on ethnic and regional marginalization and political organizing, see Gaige (1975); Gellner (2003b); Gellner, Pfaff-Czarnecka, and Whelpton (1997); Guneratne (2002); Hangen (2010); Jha (2014a); Lawoti (2005); and Shneiderman (2009a).

2 The seven that participated in the Movement Against Regression were NC (K), CPN-UML, CPN (Unity Centre–Masal) People's Front Nepal, CPN-ML, NCP-ML, the Nepal Sadbhavana Party (Anandidevi), and the Majdūr Kisān party.

3 The RPP split in 2006 when Kamal Thapa created the breakaway party National Democratic Party–Nepal (Rāstriya Prajātantra Parishad–Nepal [RPP-N]), which focused intently on reinstating the Hindu monarchy and reversing secularism. The RPP-N became the fourth-largest party in the second CA based on this platform. In 2016, the RPP and RPP-N reunited.

4 See Hoftun, Raeper, and Whelpton (1999: 392) for a detailed diagram of the CPN's complicated history of splits and mergers from 1960 to 1995; and see Thapa and Sijapati (2003: 44) for a detailed diagram on the origins of the UCPN (Maoist).

5 At the time, they were just the CPN (Maoist).

Bibliography

Abrams, P. 1988. "Notes on the Difficulty of Studying the State (1977)." *Journal of Historical Sociology* 1, no. 1: 58–89.

Adams, V. 1995. *Tigers of the Snow and Other Virtual Sherpas.* Princeton, NJ: Princeton University Press.

Adhikari, A. 2014. *The Bullet and the Ballot Box: The Story of Nepal's Maoist Revolution.* London: Verso.

Adhikari, K. P., and D. N. Gellner. 2016. "New Identity Politics and the 2012 Collapse of Nepal's Constituent Assembly: When the Dominant Becomes 'Other.'" *Modern Asian Studies* 50, no. 6: 2009–40.

Adhikari, K. R. 1996. "Naming Ceremonies as Rituals of Development." *Studies in Nepali History and Society* 1, no. 2: 345–64.

Ahearn, L. 2001. *Invitations to Love: Literacy, Love Letters, and Social Change in Nepal.* Ann Arbor: University of Michigan Press.

Allen, J., and A. Cochrane. 2007. "Beyond the Territorial Fix: Regional Assemblages, Politics, and Power." *Regional Studies* 41, no. 9: 1161–75.

Altbach, P. 1967. "Students and Politics." In *Student Politics*, edited by S. M. Lipset, 74–96. New York: Basic Books.

Amatya, S. L., J. Agrawal, and K. Pradhan. 1980. *A Study on the Nature of Student Problem in Tribhuvan University.* Kirtipur: Tribhuvan University, Rector's Office, Research Division.

Amit-Talai, V. 1995. "Conclusion: The 'Multi' Cultural of Youth." In *Youth Cultures: A Cross-Cultural Perspective*, edited by V. Amit-Talai and H. Wulff, 223–37. New York: Routledge.

Anthias, F. 2006. "Belongings in a Globalising and Unequal World." In *The Situated Politics of Belonging*, edited by N. Yuval-Davis, K. Kannabiran, and U. Vieten, 17–31. London: Sage.

Arendt, H. 2000. *The Portable Hannah Arendt.* London: Penguin.

Aryal, B. R., and V. M. Inchley. 2005. *Maps of Nepal.* Kathmandu: Shisam Prakashan.

Asad, T. 1993. *Genealogies of Religion: Discipline and Reasons of Power in Christianity and Islam.* Baltimore: Johns Hopkins University Press.

———. 2003. *Formations of the Secular: Christianity, Islam, and Modernity.* Stanford, CA: Stanford University Press.

Asia-Pacific Interagency Group on Youth. 2011. *Investing in Youth Policy.* New York: UNICEF.

Baker, R., and R. Hinton. 2001. "Approaches to Children's Work and Rights in Nepal." *Annals of the American Academy of Political and Social Science* 575: 176–93.

Bangstad, S. 2009. "Contesting Secularism/s: Secularism and Islam in the Work of Talal Asad." *Anthropological Theory* 9, no. 2: 188–208.

Baral, L. R. (1977) 2006. *Oppositional Politics in Nepal*. Kathmandu: Himal Books.

———. 1995. "The 1994 Elections: Emerging Trends in Political Parties." *Asian Survey* 35, no. 5: 426–40.

Bennett, L.1983. *Dangerous Wives and Sacred Sisters: Social and Symbolic Roles of High Caste Women in Nepal*. Kathmandu: Mandala Book Point.

Béteille, A. 1983. "The Backward Classes and the New Social Order." In *The Idea of Natural Inequality and Other Essays*, edited by A. Béteille, 83–120. Delhi: Oxford University Press.

———. 1991. "Distributive Justice and Institutional Well-Being." *Economic and Political Weekly* 26, nos. 11–12: 591–600.

———. 1992. "The Future of the Backward Classes: The Competing Demands of Status and Power." In *Society and Politics in India: Essays in a Comparative Perspective*, edited by A. Béteille, 151–91. London: Athlone Press.

Bhatta, P. 2011. "Aid Agency Influence in National Education Policy-Making: A Case from Nepal's 'Education for All' Movement." *Globalisation, Societies and Education* 9, no. 1: 11–26.

Bhatta, P., L. Adhikari, M. Thada, and R. Rai. 2008. "Structures of Denial: Student Representation in Nepal's Higher Education." *Studies in Nepali History and Society* 13, no. 2: 235–63.

Bhatta, S. D. 2004. "Disparities in School Performance in the SLC Exams: An Exploratory Analysis." *Studies in Nepali History and Society* 9, no. 2: 293–343.

Bhattarai, B. 2005. "The Effectiveness of Foreign Aid: A Case Study of Nepal." PhD thesis, University of Western Sydney.

Bhusal, T. 2013. "Anarchy Vitiates Beleaguered Students' Organizations." *República*, February 1.

Bista, D. B. 1991. *Fatalism and Development: Nepal's Struggle for Modernization*. Calcutta: Orient Longman.

Bloch, E. (1959) 1986. *The Principle of Hope*. Translated by N. Plaice, S. Plaice, and P. Knight. Vol. 1. Cambridge, MA: MIT Press.

Bloch, J. Chang. 2005. "Nepal: The End of Shangri-La." *Liberal Democracy Nepal Bulletin* 1, no. 1: 1–13. Published by Nepal Study Center, University of New Mexico.

Bohara, A., N. Mitchell, and M. Nepal. 2006. "Opportunity, Democracy, and the Exchange of Political Violence." *Journal of Conflict Resolution* 50, no. 1: 108–28.

Borre, O., S. R. Panday, and C. K. Tiwari. 1994. *Nepalese Political Behavior*. New Delhi: Sterling Press.

Breines, W. 1989. *Community and Organization in the New Left, 1962–1968: The Great Refusal*. New Brunswick, NJ: Rutgers University Press.

Breuilly, J. 1993. *Nationalism and the State*. Manchester: Manchester University Press.

Brubaker, R. 1996. *Nationalism Reframed: Nationhood and the National Question in the New Europe*. Cambridge: Cambridge University Press.

Bucholtz, M. 2002. "Youth and Cultural Practice." *Annual Review of Anthropology* 31: 525–52.

Burghart, R. 1984. "The Formation of the Concept of Nation-State in Nepal." *Journal of Asian Studies* 44, no. 1: 101–25.

———. 1994. "The Political Culture of Panchayat Democracy." In *Nepal in the Nineties: Versions of the Past, Visions of the Future*, edited by M. Hutt, 1–13. New Delhi: Oxford University Press.

———. 1996. *The Conditions of Listening: Essays on Religion, History, and Politics in South Asia*. New Delhi: Oxford University Press.

Byrne, S. Forthcoming. "Authorising Bureaucracy and Other Projects in Nepal's Permanent Transition." *Modern Asian Studies*.

Byrne, S., and G. Shrestha. 2014. "A Compromising Consensus? Legitimising Local Government in Post-Conflict Nepal." *International Development Planning Review* 36, no. 4: 435–53.

Caddell, M. 2002. "'Outward Looking Eyes': Visions of Schooling, Development, and the State in Nepal." PhD diss., University of Edinburgh.

———. 2005. "Discipline Makes the Nation Great: Visioning Development and the Nepali Nation-State through Schools." In *Manufacturing Citizenship: Education and Nationalism in Europe, South Asia, and China*, edited by V. Bénéï, 76–103. London: Routledge.

———. 2006. "Private Schools as Battlefields: Contested Visions of Learning and Livelihood in Nepal." *Compare: A Journal of Comparative and International Education* 36, no. 4: 463–79.

Carney, S., and M. B. Bista. 2009. "Community Schooling in Nepal: A Genealogy of Education Reform since 1990." *Comparative Education Review* 53, no. 2: 63–88.

Carney, S., and U. A. Madsen. 2009. "A Place of One's Own: Schooling and the Formation of Identities in Modern Nepal." In *Nation-Building, Identity, and Citizenship Education: Cross-Cultural Perspectives*, edited by J. Zajda, H. Daun, and L. Saha, 171–87. Dordrecht: Springer.

Carter Center. 2013. "Observing Nepal's 2013 Constituent Assembly Election: Final Report." Atlanta: Carter Center.

CEHURDES (Center for Human Rights and Democratic Studies). 2001. "Status of Press Freedom and Freedom of Expression: Nepal Report." Edited by Y. Bhagirath and P. Ghimire. Kathmandu: CEHURDES.

Central Bureau of Statistics. 2011. *Nepal Living Standards Survey, 2010/11: Statistical Report*. Vol. 1. Kathmandu: Central Bureau of Statistics, National Planning Commission Secretariat, Government of Nepal.

———. 2012. *National Population and Housing Census*. Kathmandu: Central Bureau of Statistics, National Planning Commission Secretariat, Government of Nepal.

Chakrabarty, D. 1992. "Postcoloniality and the Artifice of History: Who Speaks for 'Indian' Pasts?" *Representations*, no. 37: 1–26.

Chalmers, R. 2003. "'We Nepalis': Language, Literature, and the Formation of a Nepali Public Sphere in India, 1914–1940." PhD thesis, School of Oriental and African Studies, University of London.

Channa, S. M. 2010. "What Do People Live On? Living Wages in India." *Anthropology of Work Review* 31, no. 1: 15–29.

Chatterjee, P. (1986) 1993. *Nationalist Thought and the Colonial World: A Derivative Discourse*. New Delhi: Oxford University Press.

———. 2004. *Politics of the Governed: Reflections on Popular Politics in Most of the World*. New York: Columbia University Press.

Chua, J. 2011. "Making Time for the Children: Self-Temporalization and the Cultivation of the Antisuicidal Subject in South India." *Cultural Anthropology* 26, no. 1: 112–37.

Clarke, G. 1997. "Development (*Vikās*) in Nepal: Mana from Heaven." In *Les habitants du toit du monde: Études recueillies hommage à Alexander W. Macdonald*, edited by S. Karmay and P. Sagant, 583–608. Nanterre: Société d'Ethnologie.

Cohn, B. 1996. *Colonialism and Its Forms of Knowledge: The British in India*. Princeton, NJ: Princeton University Press.

Cole, J., and D. Durham, eds. 2007. *Generations and Globalization: Youth, Age, and Family in the New World Economy*. Bloomington: Indiana University Press.

Collier, P., A. Hoeffler, and M. Söderborn. 2008. "Post-Conflict Risks." *Journal of Peace Studies* 45, no. 4: 461–78.

Corrigan, P., and D. Sayer. 1985. *The Great Arch: English State Formation as Cultural Revolution*. Oxford, UK: Blackwell.

Cowan, J. K., M.-B. Dembour, and R. A. Wilson, eds. 2001. *Culture and Rights: Anthropological Perspectives*. Cambridge: Cambridge University Press.

Cox, K., and A. Mair. 1988. "Locality and Community in the Politics of Local Economic Development." *Annals of the Association of American Geographers* 78: 307–25.

Czarniawska, B. 2005. "Karl Weick: Concepts, Style, and Reflection." In *Contemporary Organization Theory*, edited by C. Jones and R. Munro, 267–78. Malden, MA: Blackwell.

Dahal, D. R. 2006. "Social Composition of the Population: Caste/Ethnicity and Religion in Nepal." In *Population Monograph of Nepal*, 1:87–135. Kathmandu: Central Bureau of Statistics.

De Sales, A. 2003. "The Kham Magar Country: Between Ethnic Claims and Maoism." In *Resistance and the State: Nepalese Experiences*, edited by D. N. Gellner, 326–57. New Delhi: Social Science Press.

Des Chene, M. 1996. "Ethnography in the Janajati-yug: Lessons from Reading Rodhi and Other Tamu Writings." *Studies in Nepali History and Society* 1, no. 1: 97–162.

Desouza, N. 2015. "Nepal: The Struggle for Equal Citizenship Rights for Women." openDemocracy 50.50, December 2. www.opendemocracy.net/5050/nicoal-desouza/nepal-struggle-for-equal-citizenship-rights-for-women.

Dhital, M. 2013. "One Step Back." *Kathmandu Post*, October 21. http://kathmandupost.ekantipur.com/printedition/news/2013-10-21/one-step-back.html.

Dixit, S. 2002. "Education, Deception, State, and Society." In *State of Nepal*, edited by K. M. Dixit and S. Ramachandaran, 193–211. Kathmandu: Himal Books.

Djilas, M. 1957. *The New Class: An Analysis of the Communist System*. New York: Praeger.

Doolin, D., and P. Golas. 1964. "On Contradiction in the Light of Mao Tse-tung's Essay on 'Dialectical Materialism.'" *China Quarterly* 19: 38–46.

Dubin, J. 2004. "Nepal—End of Shangri-La." *Newsweek*, international edition, November 22, 54–55.

Durham, D. 2004. "Disappearing Youth: Youth as a Social Shifter in Botswana." *American Ethnologist* 31, no. 4: 589–605.

Edwards, R. M. 2011. "Disconnect and Capture of Education Decentralisation Reforms in Nepal: Implications for Community Involvement in Schooling." *Globalisation, Societies and Education* 9, no. 1: 67–84.

Elias, N. 1978. *The Civilizing Process: The History of Manners.* Oxford, UK: Blackwell.

Evans-Pritchard, E. E. 1940. *The Nuer: A Description of the Modes of Livelihood and Political Institutions of a Nilotic People.* Oxford: Oxford University Press.

Ferguson, J. 2006. *Global Shadows: Africa in the Neoliberal World Order.* Durham, NC: Duke University Press.

Fisher, W. 2001. *Fluid Boundaries: Forming and Transforming Identity in Nepal.* New York: Columbia University Press.

Forbes, A. A. 1999. "Mapping Power: Disputing Claims to Kipat Lands in Northeastern Nepal." *American Ethnologist* 26, no. 1: 114–38.

Foucault, M. (1984) 1992. "Space, Knowledge, and Power." In *The Foucault Reader*, edited by P. Rabinow, 239–56. New York: Pantheon.

Fujikura, T. 2003. "The Role of Collective Imagination in the Maoist Conflict in Nepal." *Himalaya* 23, no. 1: 21–30.

Fund for Peace. 2013. Failed States Index. http://ffp.statesindex.org/nepal. Accessed September 14, 2013.

Gaenszle, M. 2000. *Origins and Migrations: Kinship, Mythology, and Ethnic Identity among the Mewahang Rai of East Nepal.* Kathmandu: Mandala Book Point.

Gaige, F. 1975. *Regionalism and National Unity in Nepal.* New Delhi: Vikas Publishing House.

Gautam, K. 2015. *Lost in Transition: Rebuilding Nepal from the Maoist Mayhem and Mega Earthquake.* Kathmandu: Nepa-Laya.

Gautam, R. 2005. *Nepali Congress.* New Delhi: Adroit Publishers.

Gellner, D. N. 2003a. "Introduction: Transformations of the Nepalese State." In *Resistance and the State: Nepalese Experiences*, edited by D. N. Gellner, 1–30. New Delhi: Social Science Press.

———, ed. 2003b. *Resistance and the State: Nepalese Experiences.* New Delhi: Social Science Press.

———. 2007. "Democracy in Nepal: Four Models." *Seminar* 576: 50–56.

———. 2009. "Introduction: How Civil Are 'Communal" and Ethno-Nationalist Movements?" In *Ethnic Activism and Civil Society in South Asia*, edited by D. N. Gellner, 1–26. London: Sage.

———. 2010. "Introduction: Making Civil Society in South Asia." In *Varieties of Activist Experience: Civil Society in South Asia*, edited by D. N. Gellner, 1–16. London: Sage.

———. 2011. "Preconditions of Democracy: An Outsider's Reflections and Their Reception in Nepal." *European Bulletin of Himalayan Research*, no. 38: 33–58

———. 2014. "The 2013 Elections in Nepal." *Asian Affairs* 45, no. 2: 243–61.

———. 2015. "Rituals of Democracy and Development in Nepal." In *Governance, Conflict, and Development in South Asia: Perspectives from India, Nepal, and Sri Lanka*, edited by S. Hettige and E. Gerharz, 99–127. New Delhi: Sage.

Gellner, D. N., S. L. Hausner, and C. Letizia, eds. 2016. *Religion, Secularism, and Ethnicity in Contemporary Nepal*. New Delhi: Oxford University Press.

Gellner, D. N., and E. Hirsch. 2001. *Inside Organizations: Anthropologists at Work*. Oxford, UK: Berg.

Gellner, D. N., and M. B. Karki. 2010. "Surveying Activists in Nepal." In *Varieties of Activist Experience: Civil Society in South Asia*, edited by D. N. Gellner, 131–58. London: Sage.

Gellner, D. N., and C. Letizia. 2016. "Introduction: Religion and Identities in Post-Panchayat Nepal." In *Religion, Secularism, and Ethnicity in Contemporary Nepal*, edited by D. N. Gellner, S. L. Hausner, and C. Letizia, 1–34. New Delhi: Oxford University Press.

Gellner, D. N., J. Pfaff-Czarnecka, and J. Whelpton, eds. 1997. *Nationalism and Ethnicity in a Hindu Kingdom: The Politics of Culture in Contemporary Nepal*. Amsterdam: Harwood Academic Publishers.

Gellner, D. N., and D. Quigley, eds. 1999. *Contested Hierarchies: A Collaborative Ethnography of Caste among the Newars of the Kathmandu Valley, Nepal*. New Delhi: Oxford University Press.

Gramsci, A. 1924. "Contro il pessimismo." *L'Ordine Nuovo: Rassegna Settimanale di Cultura Socialista*, March 15. Published as "Against Pessimism," in *Antonio Gramsci: Selections from Political Writings (1921–1926)*, trans. and ed. Q. Hoare (London: Lawrence and Wishart, 1978).

Guha, R. 1989. "Dominance without Hegemony and Its Historiography." In *Subaltern Studies VI: Writings on South Asian History and Society*, edited by R. Guha, 210–309. Delhi: Oxford University Press.

Guneratne, A. 2002. *Many Tongues, One People: The Making of Tharu Identity in Nepal*. Ithaca, NY: Cornell University Press.

Hachhethu, K. 2000. "Nepali Politics: Political Parties, Political Crisis, and Problem of Governance." In *Domestic Conflict and Crisis of Governability in Nepal*, edited by D. Kumar, 90–116. Kathmandu: Centre for Nepal and Asian Studies, Tribhuvan University.

———. 2002. *Party Building in Nepal: Organization, Leadership, and People*. Kathmandu: Mandala Book Point.

———. 2008. "Local Democracy and Political Parties in Nepal: A Case Study of Dhanusha District." In *Local Democracy in South Asia: Microprocesses of Democratization in Nepal and Its Neighbours*, edited by D. N. Gellner and K. Hachhethu, 45–70. New Delhi: Sage.

———. 2009. "The Communist Party of Nepal (Maoist): Transformation from an Insurgency Group to a Competitive Political Party." *European Bulletin of Himalayan Research*, nos. 33–34: 29–73.

Hachhethu, K., T. N. Shah, and R. K. Kamat. 2015. *Politics of Representation in Nepal*. Kathmandu: Nepal Madhesh Foundation.

Hangen, S. 2007. *Creating a "New Nepal": The Ethnic Dimension*. Washington, DC: East-West Center.

———. 2010. *The Rise of Ethnic Politics in Nepal*. London: Routledge.

Hannan, M. T., and J. Freeman. 1986. "Where Do Organizational Forms Come From?" *Sociological Forum* 1, no. 1: 50–72.

Harper, I., and C. Tarnowski. 2002. "A Heterotopia of Resistance: Health, Community Forestry, and Challenges to State Centralization in Nepal." In *Resistance and the State: Nepalese Experiences*, edited by D. N. Gellner, 33–82. New Delhi: Social Science Press.

Harris, J. 2005. "The Ordering of Things: Organization in Bruno Latour." In *Contemporary Organization Theory*, edited by C. Jones and R. Munro, 165–77. Malden, MA: Blackwell.

Harvey, D. 2000. *Spaces of Hope*. Berkeley: University of California Press.

———. 2003. *The New Imperialism*. Oxford: Oxford University Press.

Haviland, C. 2005. "Top Nepal Student Leader Arrested." BBC, April 26. http://news .bbc.co.uk/1/hi/world/south_asia/4485291.stm.

Hayes, L. 1976. "Educational Reform and Student Political Behavior in Nepal." *Asian Survey* 16, no. 8: 752–69.

Heaton Shrestha, C. 2010. "Activists and Development in Nepal." In *Varieties of Activist Experience: Civil Society in South Asia*, edited by D. N. Gellner, 181–216. London: Sage.

Henslin, J. M. 1972. "Studying Deviance in Four Settings: Research Experiences with Cabbies, Suicides, Drug Users, and Abortionees." In *Research on Deviance*, edited by J. Douglas, 35–70. New York: Random House.

Herzfeld, M. 2002. "Uncanny Success: Some Closing Remarks." In *Elites: Choice, Leadership, and Succession*, edited by J. Pina-Cabral and A. Pedroso de Lima, 227–35. Oxford, UK: Berg.

Himalayan Times. 2014. "Editorial: Action Counts." June 18. www.thehimalayantimes .com/fullNews.php?headline=EDITORIAL%3A+Action+counts&NewsID=418548.

Hindman, H. 2014a. *Mediating the Global: Expatria's Forms and Consequences in Kathmandu*. Stanford, CA: Stanford University Press.

———. 2014b. "Post-Political in the Post-Conflict: DIY Capitalism, Anarcho-Neoliberalism, and Nepal's Ungovernable Mountains." Fieldsights—Hot Spots, *Cultural Anthropology Online*, March 24. www.culanth.org/fieldsights/507-post-political-in -the-post-conflict-diy-capitalism-anarcho-neoliberalism-and-nepal-s-ungovernable -mountains.

Hirslund, D. 2012. "Sacrificing Youth: Maoist Cadres and Political Activism in Post-War Nepal." PhD diss., University of Copenhagen.

———. 2014. "The Politics of Post-Conflict Democratization: Justice and Insurgency after the War." Fieldsights—Hot Spots, *Cultural Anthropology Online*, March 24. www.culanth.org/fieldsights/508-the-politics-of-post-conflict-democratization -justice-and-insurgency-after-the-war.

HMG (His Majesty's Government), High Level Commission. 1996. *Yuba Kriyaakalaaph sambandhi*. Internal report commissioned by the Ministry of Youth, Culture, and Sports, Kathmandu.

HMG (His Majesty's Government), Ministry of Education. 1971. *The National Education System Plan for 1971–76*. Kathmandu: Bureau of Publications.

Höfer, A. 1979. *The Caste Hierarchy and the State in Nepal: A Study of the Muluki Ain of 1854*. Khumbu Himal, vol. 13, pt. 2. Innsbruck, Austria: Universitätsverlag Wagner.

Hoftun, M., W. Raeper, and J. Whelpton. 1999. *People, Politics, and Ideology: Democracy and Social Change in Nepal.* Kathmandu: Mandala Book Point.

Holmberg, D. H. 1989. *Order in Paradox: Myth, Ritual, and Exchange among Nepal's Tamang.* Ithaca, NY: Cornell University Press.

———. 2000. "Derision, Exorcism, and the Ritual Production of Power." *American Ethnologist* 27, no. 4: 1–23.

———. 2011. "Contingency, Collaboration, and the Unimagined over Thirty-Five Years of Ethnography." In *Returns to the Field: Multitemporal Research and Contemporary Anthropology,* edited by S. Howell and A. Talle, 95–123. Bloomington: Indiana University Press.

Huber, M. T., and J. Emel. 2009. "Fixed Minerals, Scalar Politics: The Weight of Scale in Conflicts over the '1872 Mining Law' in the United States." *Environment and Planning A* 41, no. 2: 371–88.

Huizer, G. 1973. *Peasant Rebellion in Latin America.* Harmondsworth: Penguin.

Hutt, M. 1997. "Being Nepali without Nepal: Reflections on a South Asian Diaspora." In *Nationalism and Ethnicity in a Hindu Kingdom: The Politics of Culture in Contemporary Nepal,* edited by D. N. Gellner, J. Pfaff-Czarnecka, and J. Whelpton, 101–44. Amsterdam: Harwood Academic Publishers.

———, ed. 2004. *Himalayan People's War: Nepal's Maoist Rebellion.* Bloomington: Indiana University Press.

———. 2012. "Reading Maoist Memoirs." *Studies in Nepali History and Society* 17, no. 1: 107–42.

ICG (International Crisis Group). 2005. "Nepal's New Alliance: The Mainstream Parties and the Maoists." ICG Asia Report 106. Brussels: ICG.

———. 2012a. "Nepal's Constitution (I): Evolution Not Revolution." ICG Asia Report 233. Brussels: ICG.

———. 2012b. "Nepal's Constitution (II): Political Matrix." ICG Asia Report 234. Brussels: ICG.

———. 2016. "Nepal's Divisive New Constitution: An Existential Crisis." ICG Asia Report 276. Brussels: ICG.

Ismail, F. 2014. "The Consequences of Co-option: NGOs, the Left, and Social Change in Nepal." PhD thesis, School of Oriental and African Studies, University of London.

Jaffrelot, C. 2007. *Hindu Nationalism: A Reader.* Princeton, NJ: Princeton University Press.

Jeffrey, C. 2010. *Timepass: Youth, Class, and the Politics of Waiting in India.* Stanford, CA: Stanford University Press.

Jha, P. 2014a. *Battles of the New Republic: A Contemporary History of Nepal.* New Delhi: Aleph Book Company.

———. 2014b. "Nepal's Constitution Making: Bringing Consensus Back to Kathmandu." *Hindustan Times,* November 17.

Johnson-Hanks, J. 2002. "On the Limits of Life Stages in Ethnography: Toward a Theory of Vital Conjunctures." *American Anthropologist* 104, no. 3: 865–80.

———. 2005. "When the Future Decides: Uncertainty and Intentional Action in Contemporary Cameroon." *Current Anthropology* 46, no. 3: 363–85.

Joshi, B., and L. Rose. (1966) 2004. *Democratic Innovations in Nepal: A Case Study of Political Acculturation*. Kathmandu: Mandala Publications.

Kathmandu Post. 2012. "Youth Self-Employment Programme." April 26. http://kath mandupost.ekantipur.com/printedition/news/2012-04-26/youth-self-employment -programme.html.

Katz, C. 2004. *Growing Up Global: Economic Restructuring and Children's Everyday Lives*. Minneapolis: University of Minnesota Press.

Kaviraj, S. 1998. "The Culture of Representative Democracy in India." In *Wages of Freedom: Fifty Years of the Indian Nation-State*, edited by P. Chatterjee, 147–78. Delhi: Oxford University Press.

K.C., S. 1999. *Nepalma Communist Andolan ko Itihas*. Kathmandu: Vidyārthī Pustak Bhandar.

Keck, M. E., and K. Sikkink. 1998. *Activists beyond Borders: Advocacy Networks in International Politics*. Ithaca, NY: Cornell University Press.

Keniston, K. 1968. *Young Radicals: Notes on Committed Youth*. New York: Harcourt, Brace and World.

Khadka, N. 2000. "U.S. Aid to Nepal in the Cold War Period: Lessons for the Future." *Pacific Affairs* 73, no. 1: 77–95.

Khanal, K. 1995. "Party Politics and Governance: The Role of Leadership." In *State, Leadership, and Politics in Nepal*, edited by D. Kumar, 50–67. Kathmandu: Centre for Nepal and Asian Studies, Tribhuvan University.

Krauskopff, G., and M. Lecomte-Tilouine, eds. 1996. *Célébrer le pouvoir: Dasaï, une fête royal au Népal*. Paris: CNRS Éditions / Éditions de la Maison des Sciences de l'Homme.

Kunreuther, L. 2014. *Voicing Subjects: Public Intimacy and Mediation in Kathmandu*. Berkeley: University of California Press.

Lakier, G. 2007. "Illiberal Democracy and the Problem of Law: Street Protest and Democratization in Multiparty Nepal." In *Contentious Politics and Democratization in Nepal*, edited by M. Lawoti, 251–72. New Delhi: Sage.

Latour, B. 1987. *Science in Action: How to Follow Scientists and Engineers through Society*. Cambridge, MA: Harvard University Press.

———. 1994. "On Technical Mediation: Philosophy, Sociology, Genealogy." *Common Knowledge* 3, no. 2: 29–64.

Latschan, T. 2015. "Stateless in Nepal—How a Patriarchal System Denies Citizenship to Millions." Deutsche Welle, January 29. www.dw.com/en/stateless-in-nepal-how -a-patriarchal-system-denies-citizenship-to-millions/a-18223750.

Lawoti, M. 2005. *Towards a Democratic Nepal: Inclusive Political Institutions for Multicultural Society*. New Delhi: Sage.

Lawoti, M., and A. Pahari, eds. 2010. *The Maoist Insurgency in Nepal: Revolution in the Twenty-First Century*. Routledge Contemporary South Asia Series. London: Routledge.

Leach, E. (1954) 1970. *Political Systems of Highland Burma: A Study of Kachin Social Structure*. London: Athlone Press.

Lecomte-Tilouine, M. 2005. "The Transgressive Nature of Kingship in Caste Organization: Monstrous Royal Doubles in Nepal." In *The Character of Kingship*, edited by D. Quigley, 101–21. Oxford, UK: Berg.

————. 2006. "'Kill One, He Becomes One Hundred': Martyrdom as Generative Sacrifice in the Nepal People's War." *Social Analysis* 50, no. 1: 51–72.

————, ed. 2013. *Revolution in Nepal*. Oxford: Oxford University Press.

Lecomte-Tilouine, M., and P. Dolfus, eds. 2003. *Ethnic Revival and Religious Turmoil: Identities and Representations in the Himalayas*. New Delhi: Oxford University Press.

Lenin, V. I. (1920) 1971. "Left-Wing Communism, an Infantile Disorder." In *V. I. Lenin, Selected Works*, vol. 1. New York: International Publishers.

Letizia, C. 2012. "Shaping Secularism in Nepal." *European Bulletin of Himalayan Research*, no. 39: 66–104.

Leve, L. 2007. "'Secularism Is a Human Right!': Double-Binds of Buddhism, Democracy, and Identity in Nepal." In *The Practice of Human Rights: Tracking Law between the Global and the Local*, edited by M. Goodale and S. E. Merry, 78–113. Cambridge: Cambridge University Press.

Levine, N. E. 1987. "Caste, State, and Ethnic Boundaries in Nepal." *Journal of Asian Studies* 46, no. 1: 71–88.

LeVine, S. 2006. "Getting in, Dropping out, and Staying On." *Anthropology and Education Quarterly* 37, no. 1: 21–41.

Liechty, M. 1995. "Media, Markets, and Modernization: Youth Identities and Experience of Modernity in Kathmandu, Nepal." In *Youth Cultures: A Cross-Cultural Perspective*, edited by V. Amit-Talai and H. Wulff, 185–202. New York: Routledge.

————. 2003. *Suitably Modern: Making Middle-Class Culture in a New Consumer Society*. Princeton, NJ: Princeton University Press.

MacKinnon, D. 2010. "Reconstructing Scale: Towards a New Scalar Politics." *Progress in Human Geography* 35, no. 1: 21–36.

Madsen, U. A., and S. Carney. 2011. "Education in an Age of Radical Uncertainty: Youth and Schooling in Urban Nepal." *Globalisation, Societies and Education* 9, no. 1: 115–33.

Mains, D. 2007. "Neoliberal Times: Progress, Boredom, and Shame among Young Men in Urban Ethiopia." *American Ethnologist* 34, no. 4: 659–73.

Malagodi, M. 2013. *Constitutional Nationalism and Legal Exclusion*. Oxford: Oxford University Press.

Manchanda, R. 2008. "Waiting for 'Naya' Nepal." *Economic and Political Weekly* 43, no. 29: 23–26.

Mannheim, K. 1952. "The Problem of Generations." In *Essays on the Sociology of Knowledge*, edited by P. Kecskemeti, 276–320. London: Routledge and Kegan Paul.

March, K. 2002. *"If Each Comes Halfway": Meeting Tamang Women in Nepal*. Ithaca, NY: Cornell University Press.

Masquelier, A. 2005. "The Scorpion's Sting: Youth, Marriage, and the Struggle for Social Maturity in Niger." *Journal of the Royal Anthropological Institute* 11, no. 1: 59–83.

Mathema, K. B. 2007. "Crisis in Education and Future Challenges for Nepal." *European Bulletin of Himalayan Research*, no. 31: 46–67.

Mead, M. 1928. *Coming of Age in Samoa: A Psychological Study of Primitive Youth for Western Civilization*. New York: William Morrow.

Mehta, U. S. 1999. *Liberalism and Empire*. Chicago: University of Chicago Press.

Memmi, A. 1965. *The Colonizer and the Colonized*. Boston: Beacon Press.

Merry, S. E. 2006. *Human Rights and Gender Violence: Translating International Law into Local Justice*. Chicago: University of Chicago Press.

Messerschmidt, D., Y. Gautam, and B. Silwal. 2007. "History and Significance of National Development Service (NDS): Creating 'Civil Space' and Commitment to Service in Nepal during the 1970s." *Occasional Papers in Sociology and Anthropology* 10: 174–207.

Miller, C. 1990. *Decision Making in Village Nepal*. Kathmandu: Sahayogi Press.

Mines, M. 1994. *Public Faces, Private Voices: Community and Individuality in South India*. Berkeley: University of California Press.

Ministry of Education and Sports. 2000. *School Level Educational Statistics, 1999*. Kathmandu: Ministry of Education and Sports.

———. 2004. *School Level Educational Statistics*. Kathmandu: Ministry of Education and Sports.

Ministry of Youth and Sports. 2010. *National Youth Policy, 2010*. Kathmandu: Government of Nepal.

Minkoff, D., and J. D. McCarthy. 2005. "Reinvigorating the Study of Organizational Processes in Social Movements." *Mobilization* 10, no. 2: 289–308.

Mitchell, T. 1991. *Colonizing Egypt*. Berkeley: University of California Press.

Miyazaki, H. 2004. *The Method of Hope: Anthropology, Philosophy, and Fijian Knowledge*. Stanford, CA: Stanford University Press.

Mocko, A. 2015. *Demoting Vishnu: Ritual, Politics, and the Unraveling of Nepal's Hindu Monarchy*. Oxford: Oxford University Press.

Mouffe, C. 2000. *The Democratic Paradox*. London: Verso.

———. 2005. *On the Political*. London: Routledge.

Nash, J. 1976. "Ethnology in a Revolutionary Setting." In *Ethics and Anthropology: Dilemmas in Fieldwork*, edited by M. Rynkiewich and J. Spradley, 148–73. London: Routledge and Kegan Paul.

National Planning Commission. 1998. *Ninth Plan (1997–2002)*. Kathmandu: National Planning Commission.

———. 2008. *National Plan of Action for Youth Employment (2008–2015)*. Kathmandu: National Planning Commission.

Nelson, Dean. 2015. "'Where Is Our Government?' Ask Survivors of Nepal Earthquake." *Telegraph*, April 28.

Nepali Times. 2003. "Keep the Window Open." May 9. http://nepalitimes.com/news.php?id=2939#.WX-wENPyufc.

NEPC (National Education Planning Commission). 1956. *Education in Nepal: Report of the Nepal National Education Planning Commission*. Kathmandu: Bureau of Publications, College of Education.

Nightingale, A. J. 2005. "'The Experts Taught Us All We Know': Professionalisation and Knowledge in Nepalese Community Forestry." *Antipode* 37, no. 3: 581–604.

Nightingale, A. J., A. Bhatterai, H. Ojha, T. Sigdel, K. N. Rankin, and P. Hamal. Forthcoming. "Fragmented Public Authority and State Un/making in the 'New' Republic of Nepal." *Modern Asian Studies*.

Ogura, K. 2001. *Kathmandu Spring: The People's Movement of 1990*. Kathmandu: Himal Books.

———. 2008. "Maoist People's Governments, 2001–05: The Power in Wartime." In *Local Democracy in South Asia: Microprocesses of Democratization in Nepal and Its Neighbours*, edited by D. N. Gellner and K. Hachhethu, 175–231. New Delhi: Sage.

Ojha, M. 2012. *Student Politics and Democracy in Nepal*. New Delhi: Nirala Publications.

Ollieuz, A. 2011. "The Political History of Indagru VDC." *New Angle: Nepal Journal of Social Science and Public Policy* 1, no. 1: 32–48.

Onta, P. 1996. "Ambivalence Denied: The Making of Rastriya Itihas in Panchayat Era Textbooks." *Contributions to Nepalese Studies* 23, no. 1: 213–54.

———. 2002. "Critiquing the Media Boom." In *State of Nepal*, edited by K. M. Dixit and S. Ramachandaran, 253–69. Kathmandu: Himal Books.

Ortner, S. 1989. *High Religion: A Cultural and Political History of Sherpa Buddhism*. Princeton, NJ: Princeton University Press.

Osuri, G. 2013. *Religious Freedom in India: Sovereignty and (Anti) Conversion*. London: Routledge.

Paley, J. 2002. "Toward an Anthropology of Democracy." *Annual Review of Anthropology* 31: 469–96.

Panday, D. R. 1999. *Nepal's Failed Development: Reflections on the Mission and the Maladies*. Kathmandu: Nepal South Asia Centre.

Paramanand, B. 1982. *The Nepali Congress since Its Inception*. Delhi: B. R. Publishing.

Parish, S. 1994. *Moral Knowing in a Hindu Sacred City: An Exploration of Mind, Emotion, and Self*. New York: Columbia University Press.

Parry, J. 1999. "Two Cheers for Reservation: The Satnamis and the Steel Plant." In *Institutions and Inequalities: Essays in Honour of André Béteille*, edited by R. Guha and J. Parry, 128–69. Delhi: Oxford University Press.

Pettigrew, J. 2014. *Maoists at the Hearth: Everyday Life in Nepal's Civil War*. Philadelphia: University of Pennsylvania Press.

Pettigrew, J., and S. Shneiderman. 2004. "Women and the Maobaadi: Ideology and Agency in Nepal's Maoist Movement." *Himal South Asian*, January, 19–29.

Pfaff-Czarnecka, J. 2004. "High Expectations, Deep Disappointments: Politics, State, and Society in Nepal after 1990." In *Himalayan People's War: Nepal's Maoist Rebellion*, edited by M. Hutt, 166–90. Bloomington: Indiana University Press.

———. 2008. "Distributional Coalitions in Nepal: An Essay on Democratization, Capture, and (Lack of) Confidence." In *Local Democracy in South Asia: Microprocesses of Democratization in Nepal and Its Neighbours*, edited by D. N. Gellner and K. Hachhethu, 71–104. New Delhi: Sage.

Pherali, T. J. 2011. "Education and Conflict in Nepal: Possibilities for Reconstruction." *Globalisation, Societies and Education* 9, no. 1: 135–54.

Pherali, T. J., A. Smith, and T. Vaux. 2011. "A Political Economy Analysis of Education in Nepal." Kathmandu: European Commission.

Pierre, J., and B. G. Peters. 2000. *Governance, Politics, and the State*. New York: St. Martin's Press.

Pigg, S. 1992. "Inventing Social Categories through Place: Social Representations and Development in Nepal." *Comparative Studies in Society and History* 34, no. 3: 491–513.

———. 1997. "'Found in Most Traditional Societies': Traditional Medical Practitioners between Culture and Development." In *International Development and the*

Social Sciences, edited by F. Cooper and R. Packard, 259–90. Berkeley: University of California Press.

Pignède, B. (1966) 1993. *The Gurungs: A Himalayan Population of Nepal*. Kathmandu: Ratna Pustak Bhandar.

Piliavsky, A. 2014. Introduction to *Patronage as Politics in South Asia*, edited by A. Piliavsky, 1–38. Cambridge: Cambridge University Press.

Povinelli, E. 2002. *The Cunning of Recognition: Indigenous Alterities and the Making of Multiculturalism*. Durham, NC: Duke University Press.

Ragsdale, T. 1989. *Once a Hermit Kingdom: Ethnicity, Education, and National Integration in Nepal*. New Delhi: Manohar.

Ramirez, P. 2000. *De la disparition des chefs: Une anthropologie politique népalaise*. Paris: CNRS Éditions.

Rana, G. 1995. *Prajatankrik Āndolanmaa Nepali Vidyārthī Sangh*. Kathmandu: Prakashak Press.

Rancière, J. 1994. *The Names of History: On the Poetics of Knowledge*. Translated by H. Melehy. Minneapolis: University of Minnesota Press.

———. 1999. *Disagreement: Politics and Philosophy*. Translated by J. Rose. Minneapolis: University of Minnesota Press.

———. 2004. "Who Is the Subject of the Rights of Man?" *South Atlantic Quarterly* 103, nos. 2–3: 297–310.

———. 2010. *Dissensus: On Politics and Aesthetics*. Edited and translated by S. Corcoran. London: Continuum.

Rankin, K. N. 2004. *The Cultural Politics of Markets: Economic Liberalization and Social Change in Nepal*. London: Pluto Press.

Rappleye, J. 2011. "Catalysing Educational Development or Institutionalising External Influence? Donors, Civil Society, and Educational Policy Formation in Nepal." *Globalisation, Societies and Education* 9, no. 1: 27–49.

Rayamajhi, S., and B. Subedi. 1999. *Use of Language in the Nepali Press: An Investigative Report*. Kathmandu: Across Publications Nepal.

Revolutionary Worker. 2000. "Red Flag Flying on the Roof of the World: Inside the Revolution in Nepal." No. 1043 (February 20). www.revcom.us/a/v21/1040-049/1043/interv.htm.

Riaz, A., and S. Basu. 2007. *Paradise Lost? State Failure in Nepal*. Plymouth, UK: Lexington Books.

RIM Committee (Revolutionary Internationalist Movement Committee). 2001. "Open Letter to the Central Committee, Communist of Nepal (Maoist)." *A World to Win*, no. 27: 60–61. http://bannedthought.net/International/RIM/AWTW/2001-27/AWTW-27-CoRIM-to-CPNM.pdf.

Sahlins, M. 2011. "What Kinship Is (Part One)." *Journal of the Royal Anthropological Institute* 17, no. 1: 2–19.

Sayer, D. 1994. "Everyday Forms of State Formation: Some Dissident Remarks on 'Hegemony.'" In *Everyday Forms of State Formation: Revolution and Negotiation of Rule in Modern Mexico*, edited by G. M. Joseph and D. Nugent, 367–77. Durham, NC: Duke University Press.

Scott, J. C. 1985. *Weapons of the Weak: Everyday Forms of Peasant Resistance*. Hartford, CT: Yale University Press.

Sen, P. K. 2015. "Should Nepal Be a Hindu State or a Secular State?" *Himalaya* 35, no. 1: 65–90.

Shah, A., and S. Shneiderman. 2013a. "The Practices, Policies, and Politics of Transforming Inequality in South Asia: Ethnographies of Affirmative Action." In "Towards an Anthropology of Affirmative Action," edited by A. Shah and S. Shneiderman, special issue, *Focaal: Journal of Global and Historical Anthropology* 65: 3–12.

———, eds. 2013b. "Towards an Anthropology of Affirmative Action." Special issue, *Focaal: Journal of Global and Historical Anthropology*, vol. 65.

Shah, S. 2002. "From Evil State to Civil Society." In *State of Nepal*, edited by K. M. Dixit and S. Ramachandaran, 137–211. Kathmandu: Himal Books.

Shaha, R. 1982. *Essays on the Practice of Government in Nepal.* New Delhi: Manohar.

Shaha, S. 2004. "A Himalayan Red Herring? Maoist Revolution in the Shadow of the Raj." In *Himalayan People's War: Nepal's Maoist Rebellion*, edited by M. Hutt, 192–224. Bloomington: Indiana University Press.

Shakya, D., and K. Hatakeyama. 2008. "Parentocracy, Not Meritocracy, in Basic Education of Nepal." *Studies in Nepali History and Society* 13, no. 1: 1–16.

Sharma, P. 2007. *Unravelling the Mosaic: Spatial Aspects of Ethnicity in Nepal.* Kathmandu: Himal Books.

Sharma, S. 2002. "The Hindu State and the State of Hinduism." In *State of Nepal*, edited by K. M. Dixit and S. Ramachandaran, 22–38. Kathmandu: Himal Books.

Sharma, S., and B. K. Khadka. 2011. *Nepal Contemporary Political Situation—VI, VII, and VIII: Opinion Poll Report.* Kathmandu: Interdisciplinary Analysts.

Sharrock, J. 2013. "Stability in Transition: Development Perspectives and Local Politics in Nepal." *European Bulletin of Himalayan Research*, no. 42: 9–38.

Shields, R., and J. Rappleye. 2008. "Uneven Terrain: Educational Policy and Equity in Nepal." *Asia Pacific Journal of Education* 28, no. 3: 265–76.

Shneiderman, S. 2009a. "The Formation of Political Consciousness in Rural Nepal." *Dialectical Anthropology* 33, nos. 3–4: 287–308.

———. 2009b. "Rituals of Ethnicity: Migration, Mixture, and the Making of Thangmi Identity across Himalayan Borders." PhD diss., Cornell University.

———. 2010. "Creating 'Civilized' Communists: A Quarter of a Century of Politicization in Nepal." In *Varieties of Activist Experience: Civil Society in South Asia*, edited by D. N. Gellner, 46–80. London: Sage.

———. 2015. *Rituals of Ethnicity: Thangmi Identities between Nepal and India.* Philadelphia: University of Pennsylvania Press.

Shneiderman, S., and A. Snellinger. 2014. "Framing the Issues: The Politics of 'Post-Conflict.'" Fieldsights—Hot Spots, *Cultural Anthropology Online*, March 24. www.culanth.org/fieldsights/500-framing-the-issues-the-politics-of-post-conflict.

Shore, C. 2002. "Introduction: Towards an Anthropology of Elites." In *Elite Cultures: Anthropological Perspectives*, edited by C. Shore and S. Nugent, 1–21. London: Routledge.

Shrestha, P. L. 1996. *A Short History of the Communist Movement in Nepal.* Kathmandu: Pushpa Lal Memorial Academy.

Singh, A. 2013. "Higher Education in Nepal." Working paper. University of Oslo, Department of Educational Sciences. www.academia.edu/4768986/Higher_Education_Policy_in_Nepal.

Sivaramakrishnan, K., and A. Agrawal, eds. 2003. *Regional Modernities: The Cultural Politics of Development in India*. Stanford, CA: Stanford University Press.

Siwakoti, G. 2000. "Foreign Intervention in Politics through NGOs: A Case of the Left in Nepal." In *Development NGOs Facing the 21st Century: Perspectives from South Asia*, edited by J. Vartola, M. Ulvila, F. Hossain, and T. N. Dhakal, 134–43. Kathmandu: Institute for Human Development.

Skinner, D., and D. C. Holland. 1996. "Schools and the Cultural Production of the Educated Person in a Nepalese Hill Community." In *The Cultural Production of the Educated Person: Critical Ethnographies of Schooling and Local Practice*, edited by B. A. Levinson, D. E. Foley, and D. C. Holland, 273–300. Albany: State University of New York Press.

Smith, N. 2004. "Scale Bending and the Fate of the National." In *Scale and Geographic Inquiry: Nature, Society, and Method*, edited by E. Sheppard and R. B. McMaster, 192–212. Oxford, UK: Blackwell.

Snellinger, A. 2005. "A Crisis in Nepali Student Politics? Analyzing the Gap between Politically Active and Non-active Students." *Peace and Democracy in South Asia* 1, no. 2: 18–44.

———. 2006. "Commitment as an Analytic: Reflections on Nepali Student Activists' Protracted Struggle." *Political and Legal Anthropology Review* 29, no. 2: 351–64.

———. 2007. "Student Movements in Nepal: Their Parameters and Their Idealized Forms." In *Contentious Politics and Democratization in Nepal*, edited by M. Lawoti, 273–98. New Delhi: Sage.

———. 2009a. "Democratic Form: Conceptions and Practices in the Making of 'New Nepal.'" *Sociological Bulletin* (Journal of the Indian Sociological Society) 58, no. 1: 43–70.

———. 2009b. "'Yuba, Hamro Pusta': Youth and Generational Politics in Nepali Political Culture." *Studies in Nepali History and Society* 14, no. 1: 39–66.

———. 2010. "The Repertoire of Scientific Organization: Ideology, Identity, and the Maoist Student Union." In *The Maoist Insurgency in Nepal: Revolution in the Twenty-First Century*, edited by M. Lawoti and A. Pahari, 73–91. Routledge Contemporary South Asia Series. London: Routledge.

———. 2013. "Shaping a Livable Present and Future: Review of Youth Studies in Nepal." *European Bulletin of Himalayan Research*, no. 42: 75–104.

———. 2014. "Mobilizing for What? A Discursive History of Nepal's National Youth Policy." In *Proceedings from the 2013 Annual Kathmandu Conference on Nepal and the Himalaya*. Kathmandu: Social Science Baha.

———. 2015a. "Nepal's Earthquake Politics: A Call for Decentralization." Editorial, *CounterPunch*, May 4. www.counterpunch.org/2015/05/04/nepals-earthquake-politics.

———. 2015b. "The Production of Possibility through an Impossible Ideal: Consensus as a Political Value in Nepal's Constituent Assembly." *Constellations: An International Journal of Critical and Democratic Theory* 22, no. 2: 233–45.

———. 2016a. "'Let's See What Happens': Hope, Contingency, and Speculation in Nepali Student Activism." *Critical Asian Studies* 48, no. 1: 27–49.

———. 2016b. "Perspective: Nationalism and Exclusion in Postwar Nepal." *Current History: A Journal of Contemporary World Affairs* 115, no. 780: 154–59.

————. 2017. "'Pure Democracy' in 'New Nepal': Conceptions, Practices, and Anxieties." In *Democratisation in the Himalayas*, edited by V. Arora and N. Jayaram, 135–58. London: Routledge.

————. Forthcoming. "From (Violent) Protest to Policy: Rearticulating Authority through the National Youth Policy in Post-War Nepal." *Modern Asian Studies.*

Snow, D., and R. Benford. 1992. "Master Frames and Cycles of Protest." In *Frontiers in Social Movement Theory*, edited by A. Morris and C. McClurg Mueller, 133–55. New Haven, CT: Yale University Press.

Spencer, J. 2007. *Anthropology, Politics, and the State: Democracy and Violence in South Asia.* Cambridge: Cambridge University Press.

Stash, S., and E. Hannum. 2001 "Who Goes to School? Educational Stratification by Gender, Caste, and Ethnicity in Nepal." *Comparative Education Review* 45, no. 3: 354–78.

Stirr, A. 2013. "Tears for the Revolution: Nepali Musical Nationalism, Emotion, and the Maoist Movement." In *Revolution in Nepal*, edited by M. Lecomte-Tilouine, 367–92. Oxford: Oxford University Press.

Strathern, M. 1988. *Gender of the Gift.* Berkeley: University of California Press.

————. 1991. "One Man and Many Men." In *Big Men and Great Men: Personifications of Power in Melanesia*, edited by M. Godelier and M. Strathern, 197–214. Cambridge: Cambridge University Press.

Subedi, R. 2009. "Politics of Aid." *Nepali Times*, November 27–December 3.

Subramanian, A. 2009. *Shorelines: Space and Rights in South India.* Stanford, CA: Stanford University Press.

Suykens, B., and D. Stein. 2014. "Neutrality, Party Politics, and Community Mediation in the Central and West Terai, Nepal." London: Justice and Security Research Programme, International Development Department, London School of Economics and Political Science.

Tamang, M. S. 2008. "Himalayan Indigeneity: Histories, Memory, and Identity among Tamang in Nepal." PhD diss., Cornell University.

Tamang, S. 2000. "Legalizing State Patriarchy in Nepal." *Studies in Nepali History and Society* 5, no. 1: 127–56.

————. 2002. "Civilizing Civil Society: Donors and Democracy Space." *Studies in Nepali History and Society* 7, no. 2: 309–53.

————. 2012. "Historicizing State Fragility in Nepal." *Studies in Nepali History and Society* 17, no. 2: 263–95.

Tarrow, S. 1996. "States and Opportunities: The Political Structuring of Social Movements." In *Comparative Perspectives on Social Movements*, edited by D. McAdam, J. D. McCarthy, and M. N. Zald, 41–61. Cambridge: Cambridge University Press.

Thapa, D. 2004. "Radicalism and the Emergence of the Maoists." In *Himalayan People's War: Nepal's Maoist Rebellion*, edited by M. Hutt, 21–37. Bloomington: Indiana University Press.

Thapa, D., and B. Sijapati. 2003. *A Kingdom under Siege: Nepal's Maoist Insurgency, 1996 to 2003.* Kathmandu: Printhouse.

Thapa, M. 2015. "Women Have No Nationality: Why I Burned My Country's New Constitution." *Record* (Nepal), September 21. www.recordnepal.com/perspective/women-have-no-nationality.

Tilly, C. 1995. "Contentious Repertoires in Great Britain, 1758–1834." In *Repertoires and Cycles of Collective Action*, edited by M. Traugott, 15–42. Durham, NC: Duke University Press.

Turin, M. 2000. "Time for a True Population Census: The Case of the Miscounted Thangmi." *Nagarik* (Citizen) 2, no. 4: 14–19.

Turner, V. 1969. *The Ritual Process: Structure and Anti-Structure*. New York: Aldine de Gruyter.

UN (United Nations). 2007. *United Nations Development Assistance Framework for Nepal, 2008–2010*. Kathmandu: UN.

———. 2010. *World Programme of Action for Youth*. New York: United Nations.

Upadhya, S. 2002. "A Dozen Years of Democracy: The Games That Parties Play." In *State of Nepal*, edited by K. M. Dixit and S. Ramachandaran, 62–76. Kathmandu: Himal Books.

Upreti, B. R., S. K.C., R. Mallett, and B. Babajanian. 2012. "Livelihoods, Basic Services, and Social Protection in Nepal." Working Paper 7. London: National Center for Contemporary Resources.

Vaidya, T. R. 1992. "A Case Study on 'National Development Service' Nepal." In *Nepal: A Study of Socio-Economic and Political Changes*, edited by T. R. Vaidya, 128–48. New Delhi: Anmol Publications.

Valentin, K. 2011. "Modernity, Education, and Its Alternatives: Schooling among the Urban Poor in Kathmandu." *Globalisation, Societies and Education* 9, no. 1: 99–113.

van der Veer, Peter. 1994. *Religious Nationalism: Hindus and Muslims in India*. Berkeley: University of California Press.

von Einsiedel, S., D. Malone, and S. Pradhan, eds. 2012. *Nepal in Transition: From People's War to Fragile Peace*. Cambridge: Cambridge University Press.

Wagner, R. 1975. *The Invention of Culture*. Chicago: University of Chicago Press.

Weick, K. E. 1979. *The Social Psychology of Organizing*. 2nd ed. New York: Addison-Wesley.

Whelpton, J. 1991. *Kings, Soldiers, and Priests: Nepalese Politics and the Rise of Jang Bahadur Rana, 1830–1857*. New Delhi: Manohar.

———. 1997. "Political Identity in Nepal: State, Nation, and Community." In *Nationalism and Ethnicity in a Hindu Kingdom: The Politics of Culture in Contemporary Nepal*, edited by D. N. Gellner, J. Pfaff-Czarnecka, and J. Whelpton, 39–78. Amsterdam: Harwood Academic Publishers.

———. 2005. *A History of Nepal*. Cambridge: Cambridge University Press.

Winther-Schmidt, E. 2011. "Projects and Programmes: A Development Practitioner's Critique of the Transition to a Sector-Wide Approach to Educational Development in Nepal." *Globalisation, Societies and Education* 9, no. 1: 51–65.

Wood, H. 1965. *The Development of Education in Nepal*. Studies in Comparative Education 5. Washington, DC: US Department of Health, Education, and Welfare, Office of Education.

A World to Win. 1996. "Nepal: Hoisting the Red Flag to the Roof of the World." Special issue, no. 22. http://bannedthought.net/International/RIM/AWTW/1996-22/nepal _hoisting_22_eng.htm.

Yogi, B. 2012. "Role of State and Non-state Actors in Nepal's Development." In *Readings on Governance and Development*, vol. 14. Kathmandu: Institute for Governance and Development.

Zharkevich, I. 2009. "A New Way of Being Young in Nepal: The Idea of Maoist Youth and Dreams of a New Man." *Studies in Nepali History and Society* 14, no. 1: 67–105.

Zotter, A. 2016. "State Rituals in a Secular State? Replacing the Nepalese King in the Pacali Bhairava Sword Procession and Other Rituals." In *Religion, Secularism, and Ethnicity in Contemporary Nepal*, edited by D. N. Gellner, S. L. Hausner, and C. Letizia, 265–301. New Delhi: Oxford University Press.

Zournazi, M. 2002. *Hope: New Philosophies for Change*. New York: Routledge.

Index

activists (*āndolankāri*), x, 49, 59–63, 199n13. *See also* student activists
ageism, 182. *See also* generations; political regeneration
Akash (interlocutor), 13–14; ageism, 182; as activist, 62; arrests, 13, 62, 86, 162, 169; CA elections, 14, 63, 104, 151, 182; constitutions, 150, 187; democracy, 13, 119–20, 208n3; disappearances, 162; federalism, 147; FSU, 13; Hinduism, 144–45, 146; INGOS, 151; international connections, 162–64; Koirala, G. P., 14, 85, 151, 198n28; monarchy deposition, 86, 144–45, 149, 182; as Maoist, x; Movement Against Regression, 14, 144, 151, 162, 182–83; NC, 13–14, 109, 119–20, 151, 182–83, 208n2, 208n3; new Nepal, 144, 146; NSU, 5–6, 13–14, 109, 119–20; NSU (K), 151; on organization, 108–9; political parties, 6–7, 14, 151–52, 182; political pathways, 181–82; political regeneration, 181; Prachanda, 104; public support, 13, 14, 86; republicanism, 85, 144, 153, 198n28; scalar politics, 164; secularism, 144–45; social media, 171, 172; street protests, 120; as student leader, 151; on student organizations, 5–6; student unions, 151; Tri-Chandra College, 13; on working styles, 113; youth and, 151, 152, 182–83
All Nepal National Free Student Union (ANNFSU), 18, 37, 39, 41, 102, 104–6, 198n27, 208n8
All Nepal National Free Student Union (Unified) (ANNFSU [Ekikrit]), 12*table*, 71
All Nepal National Free Student Union (United) (ANNFSU [Akhil]): central committees, 119; CPN-UML, 12*table*, 119, 186; exploitation, 156; FSU, 8*fig.*; leadership, 116; Movement Against Regression, 200n15; People's Movement, 200n15; Ratna Park, 200n15; struggle and sacrifice, 72–73; World Federation of Democratic Youth, 156
All Nepal National Free Student Union– Marxist Leninist (ANNFSU-ML), 12*table*
All Nepal National Independent Student Union (Revolutionary) (ANNISU [R]): CA elections, 72, 108, 118–19; class, 64, 65, 115; committees, 114; communists, 64; CPN-RM (Baidya), 119; culture, 115; FSU, 108; hierarchical systems, 114–15; holism, 71; ideologies, 64–65, 72, 107, 115, 116; leadership, 115, 116, 118; lifestyles, 118; militarism, 115; Norwegian embassy, 209n15; organization and organizing, 115; People's War, 115; Ratna Park, 200n15; scientific organization, 98, 107, 110–12, 114–15, 118; struggle and sacrifice, 64–65; student leaders, 114–15; UCPN (Maoist), 12*table*, 119; youth and, 64
All Nepal National Independent Student Union (Revolutionary) (Baidya Faction) (ANNISU [R] [Baidya]), 12*table*
anthropology, xii, 21, 74–75, 99, 100, 197n11

aid, 38, 46, 47, 158; Hinduism, 46, 75, 201n4; Kathmandu, 46; literacy rates, 45, 46; Mahendra, 46; Maoists, 47, 48; Ministry of Education, 47, 79, 198n33; modernity, 46; monarchists, 48; multi-party democracy, 47; National Development Service, 78–79; National Education System Plan (1971), 38, 39, 46; nationalism, 48; National Planning Commission, 48; National Youth Policy, 80, 92; Nepal, 34–36, 196n4; Nepali language, 46; New National Education Act (2005), 48; Panchayat rule, 38, 46–47; Parsa district, 178; political parties, 44–45, 48, 130; politics, 48; Rana regime, 34, 35, 45–46; reservations policies, 148; resources, 47; School Leaving Certificate, 39, 199n34; service, 51; Shah monarchy, 45; South Asia, 130; student organizations, 41; Tenth National Development Plan, 48; Vedic dharmashastra system, 45; women, 134; World Programme of Action for Youth (UN), 78; youth as political category, 75, 79, 80, 92, 201n5. *See also* schools; universities

elections, 6–7, 9, 66, 139, 186, 204n15, 208n1. *See also* Constituent Assembly elections

elites, 129–32, 141–46; CA elections, 127; castes, 129; education, 44–48; filial metaphors, 136–37; Hinduism, 28; local elites, 30, 52, 57; Maoists, 124; Nepali politics, 130, 135, 206n8; the people, 122; political parties, 129–32, 147; politics, 129; secularism, 141–46; state reconstruction, 142. *See also* high-caste hill ruling elite

emergence and waiting, 77, 87–91, 93, 95, 184

employment, 78, 79, 80, 81, 178

ethnicities: constitutions, 128; Dasain, 26–27; democracy, 4, 197n10; education, 47; exclusionary tenants, 25; federalism, 126, 147–48; intercommunal

tension, 180; mainstream politics, 129–32, 188, 211n1; Muluki Ain, 27; Nepali language, 46; newspapers, 166; National Youth Policy, 202n26; political parties, 131, 195n3; protests, 31; provinces, 127; Rana regime, 188; ruling elite, 188; secularism, 142; Shah monarchy, 188, 197n10; state reconstruction, 147; student leaders, 13, 131. *See also* Janajāti

ethnography, xii–xv

Evans-Pritchard, E. E., 74–75, 89

exclusion: civil war, 129; constitutions, 28, 129, 143; education, 44–45; federalism, 147–48; Madheshi movement, 125; Maoists, 25; minorities, 131, 138; Nepal, 25; political parties, 124; political subjectification, 123–24; politics, 138; reservations policies, 148; women, 131, 138. *See also* inclusion

factionalism: Maoists, 183–84; NC, 191; Nepali politics, 182; Nepal Sadbhavana Party, 194; NSU, 103; political parties, 111, 136, 185; RPP-N, 211n3; student leaders, 82; UCPN (Maoist), 119, 193

federalism: CA, 19, 34, 112, 126, 127; castes, 126; class, 147–48; constitutions, 128; CPN-UML, 126; ethnicities, 126, 147–48; exclusion, 147–48; inclusion, 147–48; Madheshi movement, 125, 126; mainstream politics, 123; marginalization, 126, 147–48; NC, 126; Nepal, 3–4; Parsa district, 179; political parties, 123; secularism, 142–43; state reconstruction, 125, 147; student activists, 63; student leaders, 147; UCPN (Maoist), 126, 193

filial metaphors, 54, 88, 133, 136–37, 138. *See also* kinship; nepotism

foreign aid, 22, 29–30, 38, 46, 47, 127–28, 158–59, 160. *See also* international donors

freedom of expression, 110, 116. *See also* individualism

Shah, Prithvi Narayan, and Shah monarchy, 26, 27, 121; state reconstruction, 141–42; student activists, 49; women, 138; youth as political category, 75, 88
human rights, x, 22, 49, 159, 160, 162, 165, 167, 180–81. *See also* civil rights; rights

idealism, 3–4, 9, 11, 43–44, 49, 97, 119
identity politics, 126, 158
ideologies: ANNISU (R), 64–65, 72, 107, 115, 116; castes/class, 110; civil war, 31; communist ideologies, 22, 31, 69–70, 156; CPN, 156; CPN-UML, 102, 108, 110–12; gender, 110; generations, 110; institutional cultures, 100, 101; lifestyles, 119; Maoists, 70, 71, 104, 106–7, 108, 109–12, 156, 184; NC, 108, 109, 182; Nepali politics, 97, 111; Nepal Sadbhavana Party, 194; NSU, 109; NSU (K), 72; organization, 97, 98, 108–9, 118, 203n2; personal interest, 107, 111; political parties, 54, 72, 98, 102, 107, 108, 110, 111, 118, 119; political regeneration, 181; politics, 50; Prachanda, 202n10; struggle and sacrifice, 71–72; student activists, 4, 72; student organizations, 106; value orientation, 195n7; working styles, 101, 113
inclusion: CA elections, 125, 126–27; civil war, 124; constitutions, 67, 129, 181; diversity into unity principle, 148; earthquakes, 174; federalism, 147–48; Hinduism, 145; mainstream politics, 123, 211n1; Maoists, 121, 125; minorities, 140, 142; National Youth Policy, 80, 92; NC, 67–68; Nepali politics, 19, 49; political parties, 147; political subjectification, 123–24; religion, 143, 144; republicanism, 124; reservations policies, 148; secularism, 124, 141, 142, 143; South Asia, 123; state reconstruction, 123, 124; student activists, 49; student leaders, 147, 188; Tarai, 179; women, 140
India: All India Nepalese Congress, 154; All India Nepalese Students' Union, 155; Britain, 154; Communist Party India,

154; CPN, 156; democracy, 53, 154–55; Indian National Congress, 154, 208n4; Kalapani campaign, 41; Mahendra, 198n27; Maoists, 160; Nepal, 26, 28–29, 34, 35–36, 51, 128, 143, 153–55, 156, 157–58, 160, 196n3, 197n13, 198n27; Nepal sovereignty, 29, 51; political parties, 160; Quit India movement, 154; reservations policies, 207n41; service, 52; Socialist Party India, 154, 155
individualism, 103, 109, 110–11, 113, 116
institutional anarchy, 98, 108–9, 112, 119
institutional cultures, 98–101, 107, 113
international connections, 15, 160–64, 172, 173, 174–75
International Crisis Group, 159, 162
international diplomacy, 15, 159, 160, 162
international donors: civil war, 159, 206n8; disappearances, 159, 162; earthquakes, 206n8; human rights, 159, 160; National Youth Policy, 93, 94–95; Nepal, 22, 158–59, 160, 206n8; new Nepal, 33, 87; peace talks, 206n8; royal massacre, 159; student activists, 4, 87–88, 160–64; student leaders, 160; women's rights, 163; youth and, 80. *See also* development; foreign aid; international non-governmental organizations
International Labour Organization (ILO), 81, 93
international non-governmental organizations (INGOs), 30, 31, 92, 151, 156, 158, 159, 160, 163, 173. *See also* non-governmental organizations
international youth policies, 77–78, 80, 202n28
Internet, 87, 164, 166–68. *See also* media/social media

Janajāti (ethnic group), 25, 124–25, 127, 128–29, 131–32, 140, 146, 188. *See also* ethnicities
Jayatu Sanskritam Āndolan (Victory to Sanskrit Movement) (1947), 35–36, 45, 154

Tri-Chandra College, 13, 34, 35, 45, 109
twelve-point agreement, 42, 160
twenty-first century student activists,
     xiii, 81–87, 87–88, 158. *See also* student
     activists

Unified Communist Party of Nepal (Mao-
     ist) (UCPN [Maoist]): ANNISU (R),
     12*table*, 119; author and, 195n3; Bhatta-
     rai, Baburam, 112, 193; CA, 112, 135–36,
     193; CA elections, 34, 112, 118, 127; CPN
     (Maoist), 193; CPN-RM (Baidya), 112, 119,
     184; CPN-UML, 192; earthquakes, 128;
     factionalism, 119, 193; federalism, 126,
     193; leadership, 191; Movement Against
     Regression, 191; Prachanda, 112; stu-
     dent leaders, 13; Yami, Hisila, 141, 155
United Kingdom, 30, 164, 175. *See also*
     Britain; British East India Company
United Nations, 47, 77–78, 79, 80–81, 92,
     93, 159, 160
United Nations Country Team's Peace
     and Reconciliation Plan, 80–81
United Nations Development Programme
     (UNDP), 15–16, 67, 81, 173
United Nations Mission in Nepal
     (UNMIN), ix, 33, 160, 161*fig.*, 197n18
United Nations resolutions, 77, 78
United States, 29, 158, 163, 175
United States Agency for International
     Development (USAID), 15–16, 30, 45,
     46, 67
United States embassy, ix, 159, 160–61, 162,
     175, 202n16, 209n15
United States Mission in Nepal, 160–62,
     174–75, 209n15
unity in diversity, 25, 141–42, 148, 188
universities, 36, 39, 47–48, 81–82. *See also*
     education; *individual universities*
university/campus politics, 3–5, 6–9, 11,
     36, 43

value-orientated movements, 9, 11, 195n7.
     See also norm-oriented movements
vernacularization, 21, 22–23, 176

women, 46, 84, 202n26, 206n19; CA elec-
     tions, 127, 140–41; castes, 138; consti-
     tutions, 128; education, 134, 198n30;
     exclusion, 131, 138; filial metaphors, 136–
     37, 138; Hinduism, 138; inclusion, 140;
     kinship, 133–37, 138; Koirala, Sujata,
     135; leadership, 132, 134, 135, 136, 139–
     40; marginalization, 174; media, 166;
     modernity, 138; nature metaphors, 138–
     39; nepotism, 134–35, 206n21; NGOS,
     173–74; Panchayat rule, 138; political
     identity, 133; political parties, 140–41,
     195n3; politics, 131–32, 136, 137–41, 185–
     86; religion, 138, 139; social media, 171;
     as student leaders, 139–40; US Mission
     in Nepal, 161. *See also* gender; women's
     rights
Women Act (network), 15–16, 91, 173–74
women's rights, 15–16, 67, 128, 129, 133–34,
     138, 141, 163, 173–74
working styles, 97, 98, 100, 101–2, 112–16,
     195n3, 203n2, 204n15
World Federation of Democratic Youth,
     156, 208n8
World Programme of Action for Youth
     (UN), 78, 79, 80–81
youth: ANNISU (R), 64; anthropology,
     74–75; CA, 186; coming-of-age, 74–75;
     constitutions, 67, 76*fig.*, 80–81; CPN-
     UML, 87, 186; democracy, 5, 91; demo-
     graphics, 93; Deuba, Sher Bahadur,
     79–80; education, 79, 201n5; employ-
     ment, 79, 80, 81; empowerment, 81,
     87, 95–96; Gyanendra, 79–80; India,
     202n28; international donors, 80;
     international policies, 77–78, 80,
     202n28; Koirala, G. P., 76; leadership,
     184; Madheshi movement, 80; Maoists,
     80; marginalization, 174, 182; media,
     186; Ministry of Youth, Culture, and
     Sports, 79–80, 202n24; multiparty
     democracy, 79, 80, 82; National Youth
     Council, 79, 91–92, 94, 202n24;
     National Youth Policy, 79–80, 81, 91–
     96, 202n28, 209n15; NC, 182–83; Nepal,

78–81; Nepal Army, 202n28; Nepali politics, 89; new Nepal, 76*fig.*, 87, 91–92, 182; NGOS, 53, 80; Ninth Plan, 79; Panchayat rule, 78, 81, 93; peace talks, 80–81; People's War, 80; police, 202n28; political identity, 91; political movements, 96; political parties, 186–87, 195n3; political regeneration, 23; social interactions, 89–90, 96; state reconstruction, 91; student activists, 81; temporality, 20–21, 187; United Nations, 77–78, 79, 80–81; World Federation of Democratic Youth, 156, 208n8; youth as political category, 74–96, 202n28

Youth Communist League, 55, 93, 209n15

GLOBAL
SOUTH
ASIA

Padma Kaimal
K. Sivaramakrishnan
Anand A. Yang
SERIES EDITORS

GLOBAL SOUTH ASIA takes an interdisciplinary approach to the humanities and social sciences in its exploration of how South Asia, through its global influence, is and has been shaping the world.

A Place for Utopia: Urban Designs from South Asia, by Smriti Srinivas

The Afterlife of Sai Baba: Competing Visions of a Global Saint, by Karline McLain

Sensitive Space: Fragmented Territory at the India-Bangladesh Border, by Jason Cons

The Gender of Caste: Representing Dalits in Print, by Charu Gupta

Displaying Time: The Many Temporalities of the Festival of India, by Rebecca M. Brown

Banaras Reconstructed: Architecture and Sacred Space in a Hindu Holy City, by Madhuri Desai

Mobilizing Krishna's World: The Writings of Prince Sāvant Singh of Kishangarh, by Heidi Rika Maria Pauwels

The Rebirth of Bodh Gaya: Buddhism and the Making of a World Heritage Site, by David Geary

Making New Nepal: From Student Activism to Mainstream Politics, by Amanda Thérèse Snellinger